The Word of God
Has Not Failed

Paul's Use of the Old Testament in Romans 9

The Word of God Has Not Failed

Paul's Use of the

Old Testament

in Romans 9

AARON SHERWOOD

STUDIES IN
SCRIPTURE
& BIBLICAL
THEOLOGY

LEXHAM PRESS

The Word of God Has Not Failed: Paul's Use of the Old Testament in Romans 9
Studies in Scripture & Biblical Theology

Copyright 2015 Aaron Sherwood

Lexham Press, 1313 Commercial St., Bellingham, WA 98225
LexhamPress.com

Print ISBN 9781577996620
Digital ISBN 9781577996835

Lexham Editorial Team: Elliot Ritzema, Lynnea Fraser
Cover Design: Christine Gerhart
Back Cover Design: Brittany VanErem
Typesetting: ProjectLuz.com

Contents

Acknowledgments

I would like to recognize two of my mentors, Gordon D. Fee and Rikki E. Watts. The best ideas in this work should all be credited to them, and I am grateful for their investment into my training and their sufferance to bring their wisdom to bear on such a modest passage. I also want to thank the publishing staff at Lexham Press and particularly Brannon Ellis for bringing this work to publication.

List of Figures

List of Abbreviations

AB	Anchor Bible
ANE	Ancient Near East(ern)
ANTC	Abingdon New Testament Commentary
BBR	*Bulletin for Biblical Research*
BECNT	Baker Exegetical Commentary on the New Testament
Bib	*Biblica*
BibInterp	*Biblical Interpretation*
BSac	*Bibliotheca Sacra*
BT	*The Bible Translator*
BTB	*Biblical Theology Bulletin*
BZ	*Biblische Zeitschrift*
CBQ	*Catholic Biblical Quarterly*
CBQM	Catholic Biblical Quarterly Monograph Series
ETL	*Ephemerides theologicae louvanienses*
EvQ	*Evangelical Quarterly*
ExAud	*Ex Auditu*
FOTL	Forms of the Old Testament Literature
HBT	*Horizons in Biblical Theology*
IBC	Interpretation Bible Commentary
ICC	International Critical Commentary
JANES	*Journal of the Ancient Near Eastern Society*
JBL	*Journal of Biblical Literature*
JBQ	*Jewish Bible Quarterly*
JETS	*Journal of the Evangelical Theological Society*
JNSL	*Journal of Northwest Semitic Languages*
JPS	Jewish Publication Society
JSNTSup	Journal for the Study of the New Testament: Supplement Series
JSOT	*Journal for the Study of the Old Testament*
JSOTSup	Journal for the Study of the Old Testament: Supplement Series

JTS	*Journal of Theological Studies*
LNTSSup	Library of New Testament Studies Supplement Series
LXX	Septuagint
NAC	New American Commentary
MNTC	Moffatt New Testament Commentary
mss	manuscripts
MT	Masoretic Text
NIB	*New Interpreter's Bible*
NICNT	New International Commentary on the New Testament
NICOT	New International Commentary on the Old Testament
NovT	*Novum Testamentum*
OTE	*Old Testament Essays*
OTS	Old Testament Studies
PRSt	*Perspectives in Religious Studies*
RevEx	*Review and Expositor*
RTR	*Reformed Theological Review*
SBLDS	Society of Biblical Literature Dissertation Series
SBLSP	*Society of Biblical Literature Seminar Papers*
SBLSymS	Society of Biblical Literature Symposium Series
SP	Sacra Pagina
ST	*Studia Theologica*
SwJT	*Southwestern Journal of Theology*
TDOT	*Theological Dictionary of the Old Testament.* Edited by G. Johannes Botterweck, Hene Ringgren, and Heinz-Josef Fabry
TJ	*Trinity Journal*
TNTC	Tyndale New Testament Commentaries
TynBul	*Tyndale Bulletin*
VE	*Vox Evangelica*
VT	*Vetus Testamentum*
VTSup	Supplement to Vetus Testamentum
WBC	Word Biblical Commentary
WCJS	*World Congress of Jewish Studies*
WUNT	Wissenschaftliche Veröffentlichungen zum Neuen Testament
ZAW	*Zeitschrift für die alttestamentliche Wissenschaft*

ANCIENT SOURCES

1 En.	*1 Enoch*
'Abod. Zar.	*Avodah Zarah*
Abraham	Philo, *On the Life of Abraham*
Alleg. Interp.	Philo, *Allegorical Interpretation*
b.	Babylonian Talmud
Eccl. Rab.	*Ecclesiastes Rabbah*
Exod. Rab.	*Exodus Rabbah*
Gen. Rab.	*Genesis Rabbah*
Jub.	*Jubilees*
L.A.B.	*Liber antiquitatum biblicarum* (Pseudo-Philo)
Lev. Rab.	*Leviticus Rabbah*
Meg.	*Megillah*
Mek. Isa.	*Mekilta Isaiah*
Midr. Prov.	*Midrash Proverbs*
Midr. Pss.	*Midrash Psalms*
Migration	Philo, *On the Migration of Abraham*
Names	Philo, *On the Change of Names*
Ned.	*Nedarim*
Num. Rab.	*Numbers Rabbah*
Pesiq. Rab.	*Pesiqta Rabbati*
Pesiq. Rab Kah.	*Pesiqta of Rab Kahana*
Pirqe R. El.	*Pirqe Rabbi Eliezer*
QG	Philo, *Questions and Answers on Genesis*
S. Eli. Rab.	*Seder Eliyahu Rabbah*
S. Eli. Zut.	*Seder Eliyahu Zuta*
Sanh.	*Sanhedrin*
Song Rab.	*Song of Songs Rabbah*
t.	Tosefta
T. Ab.	*Testament of Abraham*
T. Job	*Testament of Job*
T. Naph.	*Testament of Naphtali*
Tanḥ Gen.	*Tanḥuma Genesis*
Tanḥ. Lev.	*Tanḥuma Leviticus*
Tg. Hos.	*Targum Hosea*
Tg. Neof.	*Targum Neofiti*
Tg. Onq.	*Targum Onqelos*
Tg. Ps.-J.	*Targum Pseudo-Jonathan*
y.	Jerusalem Talmud

Introduction

It has become routine—almost trivial—to observe that Paul's letter to the Romans is not a theological treatise. Current wisdom is that *of course* Romans is occasional: it is a particular letter addressed to a particular audience in a particular situation, even if some of those particulars remain debated. Still, even recent Romans scholarship sometimes gives the impression the most secure manner in which to decipher Paul's response to the *Israelfrage* ("Israel question") is continued reliance upon traditional, theoretical approaches to the *crux interpretum* of Romans 9–11.[1] This is in the face of not just increased awareness of the occasional nature of Romans but also the multiplication of analyses of ancient Jewish authors' use of Scripture, which has raised scholars' awareness of the use of Scripture in Romans generally and chapters 9–11 in particular.[2] This is only fitting, since Romans contains the highest frequency of

---

1. See, for example, E. Elizabeth Johnson, "Romans 9–11: The Faithfulness and Impartiality of God," in *Pauline Theology*, vol. 3, ed. David M. Hay and E. Elizabeth Johnson (Minneapolis: Fortress, 1995), 214. The question of Israel as it relates to chapters 9–11 is not just that of Israel's identity, but more specifically: what is to be made of ethnic Israel's unexpected response to the Christ event? In Calvin's words, "If [the gospel] be the doctrine of the law and the Prophets [cf. Rom 9:4–5], how comes it that the Jews so pertinaciously reject it?" *Commentaries on the Epistle of Paul the Apostle to the Romans*, trans. John Owen (Grand Rapids: Eerdmans, 1955), 333.

2. This type of perspective was first advocated by (among others) C. H. Dodd, in *According to the Scriptures: The Sub-Structure of New Testament Theology* (London: Nisbet, 1953). It was later famously championed and developed especially with regard to Pauline studies by Richard B. Hays, *Echoes of Scripture in the Letters of Paul* (New Haven, CT: Yale University Press, 1987). Consequently, Stanley E. Porter is able to identify interest in the use of Scripture by New Testament documents "an active area of contemporary New Testament research." See "The Use of the Old Testament in the New Testament: A Brief Comment on Method and Terminology," in *Early Christian Interpretation of the Scriptures of Israel: Investigations and Proposals*, JSNTSup 148, ed. Craig A. Evans and James A. Sanders (Sheffield: Sheffield Academic, 1997), 79; see further the other essays in this volume, as well as Richard B. Hays, *Echoes of Scripture in the Letters of Paul* (New Haven, CT: Yale University, 1987); D. A. Carson and H. G. M. Williamson, eds., *It is Written: Scripture Citing Scripture: Essays in Honour*

scriptural citations of all the Pauline documents. Chapters 9–11 contain over half of the citations for the entire letter, at a frequency of nearly one every three verses.[3]

Despite all this, there are comparatively few studies on Paul's use of Scripture in Romans 9–11, especially ones that take full account of the historical context of Romans and therefore Paul's communicative strategy in these chapters. This trend holds true for the first stage of Paul's argument, Romans 9:6–29, wherein he quotes the Bible in (at least) twelve of twenty-four verses.[4] Romans 9:6–29 thus contains one of the highest concentrations of scriptural quotations in Paul's letters. Along with its lead position in Romans 9–11, this entails that Paul's answer to the *Israelfrage* in these chapters depends on Paul's use of Scripture. Most interpreters try to determine what Paul means—including how he understands and means to use the Scriptures of which he avails himself—by looking at what he says in 9:6–29. But this text resists such a straightforward approach because it is so crowded with citations that, comparatively, Paul says very little of his own—not enough for him to be properly understood by focusing just upon the discourse of 9:6–29.

Romans 9:6–29 has also for centuries been a theological battleground, which creates its own interpretive momentum. For instance, much classical (and patristic) scholarship generally saw these verses as a treatise on divine sovereignty and human free will.[5] Modern scholarship almost

---

of Barnabas Lindars (Cambridge: Cambridge University Press, 1988); G. K. Beale, ed., *The Right Doctrine from the Wrong Texts? Essays on the Use of the Old Testament in the New* (Grand Rapids: Baker, 1994); Steve Moyise, ed., *The Old Testament in the New Testament: Essays in Honour of J. L. North* (Sheffield: Sheffield Academic, 2000); Craig A. Evans, ed., *The Interpretation of Scripture in Early Judaism and Christianity: Studies in Language and Tradition* (Sheffield: Sheffield Academic, 2000); Klyne Snodgrass "The Use of the Old Testament in the New," in *Interpreting the New Testament*, ed. David Alan Black and David S. Dockery (Nashville: Broadman and Holman, 2001), 407–34; and the helpful survey in J. Ross Wagner, *Heralds of the Good News: Isaiah and Paul "in Concert" in the Letter to the Romans* (Boston: Brill, 2002), 5–13 (esp. 5n18).

3. James D. G. Dunn, *Romans 9–16*, WBC 38b (Dallas: Word Books, 1988), 520.

4. Rom 9:7 = Gen 21:12; Rom 9:9 = Gen 18:14; Rom 9:12 = Gen 25:23; Rom 9:13 = Mal 1:2–3; Rom 9:15 = Exod 33:19; Rom 9:17 = Exod 9:16; Rom 9:20 = Isa 29:16; Rom 9:25 = Hos 2:23; Rom 9:26 = Hos 2:1; Rom 9:27–28 = Isa 10:22–23; Rom 9:29 = Isa 1:9.

5. See William Sanday and Arthur C. Headlam, *The Epistle to the Romans*, ICC (Edinburgh: T&T Clark, 1895), 2:269–75, for a history of classical scholarship on Rom 9:6–29, which generally supposed that Paul presented his theory of election and/or predestination to explain why some people are saved while others are damned. Romans 9:6–29—along with Exod 4–14, which Paul references in Rom 9:14–18—has long been considered a *locus classicus* for various forms of the doctrine

completely follows this agenda while also discussing the related issues of, among other things, whether the passage (and chapters 9–11 generally) is occasional or abstract; the structure and coherence of the passage (and of chapters 9–11 generally); the degree to which the passage is a treatise on election; and whether Paul's main focus is salvation (whether of individuals or groups), Israel's composition, or God's faithfulness. Much the same can be said of how almost all major commentaries for more than a century approach the passage. This is understandable, since the history of interpretation makes it necessary for commentators to address 1) whether Romans 9–11 is a systematic treatise[6] or an occasional discussion (the balance having shifted heavily to the latter option in recent decades);[7] and 2) whether these chapters are isolated and most-

---

of predestination. Conversely, Origen, Gregory of Nyssa, and Chrysostom all considered that God's election and mercy were based upon free human response (while condemnation resulted from self-abandonment into wicked inclinations). But the Augustinian tradition has since determined (or at least overshadowed) engagement with Paul's thought: Augustine understood God's wrath as merited by all humans such that the puzzle is why any receive mercy, and that God's granting of grace is ultimately inscrutable. Later (working against semi-Pelagianism), he developed the notion of God's control over the will of all those yet unredeemed. This interpretation was refined and strengthened by, e.g., Aquinas, and accepted in some form by Luther (e.g., *Commentary on the Epistle to the Romans: a new translation by J. Theodore Mueller* [Grand Rapids: Zondervan, 1954], 122–23; *Lectures on Romans*, trans. Wilhelm Pauck [Philadelphia: New Westminster, 1961], 268–70) and Calvin (e.g., *Commentaries*, 350–55). Cf. Sanday and Headlam, *Epistle*, 2:269–75; Claire Mathews McGinnis, "The Hardening of Pharaoh's Heart in Christian and Jewish Interpretation," *JTI* 6 (2012): 46–53.

6. E.g., Dodd, *The Epistle to the Romans*, MNTC (London: Hodder and Stoughton, 1932), 148–51; R. C. H. Lenski, *The Interpretation of St. Paul's Epistle to the Romans* (Minneapolis: Fortress, 1961), 16–18; and notably Douglas J. Moo, *The Epistle to the Romans*, NICNT (Grand Rapids: Eerdmans, 1996), 14.

7. E.g., C. E. B. Cranfield, *A Critical and Exegetical Commentary on the Epistle to the Romans*, ICC (Edinburgh: T&T Clark, 1975), 1:19; F. F. Bruce, *Romans*, TNTC (Grand Rapids: Eerdmans, 1985), 172–73; Dunn, *Romans 1–8*, WBC 38A (Dallas: Word Books, 1988), lv–lviii; Joseph A. Fitzmyer, *Romans: A New Translation with Introduction and Commentary*, AB 33 (New York: Doubleday, 1993), 76–80, 541.

ly parenthetical,[8] necessary but self-contained,[9] or even climactic[10] to
the structure and argument of the letter. In this, commentators largely
presume the issues to be merely whether Paul holds to election and salvation of individuals[11] or groups,[12] and whether Paul presents a doctrine
of predestination (even if the scholar disagrees with it)[13] or merely describes God's freedom to elect and showing mercy.[14]

Of course, I am open to the notion that Paul's views on such things
may be the focus, and that more than one of these items could be revealed in Romans 9:6–29 at the same time (they are not mutually exclusive). Likewise, hypothetically, it could indeed be the case that Paul
chose to answer the *Israelfrage* indirectly by way of presenting his view
on election instead. However, a major concern with these possibilities
is that few if any analyses of Romans 9 demonstrate such assumptions
to be the case before proceeding as if they were. Aside from a handful
of more recent studies (introduced below) that focus on the occasional
relevance of 9:6–29 (largely with respect to some degree of focus upon
Paul's recourse to Scripture), scholars predominantly plumb the depths
of tradition for answers regarding Paul's view on election prior to examining his logic and language within the passage's literary-historical
context. As a result, a relatively small amount of attention gets paid to

8. E.g., Sanday and Headlam, *Epistle*, 1:xlv; 2:226; Dodd, *Epistle*, xxx, 148; Rudolf Bultmann, *Theology of the New Testament*, trans. Kendrick Grobel (New York: Schribner's, 1955), 2:132.
9. E.g., Lenski, *Interpretation*, 579; Ernst Käsemann, *Commentary on Romans*, trans. Geoffrey W. Bromiley (Grand Rapids: Eerdmans, 1980), 255; Bruce, *Romans*, 172–73; Fitzmyer, *Romans*, 131; Peter Stuhlmacher, *Paul's Letter to the Romans: A Commentary*, trans. Scott J. Hafemann (Louisville: Westminster John Knox, 1994), 143–44; Brendan Byrne, *Romans*, SP 6 (Collegeville, MN: Liturgical, 1996), 283.
10. E.g., Cranfield, *Romans*, 2:445–46; Dunn, *Romans 1–8*, lxi–lxii; *Romans 9–16*, 519–20; Thomas R. Schreiner, *Romans*, BECNT 6 (Grand Rapids: Baker, 1998), 17–18; Wright, *Letter*, 403–4; Ben Witherington III, *Paul's Letter to the Romans: A Socio-Rhetorical Commentary* (Grand Rapids: Eerdmans, 2004), 237.
11. E.g., Cranfield, *Romans*, 2:471; Käsemann, *Commentary*, 260–79; Leon Morris, *The Epistle to the Romans* (Grand Rapids: Eerdmans, 1987), 365–66; Moo, *Epistle*, 548; Schreiner, *Romans*, 476–77; John E. Toews, *Romans*, Believers Church Bible Commentary (Scottdale, PA: Herald, 2004), 476.
12. E.g., Dunn, *Romans 9–16*, 547–48; Fitzmyer, *Romans*, 559; Byrne, *Romans*, 289–90.
13. E.g., Sanday and Headlam, *Epistle*, 257; John Murray, *The Epistle to the Romans*, NICNT (Grand Rapids: Eerdmans, 1968), 1:24; Käsemann, *Commentary*, 262–64; Stuhlmacher, *Paul's*, 146–47; Schreiner, *Romans*, 472; Grant R. Osborne, *Romans* (Downers Grove, IL: InterVarsity, 2003), 247–53.
14. E.g., Cranfield, *Romans*, 2:471; Dunn, *Romans 9–16*, 554–55; Fitzmyer, *Romans*, 558–60; Byrne, *Romans*, 292; Wright, *Letter*, 634.

the function and meaning of the Scriptures referenced by Paul in either their original or Romans 9 settings. Similarly, commentators naturally make some effort to explain Paul's prolific use of Scripture in 9:6–29; nevertheless, they usually offer few or no observations (often being constrained by space) regarding the contextual meanings of the traditions from which he draws, how they were understood by Paul's early Jewish contemporaries, or whether any of those features are evident in Paul's use of them.

This all brings up the question of whether scholarly interest regarding election in this text has to do with Paul's primary interest(s) after all, or whether the text directly speaks to this issue as opposed to occasional concerns. I am not trying to deny any particular theory of Paul's view of election; I am merely asking whether the cart has been put before the horse (and whether it is hitched to the *right* horse). As Ben Meyer cautions,

> How did it happen that readers installed themselves in this misconstrual, mounting and sustaining for centuries a dedicated exploration of issues that Paul himself had not raised? Whatever the worth of the inquiry into the predestination of the individual to glory, that question was not Paul's question and none of the answers given to it over more than a thousand years can be attributed to Paul.[15]

I would like to suggest that the convention of taking the various aspects of election as Paul's main focus is a shortcoming in modern interpretations of Romans 9:6–29. Commentators and other scholars are all but unanimous that Paul is indeed discussing election, usually in a manner unrelated to the occasion of Romans. While it is easy to sympathize with how this presumption arose given the nature of the material, the question of whether this topic is really what is under discussion, or is Paul's means of addressing the *Israelfrage*, is not (re)visited enough.

In light of this state of affairs, Brian Abasciano is correct in his claim that Romans 9:6–29 is in need of fresh exegetical analysis that is sensitive

---

15. "Election-Historical Thinking in Romans 9–11, and Ourselves," *ExAud* 4 (1988): 1. On modern scholarship since Sanday and Headlam, N. T. Wright reflects, "Romans has suffered for centuries from being made to produce vital statements on questions it was not written to answer. ... Like almost every part of this letter, [Romans] 9–11 has suffered from being seen as the classic treatment of certain topics—topics that interpreters have brought to Paul rather than letting him dictate his own terms." *The Letter to the Romans, NIB* 10 (Nashville: Abingdon, 2002), 403, 620.

to Paul's use of Scripture.[16] A limited amount of scholarship has focused on understanding Romans 9:6–29 in terms of both the full contextual sense and Paul's contextually sensitive usage of the Scriptures referenced in the passage. But in my estimation, no study to date gets at the heart of Paul's argument within this passage, or the manner in which it serves his larger communicative strategy.

I will argue in this study that the occasion of Romans is such that Paul had to defend himself in light of Jews' pervading rejection of his gospel. This why in Romans 9:6–29 he discusses the nature and character of contemporary Israel's relationship with God in light of the precedents and antecedents of Israel's relationship with God in select Scriptures. This interpretation is innovative in comparison with much of the interpretation of this text throughout history. To prepare for my proposed solution, a quick overview of recent relevant studies is in order.

PREVIOUS STUDIES ON PAUL'S USE OF SCRIPTURE IN ROMANS 9:6–29

One influential study that seriously engages the use of Scripture in Romans 9:6–29 is John Piper's 1983 monograph *The Justification of God*.[17] Decades on, Piper's study remains the standard for a modern critical Reformed interpretation of Romans 9—so much so that Thomas Schreiner's 1998 Romans commentary could be understood as representing to a significant degree what it might look like to expand Piper's analysis to cover the entire letter. Despite his stated goal of an unbiased approach, Piper admits bringing to his analysis the a priori dogmatic principle that biblical texts, Romans 9:6–29 included, speak directly to "God's righteousness [which] consists in his being an allglorious God, and refusing to be anything less than allglorious." He also brings to the text two questions that this tradition is presumed to answer: "Does election in Romans 9:1–23 concern nations or individuals? And does it concern historical roles or eternal destinies?"[18]

---

16. *Paul's Use of the Old Testament in Romans 9.1–9: An Intertextual and Theological Exegesis*, LNTSSup 301 (Edinburgh: T&T Clark, 2005), 1.

17. *The Justification of God: An Exegetical and Theological Study of Romans 9:1–23* (Grand Rapids: Baker, 1983).

18. Ibid., ix, 1, 201; cf. 97, 100 [203], where God's righteousness in the OT is likewise defined as his "unswerving commitment to preserve the honor of his name and display his glory." It should be noted that Piper does include an entire chapter that seeks to exegete (and exegetically justify) his view of God's righteousness in the Hebrew Bible as background to Paul's presentation of God's righteousness. Nonetheless, his

In Piper's view, Romans 9:6 and following is a non-occasional discussion of theodicy, wherein Paul believes that God has unconditionally predestined individuals to either eternal salvation or damnation.[19] This conclusion is found in other interpretations, but what is significant for this study is how Piper argues this conclusion with attention to Paul's use of Scripture in Romans 9:6-29, being the first modern study to do so in a focused manner. The intent of his approach is commendable, to "read the same text as Paul did ... [and] to avoid, as far as I can, reading Paul's theology into [the OT]," despite the a priori conditions noted above.[20] But even this language implies that what interests Paul in 9:6-29 is theology per se. Correspondingly, Piper's analyses of OT Scriptures in their original context often have curiously little influence on his final interpretation. For instance, without considering the original context (and based solely on the occurrence of ἵνα in Rom 9:11), Piper asserts that for Paul, "the divine words [of Gen 25:23] have as their *aim* ... to secure and establish God's purpose," and reasons that "the word *pre-destine* is an apt description of the divine act described in the words, 'The elder shall serve the younger.'"[21] For Piper, this being the concern of Genesis 25 means that it is also Paul's concern in citing Genesis 25. But this is sound only if it is indeed presenting such a doctrinal statement within its narrative setting. It is possible that Paul read Genesis 25 in this way, but Piper falls short of demonstrating this meaning for Genesis 25 in its original context, or that it is the understanding that Paul indeed shares (beyond the fact that his doing so would cohere with Piper's reading of Paul).

Or again, concerning Paul's use of Exodus 33:19 in Romans 9:14-18, based on parallels presumed to be relevant, Piper reads Exodus 33:19 as a shorthand reference to Exodus 34:5-6,[22] resulting in his dubious

---

presupposition is that Paul's aim—and that of the Scriptures quoted by Paul in Rom 9—is an exposition of God's righteousness and the manner in which its exercise contributes to his glorification. In that sense, Piper's work can be criticized as not being genuinely exegetical in seeking to establish the meaning of Paul's argument, or as not forming its conclusions based upon exegetical analysis.

19. Ibid., 182–83, 204–5.
20. Ibid., 56.
21. Ibid., 34, emphasis original. Likewise, when arguing for his own position on Rom 9:6-13, rather than relying on Paul's use of Scripture, Piper dogmatically imposes that Paul is arguing from "the *principle* ... that God's blessings [are] enjoyed ... only on the basis of God's sovereign, free predestination" (ad loc., 46, emphasis original).
22. Within the narrative progression of Exod 32–34, 34:5-6 resolves the tension or conflict from the episode in 33:12-23, but the concern of the latter is covenant

conclusion that Exodus 33:19 is actually a systematic articulation of the doctrine that God's essential nature to act free from external constraint is based in his gracious nature and dedication to his own greater glory. And because Exodus 33:19, so analyzed, is a biblical tradition that defines God's glory in terms of his sovereign freedom, it serves a resource (over Exod 34:5-6?) that Paul is able to locate and harness in Romans 9:14-18 to legitimate God's predestination as righteous. Moreover, this is a foregone conclusion given Piper's premise that Paul is explicating a doctrine of predestination, making redundant his analysis of Paul's use of Exodus 33:19.

The concern here is not with Piper's conclusions (let alone his interpretations of Paul's vocabulary or grammar), but that he offers interpretations that sometimes border on eisegesis. Examples like these have led Roger Omanson, among other scholars, to point out that "Piper's fundamental error here consists in making this Pauline text address theological questions of predestination and free will, when in fact Paul was facing the issue of God's faithfulness to his people Israel."[23] Piper's intention to explore Paul's meaning in light of his use of Scripture is laudable, especially in its pioneering approach. However, he understands the texts Paul quotes as only valuable to him for the theological principles they embody, presuming that these are principles of election and/ or predestination. A significant weakness of Piper's study, then, is that it neither allows the relevant scriptural traditions to speak for themselves nor engages in contextually sensitive readings of them. In terms of its exploration of Romans 9 in light of Paul's use of Scripture and its occasional and literary contexts, there is little in Piper's study to commend it.

---

renewal while that of the former is God's response to Israel's specific sin of idolatry. It is both careless and in error to read the motif of 34:5-6 back into the contextual meaning of 33:19, especially as concerns all non-Pauline early Jewish witnesses (see chapter 4 below). On this count, interpretations of Paul's argument are mistaken when they suppose that there is reason to consider that Paul is doing so, or on the basis of such a false premise to reckon that Rom 9:14-18 discusses the theological interplay between God's mercy and his election.

23. Roger L. Omanson, review of John Piper, *The Justification of God: An Exegetical and Theological Study of Romans 9:1-23*, RevEx 82 (1985): 284; cf. Sam K. Williams, review of John Piper, *The Justification of God: An Exegetical and Theological Study of Romans 9:1-23*, JBL 104 (1985): 548-51; N. T. Wright, review of John Piper, *The Justification of God: An Exegetical and Theological Study of Romans 9:1-23*, EvQ 60 (1988): 80-84, esp. 83: "I am worried about Piper's central arguments ... because I do not think that this is the way, exegetically or theologically, to defend the doctrine of the righteousness of God."

Before visiting the next relevant major study, the intervening work of G. K. Beale, N. T. Wright, and Edward Meadors merits brief mention. In 1984, Beale produced an article that, while limited in scope, provides an incisive model for examining Paul's use of Scripture, specifically in Romans 9:14–18.[24] Beale aims at a detailed analysis of the hardening of Pharaoh's heart in Exodus 4–14. Then he applies his findings to Paul's use of Exodus 9:16 in Romans 9:14–18,[25] asking the question, "How does Paul's use of Exod 9:16 argue for God's justice?"[26] A strength of Beale's study is his method, as his is the first extended analysis of Romans 9:14–18 expressly in terms of Paul's use of Scripture. His exegesis of Exodus is especially rigorous, enabling him to fill a gap in most Romans commentary analysis (even since) in demonstrating how Paul understands Exodus 9:16 as "a summary of the purpose of the hardening throughout Exodus 4–14."[27] The remainder of Paul's argument will benefit from similar examination.[28]

Wright's work is also interesting, as it is commentary analysis that in some ways stands apart from other commentaries regarding Paul's dialogue with Scripture.[29] Wright argues that in Romans 9:6–29 Paul is unconcerned with salvation per se (whether of individuals or of groups), but somewhat idiosyncratically sees Paul as offering his own creative retelling of the "single story ... of Israel, from Abraham to the exile and beyond. ... It is the story, in other words, whose climax and goal is the Messiah."[30] According to Wright, Paul seeks to argue that "what God has promised [in Scripture, properly understood], God has performed."[31] One limitation of his treatment is the unavoidable brevity of his examination. In nearly every case, Wright can devote only a single paragraph to the original meanings of Scriptures used by Paul. Wright's views on biblical-theological narrative and Paul's understanding of the gospel

---

24. "An Exegetical and Theological Consideration of the Hardening of Pharaoh's Heart in Exodus 4–14 and Romans 9," *TJ* 5 (1984): 129–54.
25. Ibid., 130.
26. Ibid., 151.
27. Ibid., 151.
28. Weakness in Beale's analysis is due mainly to its necessarily limited scope, sometimes preventing him from accounting for the wider context of Rom 9:6–29 or requiring him to rely on other scholars' material, such as that of Piper.
29. Wright, *Letter*, 634–44.
30. Ibid., 634.
31. Ibid.

are documented elsewhere,[32] but here one is left wishing he had further space for detailed exegesis in support of his interpretation. More crucially, though, Wright's discussion of Paul's Hebrew-Bible Jewish narrative tends to overshadow Paul's actual use of specific biblical traditions, resulting in more of a theological evaluation than a precise interpretation of Paul's argument.[33]

Meadors' contribution to this discussion is found in his study of the theme of hardening in biblical traditions.[34] Meadors' study most closely resembles a theological interpretation; it claims even by its subtitle to employ a biblical-theological approach, such that exegesis and critical analysis are not his main design. That being the case, when reflecting upon Romans 9 (as well as Rom 10-11) he places primacy upon Paul's use of Scripture (and that in relevant early Jewish parallels that Meadors identifies) for understanding the progression of Paul's thought.[35] In accordance with his interpretive approach, he incorporates thematically relevant Scriptures not cited by Paul that shed light on those upon which he does draw in order to clarify the paradigm of hardening and idolatry within which he considers Paul to be speaking (such as Isa 6:9–10; 65:12; and Obad 11, 15, 17–18).

Nevertheless, Meadors' approach results in a fairly standard overall reading of Romans 9, in that he aims to defend God's faithfulness by arguing that a so-called Israel within Israel was repentant and obedient to God, whose sovereignty justifies his grace toward the faithful and judgment toward the wicked.[36] Meadors' focus on the theme of idolatry in Romans 9 means that God's faithfulness to corporate "true Israel"

---

32. Cf. Wright, *The Climax of the Covenant: Christ and the Law in Pauline Theology* (Minneapolis: Fortress, 1992); and *The New Testament and the People of God* (Minneapolis: Fortress, 1992).

33. See, e.g., his argument that in Rom 9:14–18 Paul sees God as assigning national Israel Pharaoh's former historical role in spreading God's mercy. This is promising but incomplete: it does not address the question of what has changed that ethnic Israel should be assigned this new role (rather than receiving mercy, as they had formerly). In recognition of the difficulty that Wright has produced, he only states, "Reading this part of Romans is like riding a bicycle: if you stand still for more than a moment … you are liable to lose balance—or, perhaps, to accuse Paul of losing his" (ibid., 639).

34. *Idolatry and the Hardening of the Heart: A Study in Biblical Theology* (New York: T&T Clark, 2006).

35. Ibid., 121–37.

36. Meadors' reading exhibits more fruitfulness from the theme of idolatry in his scan of Rom 10, asserting a compelling interpretive reading that unbelieving Jews' aim of self-righteousness there is indeed idolatrous.

is intact while unbelieving Jews' hardening is conditional and merited, which aligns Paul theologically with those arrayed against the likes of Piper.[37] Meadors' recognition that Paul forms his response in Romans 9 in terms of the biblical background of idolatry is an exciting development, and he does well to find some parallels in other Pauline traditions (e.g., 2 Thess 1–2; 2 Tim 2).[38] But otherwise, his other-than-exegetical approach leaves something to be desired regarding Paul's use of Scripture and the resulting shape of his argument in Romans 9:6–29.

The scholars whose work compares most directly to that of Piper are Ross Wagner and, more recently, Brian Abasciano.[39] Wagner's *Heralds of the Good News* argues that Paul enlists a "revisionary rereading of Isaiah," which becomes operative for his argument in Romans 9–11.[40] According to Wagner, Paul assembles various Isaianic strands to form a "web of intratextual connection" that evinces Paul's close contextual reading of Isaianic texts as well as his attentiveness to "larger stories and motifs that run throughout [Isaiah]."[41] Paul discovered that Isaiah preached the salvation of the nations, Israel's resistance to his message, and the persistence of a remnant, which vouchsafed Israel's future redemption. Recognizing these elements in his own apostolic experience, Paul found

---

37. See, e.g., Meadors' treatment of Exod 33:19 in Rom 9:15, where God's judgment upon the idolaters was just, and equally so his mercy upon the "Israel within Israel" who repented (with reference to Exod 32:26–28) in light of God's fundamentally gracious and compassionate character (with reference to 34:9). Ibid., 128.
38. Ibid., 132–33.
39. Respectively, Wagner, *Heralds* (a revised publication of his doctoral thesis, which follows in the spirit of Hays, Wagner's doctoral advisor); and Abasciano, *Romans 9.1–9*, and *Paul's Use of the Old Testament in Romans 9.10–18: An Intertextual and Theological Exegesis*, Library of New Testament Studies 317 (New York: T&T Clark, 2012). Also sometimes relevant (and more often helpful) is Shui-Lun Shum, *Paul's Use of Isaiah in Romans: A Comparative Study of Paul's Letter to the Romans and the Sibylline and Qumran Sectarian Texts*, WUNT 156 (Tübingen: Mohr Siebeck, 2002), whose stated goal is to investigate "how the Isaianic material serves as and helps shape the substructure of the apostle's argumentation in the Letter to Romans *as a whole*" (5, emphasis original). Regarding Rom 9:6–29, it is less concerned with an interpretation of Paul's argument than establishing the *fact* of Paul's use of Isaiah in the substructure of his argument. Notably, this allows Shum to discover aspects of Paul's argument overlooked by most Romans commentaries, such as a parallel note of "Yahweh's fierce, inexorable judgment against Israel" between Isa 10:22–23 and Rom 9:27–28 (210), though perhaps without adequate argumentative support.
40. *Heralds*, 41.
41. Ibid., 184; 41.

in the prophet "a fellow preacher of the good news," and came to understand his Gentile mission after the pattern of Isaiah.[42]

Concerning Romans 9:6–29 in particular, Wagner's study offers some helpful—if often perfunctory—observations. For instance, he argues that in Romans 9:14–18 Paul discusses God's freedom only relative to his relationship with Israel, and that Paul seems to draw on the dynamic whereby God chose "to keep his covenant with his people even in the face of their unfaithfulness and idolatry" but was free with Pharaoh "*not* to show mercy, but to turn human rebellion to his own purposes."[43] In addressing Paul's use of Isaiah in Romans 9:6–29 (and all of Rom 9–11), Wagner always offers an in-depth comparison between Paul's verbiage and that of his source.

However, Wagner's study has problems of both scope and method that detract from his interpretation of Paul's argument. On one hand, he maintains that Paul did not plunder Scripture for texts that would superficially meet his needs; he argues that "Paul's reading of Isaiah cannot be fully understood apart from his interpretation of key texts from the Torah, Psalms, and other prophetic books."[44] Nevertheless, in places he claims that Paul interpreted Isaiah in terms of his own missionary experience instead of vice versa.[45] Wagner's method leads him to state that Paul sometimes engages in "stunning misreading[s]" and "shocking" interpretive moves.[46] Such conclusions only apply if there is genuine disjunction between Paul's meaning and that of the Scriptures with which he engages. Additionally, Wagner's in-depth analysis is reserved for the Isaianic texts appearing in Romans 9:6–29; the non-Isaianic biblical traditions do not get comparable consideration.[47] Since Paul aims to make an argument rather than an uninterrupted interpretation of Isaiah, it seems that studying Paul's argument holistically is the soundest

---

42. Ibid., 1.
43. Ibid., 53, emphasis original.
44. Ibid., 43.
45. Ibid., 43.
46. Ibid., 155, 82.
47. Isaianic traditions account for only three of eleven biblical traditions appearing in Rom 9:6–29. Furthermore, it may be that in his eagerness to identify an "intratextual web" in Paul's use of Isaiah, Wagner relies too heavily on linguistic similarities between Romans and possible Isaianic source(s): for example, in Rom 9:20 he has Paul simultaneously using both Isa 29:16 and 45:9, regardless of the significant dissimilarities of their contexts. Similarly, in Rom 9:27–29 he has Paul using both Isa 10:22–23 and 28:22, again with their disparate contexts.

method for establishing his meaning. That is, it is inadvisable to offer a perhaps-insufficient analysis of Romans 9:6–18 and then rely on the resultant understanding of Paul's discussion to that point as the basis for analyzing verses 19–29, in which Isaianic traditions finally occur.[48]

As a result, despite his focus on Paul's use of Scripture, Wagner's conclusions are remarkably similar to those of previous scholars such as Piper. They also essentially align with the less-attentive analyses in standard commentaries. Wagner rather simplistically finds that Romans 9:6–13 is Paul's argument for God's freedom in electing Israel, and that Romans 9:14–18 is Paul's discussion of God's sovereignty in dispensing mercy or judgment. Consequently, rather than producing an incisive reading of Paul's argument and use of Isaiah in Romans 9:19–29, Wagner catalogues "echoes" of the Jewish potter/clay metaphor that "whisper suggestively around the edges," the combined weight of which is somehow meant to defend God's faithfulness through his divine right to "form" ethnic Israel as he sees fit.[49] Further, he offers the debatable conclusion that Romans 9:6–29 ends with a hopeful conflation of Scriptures regarding Jews' and Gentiles' foretold salvation. Wagner's interest in Paul's use of Scripture would benefit from giving equal weight to the various traditions used, not prioritizing those from Isaiah.

The final relevant study is Abasciano's project of analyzing Romans 9 in terms of the Scriptures Paul employs. So far he has produced in two volumes over 250 pages of detailed analysis of both Paul's writing and the biblical traditions upon which Paul draws in their original contexts.[50] Abasciano has to date completed his work on Romans 9:1–18, and

---

48. Although the interpretation of Rom 9:6–29 offered in the present study differs from that of Wagner, his attention to Paul's use of Scripture rightly brings him to recognize motifs present in the Isaianic traditions upon which Paul draws, such as God's justice, his chosen means of redemption, and the so-called wisdom debate. Many of these are applicable to the problem of the rejection of God's wisdom by first-century unbelieving Jews in Romans. But on the negative side, Wagner fails to recognize or sufficiently explore the theme of God's faithfulness in the Genesis texts quoted in Rom 9:6–13, the theme of idolatry in the Exodus texts, and the possible parallels between the rebellion of Israel in the biblical traditions quoted by Paul and that of contemporary Israel.

49. Ibid., 71.

50. Between Abasciano's most recent and forthcoming volumes comes David R. Wallace, *Election of the Lesser Son: Paul's Lament-Midrash in Romans 9–11* (Minneapolis: Fortress, 2014). Wallace works from the assumption that Paul's use of Scripture contains midrashic elements, reckoning that Paul's technique in passages such as Rom 9:6–18 is "commentary with proof texts" (albeit "*with the Old Testament context in mind*"; ad loc., 13–14, emphasis original). That is, he sees it as commentary on one

intends to finish with a forthcoming volume on 9:19-33. One distinctive
of Abasciano's investigation is the extent to which he is able to overview, detail, and interpret not just the biblical traditions quoted by Paul
but their contexts. Yet this is usually instrumental to his analysis, since
Abasciano more often than not finds that the precise text that Paul quotes
captures in a nutshell the thematic whole of a much larger context.[51] It is
also noteworthy that Abasciano openly writes from an Arminian perspective, hoping to provide an interpretation that defeats the doctrinal
positions found in Romans 9 by scholars such as Piper and Schreiner.
That is, one of Abasciano's concerns is to condition election on an individual's choice over God's choice or mercy, making his work seem like an
invested theological interpretation based on exegetical analysis rather
than an actual exegetical analysis of Paul's argument within its context.
In this it is not dissimilar to Piper's study, for instance.

The larger portion of Abasciano's first volume, *Romans 9:1-9*, is devoted to Romans 9:1-5. After situating both Romans 9-11 in general and
chapter 9 in particular within the entire letter, he argues that the allusion to Exodus 32:32 in Romans 9:3 identifies Paul with Moses, agonizing

---

text using a secondary text, like Gen 18:10 for 21:12 in Rom 9:6-9. His method leads
him to break down Romans 9 into midrashic argument, diatribe, and then testi-
monia, i.e., a list of Scriptures that functions as an argument *a fortiori* (ad loc., 57).
And this in turn leads Wallace to presume that Rom 9:6-29 is a treatise upon election,
whereby his contribution is to argue that Paul's midrash shows that God's nature is
merciful amid Israel's election. Namely (as indicated in the title of his monograph),
God punishes the elder son as a merciful object lesson for Israel, such that God's
election of the "lesser son" might promote Israel's obedience to avoid God's wrath
(ad loc., 71-72). Consequently, God's election remains righteous regardless of Israel's
unfaithfulness, as per Rom 9:14-18 (ad loc., 77-79), and ultimately God is merciful
in election in intending the mercy of Israel's election (and the forbearance of his
own wrath) for both Jews and Gentiles (ad loc., 93-95). Wallace's reading is creative
and not inarticulate, but his recourse to midrashic elements and resultant analysis
of the structure of 9:6-29 are problematic. But even more so is his *a priori* stance
that Paul is presenting a treatise upon election (regardless of the meanings of the
Scriptures to which Paul refers). Essentially, he is describing Paul's assumed use
of Scripture to legitimate his position rather than actually investigating the nature
and content of Paul's discussion both in general and in light of his use of Scripture.
51. With an examination extending over multiple volumes, Abasciano is often able
to devote several pages to evaluating numerous plausible disambiguations of a
single term or clause. Then he frequently bases his reading of the relevant biblical or Romans 9 tradition on his favored meaning. The length of this present study
does not permit such a luxury, but I will make up for that envious level of detail by
demonstrating compelling readings of sentences and theological contexts, if not of
semantic range and syntax.

over ethnic Israel's "accursed" (ἀνάθεμα) condition just as Moses ag-
onized over God's rejection of Israel in Exodus 32–34.[52] One benefit of
Abasciano's scripturally sensitive approach is that it brings him to see a
richer theological context to Paul's upcoming discussion in 9:6–29 than
most any other scholar has recognized, including motifs of "idolatry,
grief, ... merciful judgment, the faithfulness of God, divine sovereignty,
and human free will."[53]

Abasciano's examination of Romans 9:6–13 is divided across two volumes. In his consideration, Genesis 18:10/14 (the traditions quoted by
Paul in Rom 9:9) is the hermeneutical key for all of Genesis 18–19, which
demonstrates that God's faithfulness to Abraham proves that he can
be trusted to do what is good and just.[54] Likewise, Abasciano reckons
that Genesis 21:12 (Paul's source for Rom 9:7) sets a universally applicable precedent for God's sovereignty in election, wherein any sadness
at God's non-inclusive choice is mitigated by the joy at who is chosen.
This relies on reading Genesis 21:12 both as exploiting the Abrahamic
promise of greater good for the world (Gen 12:1–3, relying strongly on
a similar move made by *Jub.* 16:16–18), and the notion that this tradition
proves God's attributes of divine faithfulness and justness by reiterating
the principle found in Genesis 18–19.[55] So by quoting these traditions in
Romans 9:6–9, Abasciano concludes Paul's argument to be that national
Israel's rejection of the gospel aligns with the fact that God sovereignly
elects to covenantal identity (not salvation). This is joyous because of its
facilitation of the Abrahamic promise, and because it resolves worries

---

52. Abasciano, *Romans 9.1–9*, 32–33, rightly judges that the *object* of Paul's grief is national Israel's alienation from God (which he presumes to be God's *rejection* of them),
not the fact of their unbelief. This should not be confused with the *reason* for Rom
9–11. However, Abasciano's position may be somewhat at odds with his view that
Rom 9:1–5 is a proleptic summary of Rom 9–11, e.g., leading him to take 9:6a, "But it
is not as though the word of God has failed" (widely recognized as the thesis statement for Rom 9–11; see chapter 3 below) to mean that it is not as though all true Israel
is accursed. On a separate note, Abasciano's exegesis of Exod 32:32 and its environs
is typically detailed, though its extensiveness and the degree to which Abasciano
must strive to demonstrate a substantial connection with Rom 9:3 may suggest special pleading.

53. *Romans 9.1–9*, 101, section heading 3.4.b.3.

54. Ibid., 152–54. Important for Abasciano is that "YHWH's election of Jacob (and
his descendants) and its justification (not cause) [is] based on the despising of the
birthright and covenant blessings by the original heir" (13).

55. Ibid., 165–72.

about theodicy in that God is proving himself faithful and just by continuing to elect some and not all.

For the remainder of the pericope, Abasciano similarly examines in their original contexts Paul's citations from Genesis 25:23 and Malachi 1:2–3. He finds the former to be a proleptic summary of the Genesis Isaac cycle, whose point is that God's election is both corporate and his own prerogative (in response to individuals' choices to accept or refuse God's mercy).[56] The latter Abasciano finds to be essentially an emphatic re-iteration of or even commentary on Genesis 25:23, being for Paul a redundant but more pointed resource.[57] Thus he concludes his treatment of Romans 9:6–13 by saying that Paul has now offered two proofs "that covenant heirship has always depended on God's call and purpose rather than ancestry."[58]

At the end of his second volume, Abasciano turns to Exodus 33:19 and 9:16 in Romans 9:14–18. For the first passage, he refers back to his work on Exodus 32–34 in Romans 9:3, wherein it was concluded that those chapters boil down to God's sovereignly choosing repentance as the condition for the bestowal of his mercy (those who repent receive both mercy and covenantal identity).[59] Abasciano injects all of this into Exodus 33:19, and then sees Paul as importing it into Romans 9:15.[60] Abasciano then provides a lengthy exegesis of Exodus 4–14 that aims to produce the meaning of Exodus 9:16 (Paul's source for Rom 9:17) in context.[61] He concludes that the narrative presents Pharaoh's hardening as globally presenting "God's actions … as conditional on Pharaoh's unjust oppression of Israel and Israel's prayer for divine deliverance … an expression of his [God's] faithfulness to his covenant promises," once again in relation to Genesis 12:1–3.[62] For Abasciano, all of this is summed up in the rhetoric of Exodus 9:14–16—hence Paul's citation, which is thought to be a reference to the above theological principle.

To this point, Abasciano's reading of Paul's argument is that it is God's prerogative to freely elect his corporate people (Rom 9:6–13). In response

---

56. Abasciano, *Romans 9.10–18*, 3–8, 10–13.
57. Ibid., 17–19.
58. Ibid., 42–43.
59. Abasciano, *Romans 9.1–9*, 66–69.
60. Abasciano, *Romans 9.10–18*, 75n1.
61. Ibid., 77–138, with Exod 9:14–16 receiving focused attention on pp. 128–29.
62. Ibid., 138–39, equating hardening with resisting God's purposes, and accounting Pharaoh's hardening as strategic rather than supernatural, wherein God lured Pharaoh out of position and to stand against him to Pharaoh's own detriment.

to the objection that his doing so is unrighteous, Paul calls attention to the historical precedent and type of Israel's exodus experience in which God is wholly faithful in electing the elect-worthy (including even Gentiles)—even if not all ethnic Jews fit that category (those who refuse to accept that God would ever use faith alone as the means for determining the election of his people).[63] Abasciano's take on the remainder of Romans 9:6–29 awaits the publication of his next volume.

The basic worry about Abasciano's method is that in its application he may be majoring on the minors. In many ways, he offers not an independent, fresh reading but a reactionary over-reading in response to the likes of Piper, accepting a playing field on which it is agreed that Paul addresses the *Israelfrage* by means of God's election, justice, and mercy (which are also thought to be present in the Scriptures upon which Paul draws). It is regrettable how he does so much right with regard to approach and yet relinquishes so much in terms of getting at the heart of Paul's communicative strategy in Romans 9:6–29.

ORIENTATION OF THE PRESENT STUDY

The preceding survey of works related to the study of Paul's argument in Romans 9:6–29 in light of his use of Scripture reveals some broad areas of consensus. There is a growing acknowledgment of the need to understand Paul's scriptural dependence in order to understand his argument in 9:6–29. There is also a growing awareness of parallel motifs between Paul's description of present national Israel's circumstances and the original contexts of his various biblical quotations, including God's faithfulness and Israel's calling, rebellion, idolatry, and judgment. Scholars are also increasingly recognizing that national Israel's predicament and Paul's argument relate directly to a defense of God's faithfulness: the answer to the *Israelfrage* is *not* that God's word has failed.

However, work remains to be done. No study: 1) covers Paul's entire argument in Romans 9:6–29; 2) carries out sufficient contextual analyses of all Paul's scriptural quotations and the way in which they function in Romans; *and* 3) offers a final interpretation of Paul's argument

---

63. I.e., God conditionally bestows divine mercy on those who repent, and this repentance-mercy mechanism is the basis of election into covenantal identity (Exod 33:19//Rom 9:15), the very principle that is instantiated in both Pharaoh's recalcitrance and Israel's exodus deliverance as "renewed election" (ibid., 202; Exod 9:16//Rom 9:17), such that God's mercy can only be accepted by faith and neither willing nor striving (cf. Rom 9:16); Abasciano, *Romans 9.10–18*, 173–204.

(rather than just theological implications) in light of his use of Scripture. It is true that none of the studies surveyed above set out to do all these things, but many of them have weaknesses that are traceable to the neglect of one or more of these elements. As a result, the force of their arguments are often blunted. And because 9:6–29 constitutes the first stage of Paul's argument in Romans 9–11, and given the prominence of these chapters, a sound interpretation of 9:6–29 is important for understanding chapters 9–11, the letter as a whole, and the question of Israel in all of Pauline studies.

Consequently, this study aims to analyze Paul's argument in Romans 9:6–29—not necessarily its resultant or derivable theology—specifically in light of his use of Scripture, giving necessary weight to the argument's occasional and literary context, and also investigating the biblical traditions that Paul employs within their original contexts. To be clear, I do not begin by presuming standard approaches to 9:6–29 to be wrong in taking the view that Paul defends God's faithfulness indirectly by discussing the nature of election to salvation (and delimiting this in some way to a certain definition of Israel such that God's actions are consistent with Scripture). Theoretically, this would be a viable strategy that Paul might choose to adopt. Rather, I mean to say that I shall examine 9:6–29 empirically, with proper consideration of its place within the letter, the occasion of the letter, and Paul's first-century Hellenistic-Jewish setting. As it happens, in so doing I find that the data do not after all show Paul's discussion to be about election, as classical (and most modern) interpretations usually surmise. In other words, most interpreters argue over whether Paul is presenting the Arminian or Calvinist view of election unto salvation (or some combination of both). I will attempt to demonstrate that Paul presents neither the Arminian nor the Calvinist view in 9:6–29 (and Rom 9–11, generally) simply because he is not discussing—let alone presenting a model of—election at all.

Instead, this study shows how in Romans 9:6–29 Paul defends God's faithfulness both by identifying present national Israel's unbelief as idolatry and by arguing that God's subsequent response to their unbelief is his judgment on their idolatry.[64] More specifically, through his use of Scripture Paul argues that, possible appearances aside:

---

64. There is no consensus among scholars regarding how to refer to non-Christian Jews of the Pauline era; options include *ethnic Israel, national Israel, unbelieving Jews,* etc. Sensitivity is needed, and anachronism and ideological bias should be eschewed, but there is no single best option. The polyvalence of the terminology even in the

1. God fundamentally remains faithful to his covenant, indepen-
    dent of and even despite national Israel's rebellious rejection
    of Christ and the gospel;
2. God has discretion in dispensing either mercy or judgment,
    specifically in response to idolatry, and his judgment on na-
    tional Israel is in continuity with his response to idolatry
    throughout Israel's biblical history; and
3. God's faithfulness to his original covenantal purpose is seen
    in how he ironically makes use of his judgment upon national
    Israel in the redemption of his people, among whom is includ-
    ed representatives of the nations.

Paul argues this over three pericopes. These hold together as a single, coherent argument in support of his thesis statement for both Romans 9:6–29 and chapters 9–11 as a whole: "It is not as though the word of God has failed" (9:6a). The nature of national Israel's idolatry is found in their rejection of the Christ event. But Paul does not detail this until the next stage of his argument in Romans 9:30–10:4, since the immediate issue in 9:6–29 is that of God's apparent unfaithfulness (see chapter 6).

Generally, my method will follow the example set out by Richard Hays and others regarding Paul and other New Testament writers' use of Scripture. This has increasingly shown them to employ a contextu- ally sensitive use of Scripture within a framework of Jewish thinking. It is also roughly the same approach attempted with regard to Romans 9:6–29 by Wagner and Abasciano (and, to a lesser extent, Piper). For this study, this means a standard literary-historical analysis of Romans 9:6–29, but also involves asking about *Paul's* understanding of—and therefore intent in using—the Scriptures that he quotes.

The ideal is subtle and may seem infelicitous to scholars who are skeptical of this approach. Naturally, Paul cannot be made to look like a twenty-first century grammatical-historical exegete (let alone of the critical edition of a received canon). Likewise, as a native speaker of the language(s) of the Scriptures, Paul would not have labored over the syntactical possibilities inherent in a given participle or preposition the way that modern interpreters must do by virtue of their separation from Paul's context by time and distance. Also it would be ideal if parallel

---

first century allows Paul to make a subtle (and debated; see chapter 3) distinction in Rom 9:6a. Because of the biblical heritage of early Judaism(s), this study elects to employ the language of *national Israel*, and also intentionally to avoid introduction of expressions that may smack of supercessionism such as *true Israel*.

interpretation of the same Scriptures from Paul's Second Temple Jewish contemporaries could provide a baseline for comparison. This would enable us to identify currents of interpretation that may have influenced or been contemporaneous to Paul's use of those biblical traditions, but unfortunately few such examples are to be found. In each case below, I will conclude the analysis of the biblical tradition in question by discussing comparable references to it in Second Temple (when available) and other early Jewish usage. However, interpretation of Paul's argument is largely limited to analyzing the Scriptures that Paul employs in their original context, and then exploring whether those contextually sensitive readings make the best possible sense of Paul's discussion.

Because of our limited access to both the past and the mind of Paul (as well as his contemporaries and the minds of the authors and redactors of the biblical texts that Paul references), I propose to make full use of modern critical methods. In using these methods, we may arrive at the meaning of Paul's scriptural quotations, which he would have apprehended much less artificially than we. Therefore, my ascription to Paul of the meanings of the biblical traditions in question necessarily contains an element of inference and subjectivity, but possibly no more than any other modern critical effort in biblical studies.

The present study attempts to contribute to both the understanding of the *Israelfrage* and the burgeoning interest in Paul's use of Scripture in Romans 9–11 by building on the work of the scholars listed above. This study does *not* attempt a full exegesis of Romans 9:6–29, nor is it primarily interested in the theological implications of Paul's argument. Instead, it is a selective exegetical analysis focusing on Paul's use of biblical traditions and an interpretation of his argument in light of that use.

The organization is as follows: Chapter 2 examines the historical and literary contexts of Romans 9–11 in general and Romans 9:6–29 in particular, and offers a provisional description of the structure of 9:6–29. Chapters 3–5 investigate Paul's use of the OT and interpret his argument in the three distinct pericopes of 9:6–13 (chapter 3); 9:14–18 (chapter 4); and 9:19–29 (chapter 5). Chapter 6 begins with a summary of Paul's argument in Romans 9:6–29. I then conclude by remarking on the function of Romans 9:6–29 within Romans 9–11 and drawing out implications for the *Israelfrage* in Pauline studies.

1

The Context and Structure of Romans 9:6–29

THE HISTORICAL CONTEXT AND OCCASION OF ROMANS

In order to analyze Paul's argument and use of Scripture in Romans 9:6–26, it is first necessary to give an overview of both the historical context of Romans and the literary context of 9:6–29. Paul wrote his letter to the Romans in the mid- to late fifties, to a church he had not met and for whom he was not responsible (see, e.g., Rom 1:11–13; 15:22). The audience of Romans consisted of Christians of mixed ethnicity who were predominantly Gentile believers.[1] At the time Paul wrote his letter, Jews (both believing and unbelieving) had begun to reestablish themselves in Rome following Claudius' death in AD 54, having been expelled by his imperial edict in AD 49.[2]

---

1. Dunn, *Romans 1–8*, xlv; Fitzmyer, *Romans*, 32–33; James C. Walters, *Ethnic Issues in Paul's Letter to the Romans: Changing Self-Definitions in Earliest Roman Christianity* (Valley Forge, PA: Trinity Press International, 1993); Byrne, *Romans*, 10–12; Schreiner, *Romans*, 13–14; James C. Miller, *The Obedience of Faith, the Eschatological People of God, and the Purpose of Romans*, SBLDS 177 (Atlanta: Society of Biblical Literature, 2000), 107–10; Witherington, *Paul's*, 7–8, etc. There are good reasons for this consensus; still, in some quarters, the ethnic composition Paul's audience (often to do with the identity of the "strong" and the "weak" in Rom 14:1–15:13)—both years prior to and at the time of his writing Romans—is strongly contested. However, an audience of primarily Gentile believers is unproblematic for our study, since the Roman church was "likely raised on Jewish roots through the preaching of the gospel in the synagogues," and so even Gentile believers "would have had a keen knowledge of the OT Scriptures" (Schreiner, *Romans*, 14, who also cites evidence from J. Christiaan Beker and Dunn; cf. Dunn, *Romans 1–8*, l). For an adroit handling of this issue see Dunn, *Romans 1–8*, xlix–l; and Schreiner, *Romans*, 14–15.

2. Dunn, *Romans 1–8*, xlviii–xlix; Fitzmyer, *Romans*, 31–32; Walters, chapter 3 (esp. pp. 56–62); Byrne, *Romans*, 11; Schreiner, *Romans*, 13; Miller, *Obedience*, 110–11; Witherington, *Paul's*, 12. The dating and extent of the Claudian expulsion has been challenged, so Miller rightly qualifies that its impact was unquantifiable yet extensive enough to be relevant (*Obedience*, 111; cf. Abasciano, *Romans 9.1–9*, 28). Raymond

The issues of possible ethnic tension or underrepresentation of Jewish believers, Paul's various stated reasons for writing found in Romans 1:8–15 and 15:14–33, and the question of how the letterframe relates to the body in 1:16–15:13 have given rise to the question of Paul's purpose(s) for writing Romans, an area of inquiry known as the "Romans debate."[3] Recent scholarship has reached a broad consensus that what led to Paul's writing Romans were "a cluster of interlocking factors" that combined both "the present situation of the church in Rome and the present situation of Paul."[4] Paul himself states his desire to use Rome as a base of operations for his planned mission to Spain, similar to his use of Antioch for his missionary efforts in the eastern empire (Rom 1:14; 15:14–29). Paul also meant to give pastoral instruction to the Roman church (found mainly in 12:1–15:13), especially in light of their internal and external ethnic tensions.[5] Finally, Paul had an apologetic purpose

---

E. Brown proposes that the important question is not ethnic composition of the audience so much as where their theological sympathies lie on the issues of ethnicity and the gospel. "The Roman Church Near the End of the First Christian Generation (A.D. 58—Paul to the Romans)," in *Antioch and Rome: New Testament Cradles of Catholic Christianity*, ed. R. E. Brown and J. P. Meier (New York: Paulist, 1983), 109n227.

3. For a survey and introduction to the Romans debate and the issues involved, see Karl P. Donfried, "A Short Note on Romans 16," in *The Romans Debate*, ed. Karl P. Donfried (Minneapolis: Augsburg, 1977), 50–59. In addition to the other essays in this volume, see further those in Karl P. Donfried, ed., *The Romans Debate*, rev. and exp. ed. (Peabody, MA: Hendrickson, 1991); and A. J. M. Wedderburn, *Reasons for Romans* (Edinburgh: T&T Clark, 1988). For an excellent bibliography, see James C. Miller, *The Obedience of Faith, the Eschatological People of God, and the Purpose of Romans*, SBLDS 177 (Atlanta: Society of Biblical Literature, 2000), 1–2nn2–3.

4. Wedderburn, *Reasons*, 142; cf. Wedderburn, "Purpose and Occasion of Romans Again," in *The Romans Debate*, rev. and exp. ed., ed. Karl P. Donfried (Peabody, MA: Hendrickson, 1991), 195–202; Morris, *Epistle*, 7–18; Dunn, *Romans 1–8*, lv–lviii; Fitzmyer, *Romans*, 79–80; Abasciano, *Romans 9:1–9*, 30. See Miller, *Obedience*, chapter 1, for a recent description of the Romans debate. Miller's disagreement with Wedderburn's "multiple purpose" theory should be noted: he states that Wedderburn mistakenly assumes "the multiple factors prompting Paul to write necessitate multiple aims for the letter as well. ... [He] correctly recognizes the scope of information that needs to be accounted for, but offers an unsatisfactory reading of that information" (*Obedience*, 17).

5. Dunn, *Romans 1–8*, lviii–lxiii; Fitzmyer, 79–80, 541. Moo states that ethnic tension in Rome possibly "mirrored the tensions in the church at large in Paul's day" (*Epistle*, 20). Bruce worries that Jewish believers, because they resented their Gentile fellow-believers' disparagement of ethnic Jews, stressed "their continued solidarity with [non-believing Jews], to a point where they were in danger of underestimating those distinctive features of Christian faith which forged a bond between them and their Gentile brethren" (*Romans*, 172; cf. Walters, 78; Schreiner, *Romans*, 471).

to address Roman believers' apprehension about the rumored divisive effects of his gospel.

In particular, more needs to be said about Paul's apologetic purpose, since it bears so directly on Romans 9:6–29. The elaborate, run-on greeting in 1:1–7 roots Paul's apostleship in the "gospel of God," which is described as both based in the holy Scriptures (vv. 1b–2) and concerning "his son … namely, Jesus Christ our Lord." The son/Jesus is fleshed out in terms of his Israelite and vindicated messianic credentials (vv. 3–4a) and the effects of his work via Paul on behalf of all the nations (v. 5) and the Roman audience specifically (v. 6). This elaboration is related to Paul's diplomatic situation, meaning that verses 1b–6 likely present much of the referent of *gospel* for Romans—that is, what of God's gospel that is *not* controverted between he and his audience (i.e., that Jesus' identity as Messiah and Lord culminates Israel's Scriptures and is proven by the inauguration of God's kingdom, even among the audience themselves).

Paul's care in introducing himself continues in Romans 1:8–15 (clearly marked off by its beginning, "First off [πρῶτον μὲν]," v. 8). As in all of Paul's letters, this thanksgiving and prayer discloses his main communicative goals—in this case, that he would have fruit among the audience and evangelize them.[6] Additionally, Paul is employing what can be termed a rhetoric of mutuality, borne out by his statement that he and the audience may strengthen and "mutually encourage" one another through their shared faith (vv. 11–12).[7] So Paul's stated goal is strengthening the audience, particularly by sharing with them his gospel (εὐαγγελίζω, v. 15; cf. "my gospel" in the closing doxology at 16:25), which they had not yet fully apprehended. This statement (along with the focus of 1:1b–6) highlights the elephant in the room, yielding the statement in 1:16–17.[8]

---

6. So Gordon D. Fee, *God's Empowering Presence: The Holy Spirit in the Letters of Paul* (Peabody, MA: Hendrickson), 486–89; Richard N. Longenecker, "The Focus of Romans: The Central Role of 5:1–8:39 in the Argument of the Letter" in *Romans and the People of God: Essays in Honor of Gordon D. Fee on the Occasion of His 65th Birthday*, ed. Sven K. Soderlund and N. T. Wright (Grand Rapids: Eerdmans), 49–50.

7. See Marty L. Reid, "A Rhetorical Analysis of Romans 1:1–5:21 with Attention Given to the Rhetorical Function of 5:1–21," *PRSt* 19 (1995): 189–90; Erwin Ochsenmeier, "Romans 1,11–12: A Clue to the Purpose of Romans?" *ETL* 83 (2007): 398–99 (including how στηρίζω and συμπαρακαλέω entail a context of trying circumstances); cf. A.B. Toit, "Persuasion in Romans 1:1–17," *BZ* 2 (1989): 200.

8. Antoinette Clark Wire puts scholars on notice for often neglecting the treble occurrence of γὰρ in Rom 1:16–17, settling on the final clause when the focus points back to the first, and before into verses 8–15: "The structure of Paul's argument has

Numerous scholars have observed how Paul's gospel would have been controversial. His audience was likely aware that wherever Paul preached, the Jewish gospel of the Jewish Messiah was rejected by Jews but accepted by the *goyim*.[9] If Romans is something of an ambassadorial letter,[10] then in order to be successful Paul needed to give a(n extended) demonstration, to his audience's satisfaction, of why he is not ashamed of his gospel.[11] As James Wedderburn articulates it, this material best

---

been improperly identified." Wire, "'Since God is One': Rhetoric as Theology and History in Paul's Romans," in *The New Literary Criticism and the New Testament*, ed. Elizabeth Struthers Malbon, JSNTSup 109 (Sheffield: Sheffield Academic, 1994), 212.
9. E.g., Stuhlmacher argues that because Gentiles predominantly accepted Paul's gospel, it was under suspicion "of resulting in the damnation, rather than the salvation, of Israel" (*Paul's*, 143–44). Similarly, Byrne identifies Paul's intention to introduce himself via "an authentic and acceptable account of his gospel and its consequences" in light of his having become a "highly controversial figure" due to the questionable results of his gospel (*Romans*, 9; cf. pp. 2–4). Schreiner comments that Paul's teachings on the law had "precipitated disputes" among both Jews and Jewish believers, first in Galatia and Corinth, and now in Rome (*Romans*, 14). Thus, in order to even receive a hearing, Paul needed to demonstrate that his law-free gospel fulfills Scripture: "Paul wrote to the Roman church so that they would function harmoniously. Such unity could only be obtained by a thorough explication of Paul's gospel, for Paul's advice would be heeded only if the Romans were persuaded that his understanding of the gospel was on target" (Schreiner, *Romans*, 22). Accordingly, Wedderburn neatly summarizes how, since Paul and his gospel were matters of controversy, "considerable care and tact were called for" (*Reasons*, 93–94). This goes against, e.g., Neil Elliott, *The Rhetoric of Romans: Argumentative Constraint and Strategy and Paul's Dialogue with Judaism*, JSNTSup 45 (Sheffield: JSOT, 1990), 278–90; Johannes N. Vorster, "Strategies of Persuasion in Romans 1.16–17," in Stanley E. Porter and T. H. Olbricht, eds., *Rhetoric and the New Testament: Essays from the 1992 Heidelberg Conference*, JSNTSup 90 (Sheffield: JSOT, 1993): 153–54; Luke Timothy Johnson, *Reading Romans: A Literary and Theological Commentary* (New York: Crossroad, 1997), 9–10; Schreiner, *Romans*, 58–61, and others, all of whom read *gospel* as the soteriological content of chs. 1–11, and gloss 1:16 οὐ ...ἐπαισχύνομαι as Paul's (psychological) *pride* in the gospel—as in, not being embarrassed to share his faith; and also contra Hays, *Echoes*, 39; Wire, "Since," 214; Reid, "Rhetorical," 124, etc., all of whom take οὐ ... ἐπαισχύνομαι to mean pride in God's power.
10. So, e.g., George Smiga, "Romans 12:1–2 and 15:30–32 and the Occasion of the Letter to the Romans," *CBQ* 53 (1991): 262–63, 272 (whose argument demonstrates that Romans stood as a substitute for Paul's presence); Robert Jewett, "Ecumenical Theology for the Sake of Mission: Romans 1:1–17 + 15:14–16:24," *SBLSP* (1992): 598; Wright, *Climax*, 187–88, etc.
11. What Paul's audience knew or were committed to already—which concerns in the letter were theirs or his and what of the letter is Paul's corrective teaching—is partly a matter of speculation. However, the general occasion in conjunction with the structure of even the greeting dictates that Paul and his audience hold some percentage in common that serves as the starting point for their dialogue. This goes

makes sense "if *some in Rome had in fact claimed that* [Paul] *indeed ought to be ashamed of his gospel,*" and "*the argument of the rest of Romans from this point to the end of chapter 11 is a defense of Paul's message.*"[12]

Thus, both Steve Mason and, more recently, Rikki Watts have drawn a strong connection between Paul's apologetic purpose in writing Romans and his thesis statement (for at least 1:16–11:36) in Romans 1:16–17. Mason asks why Paul should have to say in his thesis that he is "not ashamed" of his gospel. In answer, he recalls how some Jewish believers "*did* think that Paul should be ashamed of his [gospel]," since, among other things, he was assumed to have "corrupted the apostles' teaching in order 'to please men' (Gal. 1.10–12), and that he had effectively written off Israel and its traditions (Acts 21.21, 28)."[13] Watts extends Mason's analysis by drawing out the relationship between Paul's thesis and the question of Israel in Romans 9–11: "Paul might be expected to be ashamed [of his gospel] precisely because of the theodicy question: How could he make the claims he did when his gospel seemed to mean the setting aside not only of Israel's traditions but also of the nation itself?"[14] This explains Paul's careful, diplomatic self-presentation and tactful substitution of mutuality for apostolic authority (partly in hope of the audience's support).

Therefore, God's covenant faithfulness is central to Paul's thesis— and therefore to the letter as a whole. Most scholars now agree that this

---

against, e.g., Jeffrey A. D. Weima, "Preaching the Gospel in Rome: A Study of the Epistolary Framework of Romans," in *Gospel in Paul: Studies on Corinthians, Galatians and Romans for Richard N. Longenecker* (ed. L. Ann Jervis and Peter Richardson; JSNTSup 108 (Sheffield: Sheffield Academic, 1994), 342–43. Weima argues that much of Romans is *pro forma*, wherein Paul as apostle to the nations has a "divine responsibility" to share his particular gospel with the (partly) Gentile audience—even if they are already believers—on general principle.

12. *Reasons*, 104, emphasis original.

13. "'For I am Not Ashamed of the Gospel' (Rom. 1.16): The Gospel and the First Readers of Romans," in *Gospel in Paul*, 280 (citing Gerd Lüdemann).

14. "'For I Am Not Ashamed of the Gospel': Romans 1:16–17 and Habakkuk 2:4," in *Romans and the People of God: Essays in Honor of Gordon D. Fee on the Occasion of His 65th Birthday*, ed. Sven K. Soderlund and N. T. Wright (Grand Rapids: Eerdmans, 1999), 22–23. As his title indicates, Watts' task is to examine Paul's use of Hab 2:4 in Rom 1:17, and my position is strengthened by his conclusion that "Paul's [revelation] concerning God's intervention clearly raises the problem of theodicy, just as did Habakkuk's vision in his day. In both cases, God's covenantally faithful action seems tantamount to the rejection of his people in favor of even more wicked Gentiles. ... The question must inevitably arise: Has the word of God fallen (9:1–5; cf. 3:1–4)?" (18).

is the primary meaning of δικαιοσύνη θεοῦ in Romans 1:17.[15] Because a majority of Jews rejected Paul's gospel, it seemed to result in the separation of national Israel from their promised covenantal blessings. This in turn appeared to be God's rejection of Israel. But the underlying assumption of God's character that he cannot break his covenantal promises entailed that it was Paul's gospel that was false and therefore shameful in both its falsity and its divisive effects. Paul is thus compelled to argue in Romans that his gospel is in fact "the righteousness of God," that is, God's covenantal faithfulness. Hence the thesis in 1:16–17 that despite national Israel's tragic (and traumatic for Paul; cf. 9:1–3) rejection of the gospel, it is "in fact the revelation ... of the mysterious fulfillment of Yahweh's purpose."[16] It is not until chapters 9–11, however, that Paul

---

15. That δικαιοσύνη θεοῦ in Rom 1:17 is a possessive subjective genitive and refers to God's righteousness in fulfilling his scriptural promises to Israel—that is, his covenantal faithfulness—is the view of a strong majority: e.g., J. Christiaan Beker, "The Faithfulness of God and the Priority of Israel in Paul's Letter to the Romans," in *Christians among Jews and Gentiles: Essays in Honor of Krister Stendahl*, ed. George Nickelsburg and George MacRae (Philadelphia: Fortress, 1986), 14; Dunn, *Romans 1–8*, 41–42 (who proposes a bothand sense, also seeing an element of an objective genitive); Wedderburn, *Reasons*, 112–13 (arguing that Rom 3:1–8 and chs. 9–11 contextually require this interpretation); Fitzmyer, *Romans*, 257; Stuhlmacher, *Paul's*, 30–31; Wright, "Romans and the Theology of Paul," in *Pauline Theology, Vol. 3: Romans*, ed. David M. Hay and E. Elizabeth Johnson (Minneapolis: Fortress, 1995), 33–34, 39; Byrne, *Romans*, 53–54, 60; Wagner, *Heralds*, 44–45 (esp. n5). Indeed, Richard P. Carlson has argued that because Paul here does not explicate δικαιοσύνη θεοῦ for an audience unfamiliar with his writings, he must be presuming a shared understanding of Scripture, which (like Rom 1:1–15, with its theocentric focus) generally presents the picture of God's "being steadfast and consistent in fulfilling divine covenantal responsibilities ... of God acting faithfully [with] respect to God's covenantal people [and] the world as its creator." Carlson, "Whose Faith? Reexamining the Habakkuk 2:4 Citation within the Communicative Act of Romans 1:1–17," in *Raising Up a Faithful Exegete: Essays in Honor of Richard D. Nelson*, ed. K. L. Noll and B. Schramm (Winona Lake, IN: Eisenbrauns, 2010), 309.

16. Watts, "Not Ashamed," 23. For this argument, we may remain neutral as to the meaning of both ἐκ πίστεως εἰς πίστιν (Rom 1:17) and the Hab 2:4 citation. However, it should be mentioned that several Romans scholars have demonstrated that Hab 2:4 in its original context (in both Hebrew and Greek) concerns living according to a trust in God's faithfulness: Watts, "Not Ashamed," 16–17; Alice Ogden Bellis, "Habakkuk 2:4b: Intertextuality and Hermeneutics," in *Jews, Christians, and the Theology of the Hebrew Scriptures*, ed. Alice Ogden Bellis and Joel S. Kaminsky, SBLSymS 8 (Atlanta: Society of Biblical Literature, 2000), 369, 372–75; John W. Taylor, "From Faith to Faith: Romans 1.17 in the Light of Greek Idiom," *NTS* 50 (2004): 338–39; cf. Carlson, "Whose," 297–99, 301–2, 314, focusing on the theocentric nature of Rom 1:1–15. (Hab 1:1–4 is a complaint in the face of unchecked violence; Hab 1:5–11 God's response to Babylon; Hab 1:12–17 a sarcastic question of why less-wicked Israel is punished

engages in detail the rejection of his gospel by most Jews and the issue of God's faithfulness.

THE LITERARY PLACEMENT, THEME, AND STRUCTURE OF ROMANS 9–11

The remainder of Romans 1–11 is Paul's theological discussion in support of his thesis statement in 1:16–17. The consensus has shifted in the past few decades, so that a majority of scholars rightly consider Romans 9–11 the climax of the argument in chapters 1–11.[17] In this argument, Paul first raises the question of Israel in 1:18–2:29. Then this indictment, especially against transgressing Jews, more directly raises in Romans 3:1–8 a number of questions: "Does [some Jews'] unfaithfulness nullify God's faithfulness? ... Is God unjust to bring forth his wrath? ... Why am I still being condemned a sinner?" But these questions Paul puts off until later,

---

prior to Babylon; and Hab 2:1–4 the exploration of God's painfully slow response.) Also noteworthy is that Benware and Taylor have soundly demonstrated that in both classical and biblical Greek (e.g., Greek Jer 9:3; Greek Psa 84:7) an expression of this form followed by ἐκ πίστεως κτλ is an idiom meaning "from beginning to end" (Wilbur A. Benware, "Romans 1.17 and Cognitive Grammar," *BT* 51 [2000]: 336–38; Taylor, "Faith," 341–42, 348). If so, then ἐκ πίστεως κτλ in Rom 1:17 is not part of the scriptural citation (which instead possesses its own introduction) and is best translated, "this being an issue wholly of faith," or, "this being [a path] that begins and ends in faith."

All this is to say that regarding the relevance of establishing Rom 1:16–17 for understanding 9:6–29, the best explanation is that, vis-à-vis his evangelization record, Paul is arguing in 1:17 parallel to Habakkuk's context: Righteous followers of righteous Yhwh will seek to know why God's covenantally faithful actions are not tantamount to his rejection of national Israel in favor of even more wicked non-Jews, trusting God throughout.

17. This is not to claim that there is a majority view of Rom 9–11 as the climax of the letter as a whole, but there is now a scholarly consensus concerning the integral role of these chapters in Romans: Neil Richardson, *Paul's Language About God*, JSNTSup 99 (Sheffield: Sheffield Academic, 1994), 26. Among others, see, e.g., Hays, 63; Beker, "Faithfulness," passim; Dunn, *Romans 1–8*, lxi–lxii; Wright, *Climax*, 234, 247; Wright, *Letter*, 408 ("It is not simply that, having written chs. 1–8, he finds he has to go on to 9–11; it is just as much that, because he wants to write chs. 9–11, he finds he must write 1–8 [in a way that properly prepares for 9–11].") ; Wagner, *Heralds*, 43–44; Witherington, *Paul's*, 237; Abasciano, *Romans 9.1–9*, 34. ("It is not that Romans 1–8 are merely preparatory for chs. 9–11. Nor is it that Romans 1–8 could not logically stand on their own with some sense of satisfaction. It is more that Romans 9–11 contain the height of what Paul wants to say.")

when he is able to address them in a single, uninterrupted discussion at the culmination of his argument (3:3//9:6; 3:5//9:14; 3:7//9:19; 3:8//6:1).[18]

Indeed, the language at the close of Romans 8 prompts Paul's discussion of God's faithfulness in light of the *Israelfrage*. The doxology closing chapter 8 declares God's faithfulness to his people, who are in context the christocentric community of believers, but doubt concerning God's faithfulness to Israel casts doubt upon his faithfulness to his people. How, exactly, is it that "God works together all things for good for those whom loves" in 8:28, given that Abraham's descendants appear to have been cut off from the blessings found in Christ? As Wagner remarks, "When, in Romans 8, Paul appropriates the terminology of *Israel's* election for his *Gentile* churches, the issue of God's faithfulness to his own people ... demands the apostle's sustained attention."[19] So starting in Romans 9 Paul finally addresses these issues that have been awaiting discussion since early in the letter.

There has emerged a further solid consensus, "almost universally held by exegetes," that unbelieving Jews' rejection of the gospel has occasioned the primary theme for Romans 9–11 of God's faithfulness to his covenant with Israel, a position that is "justified and unassailable."[20] In 9:1-5, the proem to chapters 9–11, Paul expresses his "great sorrow" and "continuous anguish" over the state of affairs (9:3; cf. 10:1). God's apparent rejection throws doubt upon his fidelity, whereupon in the rest of Romans 9–11 Paul defends God's covenantal faithfulness and his response to national Israel's unbelief.[21] That is, it is not God's rejection of Israel that Paul wishes to defend. Rather, it is more basically his covenantal faithfulness despite all appearances—without our presuming

---

18. Cf. John A. T. Robinson, *Wrestling with Romans* (London: SCM, 1979), 109 (who suggests that chs. 9–11 are parallel to the whole of ch. 3); W. S. Campbell, "Romans iii as a Key to the Structure and Thought of the Letter," *NovT* 23 (1981): 32-34.

19. Wagner, *Heralds*, 45, emphasis original. This does not commit us to the notion that Rom 8 refers exclusively to non-Jewish believers.

20. Lloyd Gaston, "Israel's Enemies in Pauline Theology," in *Paul and the Torah* (Vancouver: University of British Columbia, 1987), 92; cf. Cranfield, *Romans*, 2:473; Dunn, *Romans 9-16*, 518-21; Wright, *Climax*, 235-36 (cf. Wright, *Letter*, 621); Fitzmyer, *Romans*, 539; Byrne, *Romans*, 282; Schreiner, *Romans*, 472, 491; Wagner, *Heralds*, 45; Abasciano, *Romans 9.1-9*, 32.

21. This is so even granting Abasciano's distinction (*Romans 9.1-9*, 32-33) between Paul's anguish over national Israel's accursedness, which Paul literally references in the text, and the relationship between their unbelief and the question of God's covenantal faithfulness. The concern over their accursedness should not be taken to entail Paul's appeal to a theory of national election to uphold God's faithfulness.

that God has indeed rejected national Israel at all.[22] He therefore states up front the primary theme of God's faithfulness, which is textually contained in the thesis statement at 9:6a (see chapter 3 below).

At the conclusion of this study, I will be able to offer some brief remarks on the structure of Romans 9–11 and the function of 9:6–29 within that structure (see chapter 6 below). Provisionally, the logic of Romans 9–11 runs as follows: Paul begins with his introduction (9:1–5), stating his anguished desire that his fellow Jews would accept the gospel (9:1–3) and cataloguing of their blessings as Israelites, which culminate in the Messiah (9:4–5). Then, Paul's argument for chapters 9–11 comes in three stages: 9:6–29; 9:30–10:21; and 11:1–32. During the first stage, he defends God's faithfulness by discussing his response to national Israel's unbelief, which is identified as idolatry. During the second stage, Paul responds to a resultant—that the more wicked nations should not participate in Israel's blessings while national Israel is barred from them. Paul's response is to further detail the nature of national Israel's idolatrous commitments to Torah and their determination that God ought to continue "righteousizing" his people on the basis of Torah observance (10:3–4, 16), in light of which God has displayed constancy in "righteousizing" Gentiles on the basis of faith (10:5–13, 20–21). During the third stage, Paul argues that God's judgment upon unfaithful national Israel is not irrevocable (11:1, 11), and he is at work to restore his people (11:26; cf. 11:12, τὸ πλήρωμα αὐτῶν);[23] and a warning against arrogance on the part of non-Jewish believers (11:17–22). Paul concludes with a doxology in 11:33–36.

So the coherence of Romans 9–11 is predicated upon the meaning of 9:6–29. All three stages of Paul's argument play a role in his defense of God's faithfulness, which debuts in the first sentence of 9:6–29. Moreover, because 9:6–29 is the first stage in Paul's logic, whether chapters 9–11

---

22. On this point, Abasciano (*Romans 9.1–9*, 33) goes perhaps too far in thinking, for dogmatic reasons, that "if it is the unbelief of Israel which is the problem Paul addresses, then Romans 9–11 can tend to be read [i.e., incorrectly] as seeking to explain Israel's unbelief and God's responsibility for it. On the other hand, if it is rather God's rejection of Israel that is the issue, then … Paul is defending God's response to Israel's belief." The proper way of framing the issue is that Paul anguishes over national Israel's accursed state relating to their unbelief, and then defends God's response to their unbelief.

23. The debate on the nature, extent, and timing of national Israel's eventual restoration and/or redemption referenced here cannot be resolved within the scope of this study.

are a single argument (rather than discrete, thematically similar units) depends on how 9:6–29 carries forward to 9:30–10:21 the issue of God's faithfulness. Thus the meaning of 9:6–29 is crucial not only for its own sake, but for Paul's entire argument in chapters 9–11. Also, insofar as these chapters conclude the so-called theological portion of the letter, a sound interpretation of 9:6–29 is vital to understanding Paul's argument in Romans as a whole.

THE STRUCTURE OF ROMANS 9:6–29

I will conclude this chapter with a preliminary consideration of the structure of Romans 9:6–29 before moving on to investigate Paul's argument and use of Scripture in the passage. Paul presents his argument in diatribe fashion, beginning with a response to the challenge that the "word of God has failed" in verse 6a and supplying questions from an imaginary interlocutor in verses 14 and 19; in the latter two instances, a transitional οὖν ties what follows with the preceding material, rhetorically advancing Paul's logic. Accordingly, Paul's argument can be divided into the three uneven pericopes of 9:6–13, 14–18, and 19–29.[24] Demonstration of the content is to follow, but my outline is provisionally annotated:

Rom 9:6–13   God's covenant with his people depends on God's promise (i.e., emanates from his faithfulness), to which God has always remained faithful irrespective of Israel's merit—and in fact even despite their rebellion and unfaithfulness.

Rom 9:14–18   God is just when he now judges national Israel for their idolatry because his response to idolatry is at his discretion; therefore, whereas in the exodus he both dispensed mercy to idolatrous Israel and judgment upon idolatrous Pharaoh in order to bring glory to his name, he is now dispensing judgment upon unbelieving national Israel to bring glory to his name.

---

24. Dunn, Fitzmyer, and Schreiner divide the text into 9:6–13, 14–23, and 24–29, although they do so for different reasons. Byrne (*Romans*, 289–90) divides the final pericope into 9:19–21 and 22–29.

Rom 9:19-29   God's response to idolatry is at his discretion because of its dehumanizing consequences; but in an ironic fulfillment of his promises to Israel, God is using his judgment upon national Israel in the redemption of the nations (as he had used his judgment upon Pharaoh in Israel's deliverance).

In terms of logical structure, Paul begins with a defense of God's faithfulness—the primary theme of Romans 9-11—and carries it through to the end of this stage of the argument. The discussion of God's historical faithfulness at the conclusion of the first pericope (9:13) prompts the interlocutor's opening question to the next pericope: What has changed that God is no longer overlooking Israel's rebellion? The reversal seems arbitrary, which makes God appear unjust (9:14). So in 9:14-18 Paul picks up on this concern, thereby continuing his defense of God's faithfulness.[25] Then, the second pericope could be misunderstood as entailing God's responsibility for national Israel's rebellion, in which case they should not be held liable. So, once again, in 9:19 Paul gives voice to the interlocutor's objection in order to segue into 9:19-29, his explication of the consequences of Israel's idolatry and the conclusion to this portion of his defense of God's faithfulness.

Besides this, it needs noting that a few scholars beginning with Jean Noël Aletti have observed a chiastic arrangement to some of Paul's more provocative and thematically important (subjectively judged) terminology.[26] However, this linguistic arrangement does little by itself to explain Paul's meaning, and serves poorly as the basis of the logical structure of his thought (let alone the discrepancies between the various proposals). For example, in addition to other problems of balance, Aletti's resultant thematic interpretation of Romans 9:6-29 is unconvincing, as the chiasm compels him to bind national Israel to Abraham's covenantal

---

25. It may be noted (and will be in the conclusion of this study) that on my reading, election or lack thereof for Paul is neither under discussion nor in any way connected with the issue of idolatry.

26. Aletti, "L'argumentation Paulinienne en Rm 9," *Bib* 68 (1987): 42, finding a further chiasm within the central pieces of Rom 9:14-18, 19-20, and 21-24 (ad loc., 46), accepted by both Schreiner (*Romans*, 472) and Abasciano (*Romans 9.1-9*, 38); cf. Dunn, *Romans 9-16*, 537 (whose independent proposal further fills out that of Aletti); Jewett, *Romans: A Commentary*, Hermeneia (Minneapolis: Fortress, 2006), 571; and Pablo T. Gadenz, "'The Lord Will Accomplish His Word': Paul's Argumentation and Use of Scripture in Romans 9:24-29," *Letter & Spirit* 2 (2006): 76-77.

heirs despite Paul's contrast between these groups. Thus, the best way to account for the linguistic arrangement within 9:6–29 is that of Pablo Gadenz, who recognizes that the terminological chiasm serves the rhetorical effectiveness of Paul's argument, which logically develops as it progresses but draws his audience's ear in order to bring together his flow of thought.[27] James Dunn's analysis is that this chiastic pattern indicates the "careful composition of the paragraph," but perhaps little else.[28]

With regard to the interpretation of Romans 9:6–29, the foregoing considerations illustrate both its importance for Paul's apologetic purpose in writing Romans and its key position within the literary structure of the letter. A primary reason for Paul's writing in the way that he does is to defend his gospel to the Roman church in order to demonstrate that it was not shameful but demonstrated the righteousness of God. Romans 9:6–29 is the first stage in Paul's defense of that righteousness—that is, God's covenant faithfulness—in chapters 9–11, the climax of the argumentative portion of the letter. With this in mind, as well as the provisional structure of Romans 9:6–29 stated above, we are now in position to analyze Paul's argument in light of his use of biblical traditions within 9:6–29.

---

27. Gadenz, "Lord," 77; cf. Abasciano: "But how does this chiastic structure relate to the logical structure...? They are complementary. The logical structure is primary – content takes precedence over form" (*Romans 9.1–9*, 39).
28. So Dunn, *Romans 9–16*, 537.

2

Paul's Use of Scripture in Romans 9:6–13

[6]But it is not as though the word of God has failed.[1] For neither are all those from Israel Israel, [7]nor is it the case that Abraham's descendants are all of his children.[2] Rather, "It is through Isaac that your descendants will be called for you." [8]That is, it is not the children according to the flesh that are God's children, but rather the children according to the promise who are considered his descendants—[9]for it is a promise, this word: "About this time I will come and Sarah will have a son." [10]And not only that, but there is also Rebekah, having children from one marital relationship[3] with Isaac our patriarch—[11]for neither having yet been born nor having done anything good or inconsequential, but in order that God's according-to-election purpose might persist [12]based not upon Torah observance but rather upon him who calls, it was

---

1. Literally "fallen," which amounts to "fail" in context. It is notable that in ancient rhetoric ἐκπίπτειν τοῦ λογοῦ means to be defeated and run down into silence (Jewett, *Romans*, 573).

2. Translation here is difficult. οὐ γὰρ πάντες οἱ ἐξ Ἰσραὴλ οὗτοι Ἰσραήλ (9:6b) woodenly reads, "For all those from Israel, they are not Israel" (which does not differ greatly from the translation given; cf. Piper, *Justification*, 47–48; Dunn, *Romans 9–16*, 539; Moo, *Epistle*, 573; Schreiner, *Romans*, 493). Then, in 9:6–8, Paul distinguishes between restrictive (Ἰσραήλ, 9:6b; σπέρμα, 9:7b [= Gen 21:12]; τέκνα τοῦ θεοῦ, τὰ τέκνα τῆς ἐπαγγελίας, σπέρμα, 9:8) and less restrictive categories (οἱ ἐξ Ἰσραὴλ, 9:6b; τὰ τέκνα τῆς σαρκὸς, 9:8). The syntax obfuscates which of σπέρμα Ἀβραὰμ and πάντες τέκνα in 9:7a is restrictive, and scholars are not completely agreed. Paul's point is taken either way, and neither option greatly affects his meaning in 9:6–13, but Schreiner (*Romans*, 405) is probably correct that πάντες in πάντες τέκνα (9:7a) likely parallels the restrictive sense of that in πάντες οἱ ἐξ Ἰσραὴλ in 9:6b, creating an A/B//B′/A′ structure. This would make σπέρμα Ἀβραὰμ restrictive and πάντες τέκνα less restrictive (i.e., "and Abraham's descendants, neither are they all his children"; cf. the NRSV gloss, "Not all of Abraham's children are his true descendants").

3. Or "from one instance of marital intimacy" (literally, "from a single marriage bed").

said to her, "The elder will serve the younger"; [13]it is even written, "Jacob I loved, but Esau I hated"!

Romans 9:6–13

This chapter covers Romans 9:6–13, wherein Paul articulates the concern regarding whether God has broken faith with his people. On my reading, Paul repudiates the notion that God has rejected Israel, justifiably or no. Instead, he begins 9:6–29 by expanding upon God's record of faithfulness toward his people, a faithfulness on which their existence and identity is predicated (and therefore remains in effect so long as they exist). On examination, then, it would seem to be a misreading of Paul to think that he here presents either Israel or God as rejecting the other (since it is not until 9:14 that the issue of rejection shows its face) or to think that Paul is here unpacking the nature, character, or scope of election (since the focus is on the relevance of God's actions within Israel's history for the present situation). Rather, given the context of what (most of) national Israel's rejection of Paul's gospel seemingly implies about God's faithfulness, Paul's more modest opening point in 9:6–13 is that God's faithfulness has never been and *therefore is not now* conditional based on Israel's actions.

INTRODUCTION TO ROMANS 9:6–13

Romans 9:6–13 is the opening pericope of 9:6–29. Paul begins by rejecting an imaginary interlocutor's challenge, saying in 9:6a, "Now, it is not as though God's word has failed." This statement is the thesis for both 9:6–29 and Romans 9–11 as a whole, wherein "word" refers to God's promise(s) to Israel from 9:4–5.[4] The interlocutor's challenge expresses the concern that, according to Paul, unbelieving Jews' rejection of Christ and the gospel has excluded them from participation in Abraham's covenantal inheritance. The interlocutor reckons that, since these were promised specifically to them, it would stand to reason that national Israel's rejection of the gospel could only result first from their baseless rejection by God! If true, this would have farreaching implications for what Paul has said in Romans 1–8, since "if the gospel of God's righteousness is the gospel of God's faithfulness, does not what appear to be God's

---

4. Standouts are Sanday and Headlam, *Epistle*, 2:240, who interpret ὁ λόγος τοῦ θεοῦ as the "declared purpose of God" generally (cf. 9:12); and Cranfield, *Romans*, 2:472–73, who takes this phrase as the gospel in its entirety.

passing over of Israel cast doubt on Paul's message as a whole?"[5] Thus Paul's thesis for both 9:6-29 and chapters 9-11 is that national Israel's present circumstances, resulting from—or at least related to—their rejection of the gospel, does not prove God unfaithful (9:6a).[6]

Paul begins supporting this thesis with a pair of proofs, which creates a parallelism within the logic of the pericope. The first proof is that of Isaac and Ishmael in Romans 9:6b-9, introduced by an explanatory γὰρ. Verses 6b-7a ("neither are all those from Israel Israel, nor is it the case that Abraham's descendants are all of his children") are synonymously parallel statements that contrastively emphasize the main point of the first proof in 9:7b ("It is through Isaac..."). Paul further expands and supports this proof in verses 8-9.

Paul's second proof in Romans 9:10-13 is introduced by οὐ μόνον δέ ἀλλὰ καὶ, indicating the point of 9:10-13 is related—though not necessarily identical—to that of 9:6b-9 (i.e., that it makes an additional complementary point). The slightly awkward grammar builds to both halves of the main point, namely, the examples of Jacob and Esau in 9:12b ("...it was said to her...," the ultimate subject of the explanatory γὰρ beginning 9:11) and of the nations for which they were eponymous in 9:13, the two being conjoined by the coordinating conjunction καθώς.[7]

---

5. Dunn, *Romans 9-16*, 546; cf. Lenski, *Interpretation*, 590.
6. Note that this does not imply that I read Paul as identifying national Israel's rejection of his gospel as their rejection of God.
7. For general agreement on this structure, see Lenski, *Interpretation*, 599; Murray, *Epistle*, 2:12; Cranfield, *Romans*, 2:476; Käsemann, *Commentary*, 261; Dunn, *Romans 9-16*, 538; Moo, *Epistle*, 574; Wright, *Letter*, 637.

The taxonomy employed in this and similar diagrams in this study for analyzing the structure of the text is adopted from the helpful discussion in Peter Cotterell and Max Turner, *Linguistics and Biblical Interpretation* (Downers Grove, IL: InterVarsity, 1989), esp. pp. 188-229. Their categories for dissecting discourse are divided broadly into kernels (i.e., lexemes, clauses, or propositions/statements) that are equal in weight ("Addition Relations") and sets of kernels that are arranged hierarchically, with one kernel being (relatively) independent and the other(s) dependent in some fashion ("Support-HEAD Relations"). In the latter case, the CAPITALIZED feature is the logically and structurally dominant kernel, while the subordinate feature is the Support (ad loc. 208-216). As done here, a set of kernels may be laid out in alignment and their relationship graphically diagrammed, e.g., by the use of lines that form a tree or flowchart. Then those sets of kernels may be further diagrammed, one in relation to the others, to produce the flow of, e.g., a pericope. The degree of atomism to which this is carried out is left at the interpreter's discretion. It makes most sense for this study that the diagrams operate largely on the level of whole clauses, since the pericopes of Rom 9:6-29 are argumentative in nature and so much of their structures devolve into sets of relatively independent and subordinate

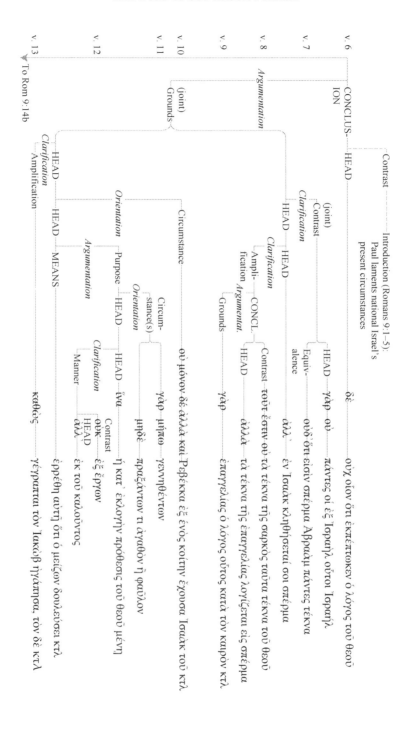

Fig. 1: Structural Analysis of Romans 9:6–13

This analysis displays how the preparatory introduction of Romans 9:1-5 is logically subordinate to this first pericope, providing a contrasting point to the dominant idea for 9:9-13, namely, the thesis in 9:6a. Most basically, Paul's logic is to *Argue* this CONCLUSION (9:6a) by appealing to both the first Grounds that Abraham's descendants are called in Isaac (9:7b, in Contrast to the idea that God's people and national Israel are synonymous, 9:6b-7a), and also to the second Grounds that Esau was to serve Jacob (9:12) along with the further *Clarification* provided by the Amplification that God has loved "Jacob" and hated "Esau" (9:13; the former half of 9:12 is further *Argued* on the basis that God's Purpose in 9:11b was to base his choice upon himself as the one who calls). The thesis successfully defended to this point, Paul's logic next points down to the pericope of 9:14-18, where a further challenge awaits.

Paul cites Scripture at the key point in each of his proofs (9:7b, 12-13). To make more manageable the breadth of material, it is best first to take the proofs in turn. And since 9:6-9 first quote Genesis 21:12 (Rom 9:7b) and then enlist further support from Genesis 18:14 (Rom 9:9), an examination of these biblical traditions in their original contexts is the proper place to begin.

GENESIS 18:14 AND 21:12 IN ROMANS 9:6-9

GENESIS 21:12 IN ITS ORIGINAL CONTEXT

As part of the Abrahamic covenant in Genesis 15, God promises to Abraham (Abram) a covenantal heir and innumerable descendants (15:2-5). In the succeeding episode, Abraham and Sarah (Sarai) attempt to fulfill God's promise by their own efforts (16:1-4a), resulting in Ishmael's birth and enmity within Abraham's household (16:4b-6).

---

clauses. The analyses in this study are largely critical and dictated by syntax, but kernel analysis is always subjective to a degree. E.g., Cotterell and Turner discuss how the difference between the Means-RESULT and MEANS-Purpose relations is one of emphasis (ad loc., 210-11). For the diagrams in this study, the dominant (relatively independent) clause (HEAD) has a line extending from it, with the line from subordinate clauses (Supports) intersecting its HEAD at a right angle; e.g., in fig. 1, the set of Rom 9:6b-7a being Support for the head of 9:7b, or again the set of 9:8-9 being Support in a lesser role (*Clarification*, minor in comparison to the main argumentative point of 9:6b-7a together) to 9:7b. For those clauses that pair together in an equivalent relation, the lines extending from them are brought to converge graphically by diagonal lines; then they as a set are related to the next most important element in the structure of Paul's language—e.g., in fig. 1, 9:6b-7a being held together, in parallel, as an element relating then to 9:7b.

Although God promises not to abandon Hagar and Ishmael (16:7–14), God's confirmation of the Abrahamic covenant in Genesis 17 (with the sign of circumcision, 17:9–14) is bracketed by a double repetition (17:1–8, 15–21) of his promise of Isaac as Abraham's heir, stating, "Concerning Ishmael, I have heard you: Behold, I will bless him by making him fruitful and exceedingly numerous. He will father twelve princes, and I shall make him into a great nation. However, my covenant I will establish with Isaac, whom Sarah will birth [ילד] to you at the appointed time, this time next year'" (17:20–21).

Finally, Isaac is indeed born in Genesis 21:1–7, in accordance with God's covenantal promise (21:1; cf. 18:10, 14). The entire scene (in addition to Isaac's annunciation scene in 18:1–15) establishes Isaac's birth as climactic and provides him with a special status over against Ishmael, whose birth received but a brief annunciation and a perfunctory report (16:4, 15).[8] However, the early occurrence of the Leitwort ילד (21:2; cf. vv. 3 [2x], 5, 7–9, 14–16) again raises in Genesis 21 the question of who is Abraham's heir. This is further underscored by the syntax of 21:3, wherein Abraham names (קרא; cf. 21:12) "his son, who was born to him— that is, whom Sarah bore him—Isaac." The question of the sons' respective statuses is finally addressed in the subsequent scene in 21:8–14.

The narrator begins by referring to Isaac as "the child" (ילד, 21:8); in contrast, Ishmael is referred to as a "lad" (נער, 21:12, 17 [2x], 18–20). Moreover, Isaac is named, whereas Ishmael remains unnamed as "the son of Hagar the Egyptian, whom she had borne [cf. ילד, Gen 16:15] to Abraham" (21:9). When Sarah catches Ishmael 'Isaac-ing' (מצחק), that is, "playing the role of Isaac" (21:9),[9] she demands, "'Drive out this slave woman and her son, for this son of a slave girl will not inherit with Isaac, with my son'" (21:10). Yet the narrator preserves dramatic tension

8. David W. Cotter, Genesis, Berit Olam (Collegeville, MN: Liturgical, 2003), 135. Cotter further argues (ad loc., 84–85, 135) a chiastic structure to the Abraham cycle; cf. Bruce K. Waltke, Genesis: A Commentary (Grand Rapids: Zondervan, 2001), 20. Genesis 21 stands out as asymmetrical, in contrast to Ishmael's birth (Gen 16), implying that once he is born Isaac's preeminence is incomparable. See further the analysis of temporal markers in Gen 16–21 in J. P. Fokkelman, "Time and Structure of the Abraham Cycle," in New Avenues in the Study of the Old Testament: A Collection of Old Testament Studies, Published on the Occasion of the Fiftieth Anniversary of the Oudtestamentisch Werkgezelschap and the Retirement of Prof. Dr. M. J. Mulder, ed. A. S. van der Woude (Leiden: Brill, 1989), 96–109, esp. p. 102.
9. Gordon J. Wenham, Genesis 16–50, WBC 2 (Waco, TX: Word Books, 1994), 82. He notes the piel of צחק implies Sarah's alarm stems from Ishmael either disdaining or, worse, presuming to supplant Isaac.

by ambiguously stating that Abraham was concerned simply about "his son," without specifying Isaac or Ishmael (21:11).[10]

In Genesis 21:12, God first directs Abraham to obey Sarah in exiling Hagar and Ishmael (whereas Abraham's "obedience" in 16:2 was rooted in misguided human initiative, here it is God's command). Continuing on, he finally resolves the narrative tension regarding Abraham's heir by explaining his command: "For in Isaac your descendants will be called [קרא] for you." Although the "precise sense of this clause is obscure, [the] general sense is clear"—Isaac is named Abraham's covenantal heir.[11] Sarah is correct in her demand in 21:10, that Ishmael "will not inherit with Isaac, with *my* son," but this happens as a result of God's decree that "the line of promise will be continued through Isaac" rather than her own spiteful designs.[12]

However, Ishmael is not excluded from God's blessing, since he is also promised provision (16:10; 21:18). Likewise, Isaac and Ishmael are not being compared or contrasted in any way. Instead, the crux of the episode is nothing more than the question of whose line will carry the Abrahamic covenant.[13] This is the case because throughout Genesis 15-21 God's covenant to Abraham is intertwined with the expectation of Isaac's birth. Finally in chapter 21, although both Isaac and Ishmael are Abraham's sons, it is only Isaac who is chosen to be blessed by and be

---

10. This tension is reinforced by intertextualities between the births in Gen 16:1-6 and 21:17. Despite God's promise of an heir in 15:2-5, in 16:1 Sarah is paradoxically characterized as a wife unable to produce a child. Likewise, in Gen 16 Hagar is referred to as a maidservant (פחשׁ) but in Gen 21 as a slave woman (אמה), violently contrasting her legal status and self-understanding as a second wife in 16:2-3. Victor P. Hamilton, *The Book of Genesis Chapters 18-50*, NICOT (Grand Rapids: Eerdmans, 1995), 80. Athalya Brenner argues that Gen 16:6 defines Hagar in terms of Sarah, to whom she is answerable, without enjoying even the limited benefits of the "legally [binding] status" as Abraham's concubine. Brenner, "Female Social Behaviour: Two Descriptive Patterns Within the 'Birth of the Hero' Paradigm," VT 36 (1986): 260.

11. Wenham, *Genesis 16-50*, 83; cf. Claus Westermann, *Genesis 12-36: A Commentary* (trans. J.J. Scullion; Minneapolis: Augsburg Publishing House, 1985), 340.

12. Hamilton, *Genesis 18-50*, 81.

13. Scholars differ to an extent on the degree to which this covenantal heritage is vocational, but the calling to be God's people is not here at all equated with salvation, whether or not the term *election* is used as a label. So, too, this episode is not focused upon and implies very little if anything about the biblical doctrine of election as such, since the focus is rather upon God's the unconventional manner in which God's activity affirms his relationship with Abraham's family. In the Bible—and arguably in early Judaism(s), as well—*election* is not a concept to argue *for* but rather to argue *from*.

a blessing to the nations (12:3). Because of Isaac's connection to God's promise to Abraham (cf. 18:10, 14)—and without Ishmael's worth or provision being a factor—God tells Abraham that Isaac is to be named his covenantal heir. Therefore, in its original context, Genesis 21:12 answers the primary question of the episode by climactically declaring that God selected Isaac to carry forward Abraham's covenantal inheritance. That the principle substantiated by this declaration has to do with God's faithfulness to Abraham's family is clear when it is recalled that Genesis 21 proves and presumes prior familiarity with its antecedent in the first half of chapter 18.

The strengths of this reading are that it is faithful to the text (particularly to the Hebrew, but to the Greek of the LXX as well) and that it is parsimonious in that it does not require Paul to hold some other speculative reading. As mentioned in chapter 1, the ideal would be to confirm this as a shared contemporary reading by its occurrence in other early Jewish traditions; this would create space in which Paul could be located as a representative Second Temple Jewish interpreter. However, also as mentioned there, there are unfortunately no such relevant parallel Second Temple references to Genesis 21:12 to use for comparison. References in the rabbis are the closest thing available.[14] To be sure, such rabbinic usage may attest interpretive traditions contemporary to Paul and his peers. But since this cannot be determined either way, rabbinic witnesses are best taken as suggestive.

Regarding (potentially) relevant rabbinic witnesses: The Tosefta depicts the choice of Isaac in terms of Ishmael's wickedness and Sarah's concern to keep Isaac from impious influences (*t. Soṭah* 5.12). The identity of Abraham's covenantal heirs is debated in the Palestinian Talmud,

---

14. Because Abasciano concludes that Gen 21:12 is emblematic of its wider context (partly comprising Gen 18–19), the central concern of which he sees as the (narrative application of the) theological principle or doctrine of election, he finds relevant references to Gen 21:12 regarding Abraham's merit over against Ishmael and Esau, as in *Jub.* 15:30–32 (*Romans 9.1–9*, 170–73). But as just demonstrated, Abasciano's criterion for selection is based on a false premise. Likewise, there are numerous references to Gen 21:12 in early Jewish and rabbinic material that are equally irrelevant: Gen 21:12 is often cited in praise of the character of one or both of Abraham or Sarah (Philo, *Alleg. Interp.* 3.87; *Tanḥ. Gen.* 4.10; 6.1; *Gen. Rab.* 47.1; 52.5; *Lev. Rab.* 4.5; *Pesiq. Rab Kah.* 14.2; *b. Meg.* 14a). Another set of traditions uses Gen 21:12 in the interpretation of the Aqedah in Genesis 22 (*y. Beṣah* 2.4; *Tanḥ. Gen.* 4.46; *Pesiq. Rab Kah.* 23.9; *Midr. Pss.* 29.1; 119.3; *S. Eli. Zut.* 145; *Pesiq. Rab.* 40.6). Still other sources use Gen 21:12 to interpret various biblical texts, e.g., *b. Sanh.* 69b in deciphering Abraham's genealogy in Gen 11:27; *Pesiq. Rab.* 32.2 on Isa 54:11; *Midr. Prov.* 108 on Gen 16:5.

suggesting that the preposition in ביצחק in Gen 21:12 refers to only a "portion" of Abraham's descendants (*y. Ned.* 3.8). Ishmael's wickedness is again the reason for his exclusion in the Targum on 21:12 (so also *Tanḥ. Gen.* 6.1). The debate over the identity of Abraham's covenantal heirs is again articulated in *Genesis Rabbah* 56.8 (cf. *Midr. Pss.* 105.1). Finally, in its engagement on the same issue, the Babylonian Talmud understands the exclusion of both Ishmael and Esau on the basis of the "portion" in Genesis 21:12 (*b. Ned.* 31a; *b. Sanh.* 59b).

Two interpretive trends emerge here. First, for the rabbis in all cases God's trustworthiness is taken for granted and left untouched in this Scripture, and is then axiomatically used in discussing Israel's inherent moral worth (for them, the crucial factor in God's choice; cf. *Tg. Ps.-J.*; *Tanḥ. Gen.* 6.1). Secondarily, Genesis 21:12 evinces an understanding of the selectivity (which is *not* to say conditionality) of participation in Israel's covenantal heritage (*y. Ned.* 3.8; *Gen. Rab.* 56.8; *Midr. Pss.* 105.1; *b. Ned.* 31a; *b. Sanh.* 59b).

This means that if Paul's logic in Romans 9 is concurrent with the above contextual interpretation of Genesis 21:12, then its use by Paul is basically in harmony with available early Jewish interpretations. He is going to agree with Scripture and the rabbis that nationality is not entirely determinative in covenantal participation, and most fundamentally that covenant is predicated upon and entirely presupposes God's faithfulness. However, after visiting Genesis 18:14, we shall see how Paul is not citing this tradition in order to discuss the character of God's election (as the rabbis sometimes do). Also, he is unique (without trying to "correct" false Jewish understanding) in applying the axiom of God's historical trustworthiness to an analysis of God's present relationship with Israel in light of a specific contemporary event—namely, unbelieving Jews' rejection of the gospel.

GENESIS 18:14 IN ITS ORIGINAL CONTEXT

Genesis 18:14 belongs to a larger literary unit encompassing Genesis 18–19.[15] Following Abraham's visitation by God and two accompanying angels in 18:1–15, God reveals his plan for Sodom and Gomorrah in 18:16–36. The succeeding chapter relates Lot's visitation by the two angelic

---

15. Wenham, *Genesis 16–50*, 40 (cf. pp. 43–44).

visitors and the destruction of Sodom (19:1–29), and the remainder of Lot's story (19:30–38).[16]

In Genesis 17 God had appeared to Abraham to confirm their covenant and his promise of an heir. In 17:15–22, God pronounced that Abraham's heir would come through withered Sarah. In response, Abraham fell on his face laughing (צחק, 17:17). Appropriately, God states Abraham's son will be called (קרא, cf. Gen 21:12) Isaac, with whom he will "establish my covenant … an eternal covenant for his descendants after him" (17:19; cf. 17:21).

With this setup, the next episode in Genesis 18:1–15 is Isaac's annunciation.[17] The proleptic summary in 18:1 reveals to the audience that one of Abraham's three visitors is God, which at first is unknown to him. After he blesses his visitors with exemplary ancient Near Eastern hospitality (18:2–8), his expectation that they will pick up and continue on their way is captured by the resumptive *wayyiqtol* in 18:9 (as per אחר תעברו in his invitation in 18:5; cf. אל־נא תעבר, 18:3). But instead, the visitors remain to bless Abraham.

In 18:10 their spokesman—namely God (explicitly identified in 18:13)—promises, "I shall certainly return to you in due season, and *hinneh* Sarah, your wife, will have a son." Sarah's (surprised? incredulous?) secret laughter in 18:12 affords God an opportunity to repeat and thereby doubly affirm his promise in 18:14.[18] Finally, his blunt rebuke in 18:15 abruptly concludes the episode and clinches the debate: Sarah will indeed have a son, who will be called Isaac.

The narrative and its use of dialogue goes out of the way to portray God's annunciation in Genesis 18:14, especially, as a divine promise.

---

16. Gen 18–19 has its own overall theme, likely to do with the effect upon the wider world of God's relationship with Abraham and Lot, the two members of another set of "brothers" (cf. אח, 13:8, 11; 14:12–14, 16), in virtue of their respective character and intimacy with him. But while wider context must always be considered, the theme of the larger unit is not determinative for the meaning of the discrete episode in Gen 18:1–15.

17. James G. Williams, following Robert Alter, specifically labels this a "promise to barren wife" annunciation biblical type-scene (cf. Judg 13:2–24; 2 Kgs 4:8–17). Williams, "The Beautiful and the Barren: Conventions in Biblical Type-Scenes," *JSOT* 17 (1980): 110.

18. LXX Gen 18:10 adds "at the appointed time" (τὸν καιρὸν τοῦτον, from Hebr למועד in v. 14). Its absence in the original is only reflected by a difference in prepositions (κατά, v. 10; εἰς, v. 14); cf. Wenham, *Genesis 16–50*, 49. Hamilton's sensible suggestion (*Genesis 18–50*, 14) is that the addition was meant to reinforce the certainty of Sarah's promised conception.

God's identity gradually unfolds to Abraham, in his speaking with "ir-resistible power and authority"[19] the promise from the immediately preceding theophany (18:10), being named Yhwh by both the narrator and himself (18:13-14), and knowing of Sarah's secret laughter (18:13). Fittingly, this identity underscores the nature of 18:14. As Gordon Wenham comments, "The promise of a son implies that the speaker is a divine messenger; the fact that he can discern Sarah's reactions without seeing her proves his status and guarantees his message."[20] Additionally, the unconventional character of Isaac's annunciation—Sarah's indirect reception, her being postmenopausal, and its uniquely long postpone-ment "filled with seemingly unrelated episodes"—further emphasizes "the difficult—indeed, miraculous—nature of the fulfillment."[21]

The proleptic summary to Isaac's birth narrative (Gen 21:1-7) in 21:1 also seizes upon 18:14, taking its fulfillment as the fulfillment of a prom-ise (poetically emphasized through synonymous parallelism): "Yhwh visited [cf. שוב(אשוב), 18:10, 14] Sarah just as he said; Yhwh did for Sarah just what he promised."[22] And in 18:14 God echoes himself from 17:21, that Sarah would birth Isaac "at the appointed time [למועד, cf. 18:14], this time next year." Accordingly, 21:2 reports that Isaac was indeed born למועד אשר־דבר אתו אלהים.[23] Likewise, God's naming of Isaac in 17:19 and Sarah's laughter in 18:12 are both fulfilled in 21:3, 6; even Sarah's wonder-ment in 18:12 is answered in 21:7.[24]

Such various threads of God's covenantal promise in Genesis 17 and its fulfillment in 21:1-7—the emphasis on God's identity as the one prom-ising, the miraculous nature of its fulfillment, the manner of its fulfill-ment at the proper time and by Isaac's naming—together pass through the bottleneck of 18:14, granting it a thematic centrality for chapters 17-21. Thus, the importance of 18:14 is such that its fulfillment is coexten-sive with the fulfillment of the covenant. In this, by making the promise in person God hangs his fidelity directly upon its fulfillment.

19. Walter Brueggemann, "'Impossibility' and Epistemology in the Faith Tradition of Abraham and Sarah (Gen 18:1-15)," ZAW 94 (1982): 618.
20. Genesis 16-50, 48; see also Hamilton, Genesis 18-50, 12, on God's use of שוב in 18:14.
21. Robert Alter, Genesis: A Translation and Commentary (New York: W.W. Norton, 1996), 78-79.
22. Cf. Gen. Rab. 53.5. See Wenham, Genesis 16-50, 80; Hamilton, Genesis 18-50, 73n5 on the significance of פקד in 21:1.
23. Cf. Wenham, Genesis 16-50, 49; Hamilton, Genesis 18-50, 14.
24. Alter, Genesis, 98.

Therefore, the narrative portrays Isaac's eventual birth as a fulfillment of the promise of 18:14. By giving Isaac to Sarah, God indisputably demonstrates his faithfulness to Abraham. In its original context—in marking out Isaac as the child of promise, the one in whom God's covenantal promise will be kept and through whom it will continue—God's words to Abraham in Genesis 18:14 demonstrate to Abraham the security of his covenantal relationship. He knows God's faithfulness to his word.

One last time it deserves mention that there are no Second Temple uses of Genesis 18:14 that are concerned with such interpretation it its original context, or that relevantly parallel Paul's usage.[25] The single relevant Second Temple tradition is *Testament of Abraham 8:6*, which is perhaps the earliest of many texts that identify Genesis 18:10 as God's promise—which is then identified as being fulfilled in Genesis 21:12. However, this impulse is likewise reflected in numerous rabbinic traditions.[26] Antedating that, Philo appeals to Genesis 18:10 in reference to the miraculous—almost transcendent (Platonic?)—nature of Isaac's birth (*Names* 47; *Abraham* 25). If considered a substantial grouping, then these data agree upon a well-recognized trajectory of promise fulfillment running from Genesis 18:10, 14 through to 21:1–7, 12 (*T. Ab.* 8:6; *Tanḥ.* 4.30; 4.36; *Gen. Rab.* 53.1; *Midr. Pss.* 80.7; *Pesiq. Rab.* 42.2). Further, expressions of this theme often highlight the miracle and importance of Isaac's birth

---

25. Again, because Abasciano concludes that Gen 18:10, 14 represent all of Gen 18–19, whose theme is God's goodness in the face of his people's/human suffering in virtue of the surety of his promise, he finds relevant various references in *Jub.* 16:16–18; *Abraham* 127, 142–143; *4 Ezra* 7:106, etc. (*Romans 9.1–9*, 170–73). But Abasciano's means of determining relevant parallels presumes an important misunderstanding of Gen 18:14. Philo does reference 18:10, but in a discussion on virtue Philo cites God's gift of Isaac in support of a virtuous characterization of Sarah (*Migration* 22). Irrelevant rabbinic sources (because they are not concerned with Gen 18:14 in its original context) include, e.g., *Tanḥ. Gen.* 4.20 in identifying Abraham's guests in Gen 18:2; *Tanḥ. Lev.* 2.10 on a discussion of peace offerings; *Pesiq. Rab.* 6.5 on extrapolating the month of Isaac's birth. Such a catalogue as that provided here and in footnote 13 above concerning Gen 21:12 could (but will not) be provided for each of the biblical traditions of which Paul makes use in Rom 9:6–29. These two examples have been provided only to illustrate the dearth of *relevant* contemporary or near contemporary parallels. As stated in chapter 1, study of Paul's argument is in many ways genuinely limited to analyses of the biblical and Pauline traditions, and wide-ranging thematic interests should not be allowed to introduce irrelevant voices into the conversation.
26. Cf. *Tanḥ.* 4.30, 36; *Gen. Rab.* 53.1; 53.2 (quoting also Num 23:18, "God is not a man that he should lie"); *Midr. Pss.* 13.1; 80.7; *Pesiq. Rab.* 42.2; and *Eccl. Rab.* 3.15 (which further expects a renewal of creation, resurrection of the dead, Zion's royal rule, and healing of the blind—of God's goodness that will be more fully realized in the eschatological "Messianic future").

as God's fulfillment of his covenant with Abraham (*Names* 47; *Abraham* 25; *Gen. Rab.* 53.2; and *Eccl. Rab.* 3.15).

We must grant the limited nature of this data. But with that said, it seems that when Paul makes use of Genesis 18:14 in reference to God's promise of upholding the Abrahamic covenant in virtue of his own faithfulness, it seems that his is likely a standard contemporary understanding of 18:14 within its original context. However, there is no evidence that other earlier Jewish interpreters combined this reflection on the nature of Isaac's birth as a promise fulfilled with discussion on the identity of Abraham's covenantal heirs—let alone in light of the Christ event (cf. *Eccl. Rab.* 3.15)—as Paul does in Romans 9:6b-9.

PAUL'S USE OF GENESIS 21:12 AND 18:14 IN ROMANS

By using Genesis 21:12 and 18:14 in the first proof of Romans 9:6-13, Paul makes use of a theological point (seen by many Romans scholars) that is implicit in the narrative of Genesis 17-21: it was never the case that all who could claim physical descent from Abraham were his covenantal heirs. This is seen in the example of Isaac and Ishmael, since both were Abraham's children (cf. τέκνον, Rom 9:7a) but God called (κληθήσεταί, Gen 21:12 = Rom 9:7b) Abraham's heirs only through Isaac. Paul's rationale for this understanding is evinced by his use of Genesis 18:14 and its inherent connection to Genesis 21:12: God has discretion in calling Abraham's heirs precisely because their calling is rooted in his promise to begin with. The operative principle is that Isaac's annunciation and the covenant in Genesis 17-21 both depend upon God's promise, and thus in a sense are coextensive. Isaac is not chosen over Ishmael because his physical descent is somehow privileged. Rather, insofar as the covenant is founded on God's faithfulness and promise, it is precisely because Isaac is the child of God's promise that it is through him God calls Abraham's covenantal heirs.

However, contrary to essentially all critical scholarship on Romans, what needs to be taken away from the above examinations is this: Paul is *not* making the point that God's people are constituted by his promise (rather than familial descent). Rather, this is the accepted biblical point that Paul is making use *of*. That God freely forms his covenantal people is not Paul's argument, but merely his understanding of Israel's calling, which he presupposes when applying Genesis 21:12 and 18:14 to present circumstances. Given his use of Scripture so far in Romans 9:6-13, *that* application is the topic of Paul's argument.

Accordingly, in Romans 9:6b–9, Paul does indeed quote Genesis 21:12 in Romans 9:7b[27] to argue that, because not all of Abraham's physical descendants are called as his covenantal heirs, national Israel's rejection of the gospel does not prove God unfaithful.[28] The LXX occurrence of καλέω is significant for Paul's use of Genesis 21:12 because, in both Jewish thought and in Romans, *calling* is an elective term referring to an act of creation,[29] one that in this instance creates the relationship between God and his people.[30] Granted that salvation and God's redemptive activity in human history are ultimately inseparable, nevertheless it is critical to note how in Romans 9:6b–7a national Israel is not being excluded from salvation any more than in Genesis 17–21 Ishmael was excluded from the blessings brought into the world by Israel.[31] Instead, Paul is speaking of God's selectivity in choosing through whom his covenantal purposes will continue. As N. T. Wright describes:

> God always intended that only some of Abraham's descendants would carry forward [the Messiah's redemptive rule]. ... Most of Paul's Jewish contemporaries would have been happy with this understanding of the patriarchal narratives; it was his [additional] application of the same principle to [present circumstances] that would have been controversial.[32]

This should not be confused with the idea of Paul claiming that *God* is rejecting some of Abraham's descendants. Paul's opening point is only that their estrangement from the covenantal promises is compatible with the enduring certainty of those promises.

---

27. Rom 9:7b follows LXX Gen 21:12 verbatim, which faithfully reflects the MT.
28. Brian Abasciano privately expressed to me the position that Paul's argument is rather that God's rejection of national Israel (for their unfaithfulness in rejecting the gospel) is given, but does not prove God unfaithful, citing in Rom 9:1–5 their (presumably imposed) exclusion from Christ. I take a more reserved approach, taking 9:1–5 as referring to their alienation from Christ—agency is indeterminate at this point. Further, I insist that the argument of 9:6–29 unfolds to establish that God has not been unfaithful precisely because he has *not* rejected national Israel, but merely judged them for their rejection of his gospel (see chapters 4 and 5 below).
29. Byrne, *Romans*, 273.
30. So Moo, *Epistle*, 582n59; cf. Schreiner, *Romans*, 499–500.
31. Cranfield correctly observes, "The Genesis narrative indicates explicitly God's care for Ishmael (cf. Gen 21.13, 17–21: also 16.10–14; 17.20). So we must not read into Paul's argument any suggestion that Ishmael, because he is not chosen to play a positive part in the accomplishment of God's special purpose, is therefore excluded from the embrace of God's mercy" (*Romans*, 2:475).
32. N. T. Wright, *Letter*, 635.

And lest his audience misunderstand, in 9:8–9 Paul clarifies (τοῦτ' ἔστιν, v. 8) he is not merely speaking of physical descent from Isaac in place of physical descent from Abraham. He introduces the citation in verse 9 by syntactically emphasizing his understanding of Genesis 18:14 as a promise, as seen in the forward placement of ἐπαγγελίας.[33]

MT Gen 18:14	LXX Gen 18:14	Rom 9:9
לַמּוֹעֵד	<u>εἰς τὸν καιρὸν τοῦτον</u>	<u>κατὰ</u> τὸν καιρὸν τοῦτον
אָשׁוּב אֵלֶיךָ	<u>ἀναστρέψω πρὸς σὲ</u>	<u>ἐλεύσομαι</u>
כָּעֵת	εἰς ὥρας	
חַיָּה וּלְשָׂרָה בֵן	καὶ ἔσται τῇ Σαρρα υἱός	καὶ ἔσται τῇ Σαρρα υἱός

Paul adapts his citation by substituting ἔρχομαι for ἀναστέφω, which (due to semantic drift) referred by the first century to personal conduct (e.g., 1 Cor 1:12; cf. Eph 2:3; 1 Tim 3:15; Heb 10:33; 13:18; 1 Pet 1:17; 2 Pet 2:18), and by dropping the second emphatic temporal clause εἰς ὥρας, likely to streamline the citation for his purposes.[34] Paul means to directly

---

33. Cf. Lenski, *Interpretation*, 555; Dunn, *Romans 9–16*, 2:596, 598; Wright, *Letter*, 636, etc.

34. See Christopher Stanley, *Paul and the Language of Scripture: Citation Techniques in the Pauline Epistles and Contemporary Literature* (Cambridge: Cambridge University Press, 1992), 104. Stanley's exhaustive study of Paul and his contemporaries' citation technique proves that Paul's citation method (including adaptations) is nearly always consistent with typical ancient/first-century citation technique.
   Paul's adaptation here of Gen 18:14 is for the sake of rhetorical smoothing (ibid., 343), made for the typical reason of ensuring that the quotation "communicates the precise point that the later author wanted to make" (ibid., 347). Paul's substitution of ἔρχομαι, when he could have chosen the contemporary synonym ὑποστρέφω (cf. Gal 1:17; or ἐπιστρέφω, cf. Gal 4:9) may indicate his intention to dehistoricize Genesis 18:14, thereby underscoring the miracle of Isaac's birth and/or first-century eschatological overtones (Dunn, *Romans 9–16*, 541; Stanley, *Paul*, 104). Regarding the change of εἰς to κατὰ, Stanley (*Paul*, 104) suggests that "no clear exegetical motive for the change can be identified." Abasciano (*Romans 9.1–9*, 155–56) contradicts Stanley, defaulting to the view that 9:9 is a composite citation of Gen 18:10 and 14 based on the presence of κατὰ in LXX Gen 18:10. However, the verbal similarities between this verse and Rom 9:9 are relatively slight otherwise, esp. in comparison with the similarity to LXX Gen 18:14. Abasciano further justifies his move only in that the pair of verses somehow "captures the essence of Gen. 18.1–15 most vividly" (ad loc., 156), even though it seems Gen 18:14 alone would suffice. If Paul intends a composite citation, then it seems that he not unreasonably views the latter as the definitive reiteration of the former (supposing that Abasciano is correct about the source of κατὰ). Since either case allows for the sound interpretation of Rom 9:6b–9, the point is hardly worth arguing—except that in, e.g., Abasciano's reading the dual

state that physical descent—being τὰ τέκνα τῆς σαρκὸς (9:8)—from either Abraham *or* Isaac is not the relevant factor in determining who are Abraham's covenantal heirs (σπέρμα, 9:7b, 8b), precisely because it was not the relevant factor in God's selection of Isaac. Rather, as with Isaac, the relevant factor lies in being children of promise (τὰ τέκνα τῆς ἐπαγγελίας, 9:8b). Moreover, Paul's identification of τὰ τέκνα τῆς ἐπαγγελίας /σπέρμα with "children of God" (τέκνα τοῦ θεοῦ, 9:8) highlights his christocentric redefinition of the scriptural promise, since he understands Jesus to be God's Son (Rom 1:3) and Abraham's ultimate covenantal heir (Rom 9:5).

Thus, Paul's citation of Genesis 18:14 in Romans 9:8-9 clarifies contrasting sides of the same point: Because Jesus is Abraham's covenantal heir par excellence, it is now in relation to him that status as "children of promise" is determined (9:8b-9). Correspondingly, because Isaac was the child of promise, physical descent even for national Israel does *not* determine whether they are Abraham's covenantal heirs (9:8a, 9). Thus Paul can quote Genesis 21:12 in Romans 9:7b to say that not all of Abraham's children are his covenantal heirs, because not all were children of promise. And coming to the present situation of national Israel's rejection of the gospel, this especially holds true since they do not identify themselves with Christ, the climactic "child of promise."

So far in this pericope, through his use of Genesis 21:12 and 18:14 in his first proof (Rom 9:6b-9), Paul's supports his thesis (9:6a) is in two ways: As with Isaac and Ishmael, it is not presently the case that "all those from Israel" participate in the blessing of carrying forward Abraham's covenantal inheritance—and this does not in any way undercut the fact of that blessing being a promise, since the promise is fundamentally rooted in none other than the character of the God who has made it. To substantiate this (still referencing Isaac), it is being a child of promise instead of physical descent that is the relevant factor in being Abraham's covenantal heir. Such a double display of constancy between patriarchal and present times cannot be said to prove unfaithfulness on God's part, and interpreted otherwise it wrongly divides the nature of the promise from God's own character. So understood, unbelieving Jews' rejection of the gospel does not signal a failure of God's promise. Subsequent to this, in Romans 9:10-13 Paul goes on to offer a second

---

citation is necessary to motivate reading Rom 9:9 as a holistic citation of the election theology of Gen 18-19.

proof that both reiterates and buttresses that of 9:6b–9. Paul first cites
Genesis 25:23 in 9:12, and then Malachi 1:2–3 in 9:13.

GENESIS 25:23 AND MALACHI 1:2–3 IN ROMANS 9:10–13

GENESIS 25:23 IN ITS ORIGINAL CONTEXT

Genesis 25:19 begins the *toledoth* of Isaac, and Jacob's birth is recounted
in verses 19–26. Although the episode serves a function within the larger context, it possesses its own meaning. Indeed, the namings of Isaac
in verses 19–20 and 26 form an inclusio around the episode indicating
that "the narrator's … interest is to set the stage and introduce the central characters of the Jacob story."[35] At the outset, Rebekah is barren just
as Sarah had been (Gen 25:21; cf. 16:1–2). Then, when she finally does
conceive in 25:22, her pain and confusion at the turmoil within her—
captured by the nearly unintelligible syntax—compel her to inquire of
God. As concerns the larger Genesis narrative, the import of the episode
lies in the continuance of Abraham's line and the covenant, once again
in the face of barrenness.[36] Yet within verses 19–26, a chiastic structure
centers the episode on God's oracle in verse 23:[37]

---

35. Jonathan Terino, "A Text Linguistic Study of the Jacob Narrative," *VE* 18 (1988): 51.
36. Hamilton, *Genesis 18–50*, 175 correctly observes that although Gen 24 confirmed
there is "no further room for doubt [that Rebekah] is indeed Isaac's wife-to-be and
the future mother of his children," now "everything is called into question. Can a
sterile woman actually … carry on the promised line?"
37. Cotter, *Genesis*, 185. Another cue of the centrality of the oracle/annunciation
may be its atypical displacement from "the period of barrenness to late pregnan-
cy" (Alter, *The Five Books of Moses: A Translation with Commentary* [New York: W. W.
Norton, 2004], 129). For analysis of Gen 25:22–23 as an oracle see Hamilton, *Genesis
18–50*, 177, who compares, e.g., 2 Kgs 8:7–15.

A Isaac's age (vv. 19–20)

    B Rebekah's barrenness, Isaac's intercession (v. 21)

        C Rebekah's conception and the twins' internal struggle (v. 22a)

Annunciation: D Rebekah requests and God grants an oracle (vv. 22b–23)

        C′ Completion of Rebekah's conception and birth of twins (v. 24)

    B′ Jacob and Esau's births and appearances (vv. 25–26a)

A′ Isaac's age (v. 26b)

Fig. 2: Literary Structure of Genesis 25:19–26

In granting her a divine oracle, God reveals to Rebekah the source of her troubles: twins! However, the burden of the oracle is not the fact of their birth but the meaning with which God invests it when he describes the future struggle between Jacob and Esau's descendants.[38] The first line of 25:23b is clear: of the two nations in Rebekah's womb, "one people will be stronger than the other people." The ambiguous syntax of the second line, though, suggests either "The elder will serve the younger" or "The elder, the younger will serve." It is only the ensuing narrative that clarifies which is the case: Jacob both obtains (steals) Esau's birthright and receives the covenantal inheritance. True to God's word, the younger son takes the place of the elder (a recurrent theme in Genesis).

In contrast to Isaac and Ishmael, Isaac's sons are born of the same mother, at the same time, and both according to God's oracle. Still, the episode neither explains nor justifies God's selection of Jacob over Esau; neither is it explained how the history of the two peoples sired by the brothers will play out. Rather, God simply announces that Jacob will have Esau's position as Isaac's heir, so that within the context of Genesis 25:19–26 Jacob's inheritance is determined by nothing more than God's

---

38. The importance of this for biblical Israel's history regarding the nations descended from the brothers extends beyond the context of Genesis. However, the importance for the narrative context of the Isaac cycle and within Genesis is to begin Jacob's character development (with Esau as a foil) as the patriarch from whom Israel draws its name. Cf. Shubert Spero, "Jacob and Esau: The Relationship Reconsidered," *JBQ* 32 (2004): 246.

decree. So even though the episode is more an introduction to the Jacob cycle than a full narrative, 25:23 relates the antepartum circumstance of God's selection of Jacob and clearly states the central point for the episode: that God chose Jacob without external constraint and for reasons as yet known only to himself.

Most early Jewish and rabbinic traditions that reference Genesis 25:23 are not relevant to this study, since rather than being interested in its contextual meaning they use it as a launching point to characterize either the historical Esau or the nation of Edom (sometimes in conjunction with Mal 1:3; see below). Often in later traditions especially, Esau/ Edom stands for Rome or the nations generally, both of which are destined for destruction.[39] Philo does engage the question of God's choice of Jacob, supplying Esau's inherent wickedness as God's reason for selecting Isaac (*Alleg. Interp.* 3.29).[40] *Tanḥuma Exodus* 7.7 stands out in not focusing upon Esau's supposed wickedness; instead, it explains how God selected Jacob exclusively on the basis of his own inclination and for his own purposes, and that no extrinsic reason can be discerned.[41] Apart

---

39. Cf. *Jub.* 19:13-31; 24:3-7; *QG* 5.157; *L.A.B.* 32.5; *Gen. Rab.* 53.7; 65.4; *Pesiq. Rab Kah.* S2.1; *Pirqe R. Eli.* 128; *b. Meg.* 6a; *b. 'Abod. Zar.* 2b. Abasciano also rightly notes how this evaluation is more difficult for *4 Ezra* 3:13-22 in light of Israel's exiled state (*Romans 9.10-13*, 27-28). Uniquely, *Pirqe R. Eli.* 128 attributes Edom's temporal dominance over Israel to Jacob's "profanity" in abasing himself before Esau in Gen 32:4. Also interesting is the interpretation in *Tg. Onq.*, which takes "the greater" to be Rome and "the lesser" to be Judea, and anticipates the "Messianic age" whereupon Rome will be "subjugated" to underdog Judea. Similarly, *Tg. Ps.-J.* conditions the subjugation of Edom on Israel's faithfulness to Torah (whereas most texts see this happening simply in virtue of Israel's being Israel).

40. Wagner notes an interesting reflection of Gen 25:23 in *T. Job* 1:5-6, where Job's second set of children are identified as being of God's people because their mother descends from Jacob, despite his own Edomite ancestry (*Heralds*, 50n21).

41. This tradition further states (in conjunction with a reference to Mal 1:2) that God's love for Jacob is evident in his reversal of primogeniture. Anthony Chadwick Thornhill has argued that 1) the Second Temple Jewish understanding of election is corporate (not individual), i.e., primarily a group who comprised individuals (which is the "lens" trough which individual members viewed themselves) rather than individuals who then constitute a group; 2) election is sometimes soteriological and other times is a description of character and/or covenantal vocation; and 3) Second Temple understandings of the remnant motif create room for and exhibit (besides Paul in Rom 9) instances of discrimation of God's people within the more inclusive category of national Israel, building up to a conscientious but (what he regards as) a warranted use of the expression *true Israel*. Thornhill, *To the Jew First: A Socio-Rhetorical and Biblical-Theological Analysis of the Pauline Teaching of "Election" In Light of Second Temple Jewish Patters of Thought* (PhD diss., Liberty Baptist Theological Seminary, 2012), 3-4; see §§2-5 on pp. 35-237. Regrettably, Thornhill

from Paul's citation in Romans 9, this single reference among all early Jewish literature appears to consider the implications of God's antepartum selection of Jacob, and the two data points reflect a common understanding of Genesis 25:23 within its original context. However, whereas *Tanḥuma* discusses in the abstract the principle of God's choice of Jacob, Paul is applying the precedent wherein that principle is recorded to his present circumstances.

Malachi 1:2–3 in Its Original Context

Malachi closes the Twelve Prophets by addressing disappointment over the apparent failure of "the 'Zion visions' of Second Isaiah [and Third Isaiah], Haggai, and Zechariah and the 'Temple visions' of Ezekiel."[42] The returning remnant's expectations of Israel's glorification, the dawning of the messianic era, and material prosperity "had been aroused but remained unrealized."[43] Persistent Persian rule, pests, and plagues led to depression, discontent, and open expression of doubt in God's faithfulness.[44] However, in a series of six disputations (besides a subsequent epilogue),[45] the prophet completes the thematic message of Haggai, Zechariah, and Malachi (the "HZM corpus") by defending God's

---

invests Paul's use of Gen 21:12 in Rom 9:7 with the meaning of *Jubilees* and *1 En.* 93:5 (wherein *Jacob* was eponymous for a corporate entity) without showing his analysis. In this, he supposes that Paul's concern is election, or at least his discussion is directly relevant to the question of Paul's understanding of election; so also with the use of Gen 25:23 in Rom 9:10–13 (ibid., 253–55).

42. Andrew E. Hill, *Malachi*, AB 25D (New York: Doubleday, 1998), 42, 164–65; cf. Pieter A. Verhoef, *The Books of Haggai and Malachi*, NICOT (Grand Rapids: Eerdmans, 1987), 198–99; Eugene H. Merrill, *Haggai, Zechariah, Malachi: An Exegetical Commentary* (Chicago: Moody, 1994), 378.

43. Beth Glazier-McDonald, *Malachi: The Divine Messenger*, SBLDS 98 (Atlanta: Scholars, 1987), 17.

44. Elie Assis considers that a date after the completion of the temple is the most precise that can be had. "Structure and Meaning in the Book of Malachi," in *Prophecy and the Prophets in Ancient Israel: Proceedings of the Oxford Old Testament Seminar*, ed. John Day, Library of Hebrew Bible/OTS 531 (New York: T&T Clark, 2010), 354–56, 265.

45. Verhoef, *Haggai and Malachi*, 162; Marvin E. Tate, "Questions for Priests and People in Malachi 1:2–2:16," *RevEx* 84 (1987): 392; Douglas Stuart, "Malachi" in *The Minor Prophets: An Exegetical and Expository Commentary, Vol. 3: Zephaniah, Haggai, Zechariah, Malachi*, ed. Thomas McComiskey (Grand Rapids: Baker, 1992), 1245; Hill, *Malachi*, 34; Richard A. Taylor and E. Ray Clendenen, *Haggai, Malachi*, NAC 21A (Nashville: Broadman and Holman, 2004), 218–22 (who prefer the term "hortatory discourse" to "disputation"). D. F. Murray, "The Rhetoric of Disputation," *JSOT* 38 (1987): 111; and J. G. Baldwin, "Mal. 1:11 and the Worship of the Nations in the Old Testament," *TynBul* 23 (1972): 122 especially argue for Mal 1:2–5 as a disputation.

covenantal loyalty (Mal 1:2-5; see below), and by condemning the people for their insincere worship (Mal 2:10-16; cf. Zech 1:4-17) and their corrupt priesthood for turning the people into a "flock for slaughter" (Zech 11:7; cf. Mal 1:6-2:9).[46] Quite likely, the three oracles are thematically linked by a concern with covenant—namely, the people's ideological erosion due to their feelings of having been rejected by God—and relate to God's justness in rewarding the righteous punishing the wicked. On this analysis, Malachi 1:2-5 is focused on the problem of Israel's identity and status in relation to God (and the nations, as especially in the following two oracles).[47]

Malachi 1:2-5 is thus the introductory disputation of the book, and polemicizes against the remnant community's doubt over both "the fact and significance of God's love."[48] Malachi 1:2a begins with the thesis of the disputation: "'I have loved you,' says Yhwh."[49] Then Israel's distrust is captured in their antagonistic response, "How have you loved us?" which "presupposes the denunciation of both election and covenant."[50] Some scholars interpret 1:2b-5 as somewhat petulant, whereby God pleads for Israel's acceptance on the basis of his general history of faithfulness.[51] But the indignant manner in which God frames Israel's response, "Yet you say," indicates a more confrontational tone.

God continues, "'Was not Esau Jacob's brother,' states Yhwh, 'yet I loved Jacob and Esau I hated?'" (Mal 1:2b-3a). *Love* (אהב) in 1:2-3 is ancient Near Eastern covenant language, referring to God's calling and

---

46. Ronald W. Pierce, "A Thematic Development of the Haggai/Zechariah/Malachi Corpus," *JETS* 27 (1984): 401-11; cf. Pierce, "Literary Connectors and a Haggai/Zechariah/Malachi Corpus," *JETS* 27 (1984): 277-89. At the conclusion of the HZM corpus, postexilic Israel is no more faithful than their ancestors just prior to exile (ad loc., 411).

47. Assis, "Structure," 359-63, whose structure is reliant upon the third oracle of 2:10-16 relating to mixed marriages, v. 10 being the prophet quoting the people's anti-particularistic stance. The implication for the setting of Malachi is that although temple had been completed for several years, the people's pre-construction perception and despair persisted and is now asserting itself as an ideology in which they are rejecting the older ideal of covenantal election, making virtue out of necessity (ad loc., 365).

48. Verhoef, *Haggai and Malachi*, 198.

49. Ibid., 195 and Stuart, *Malachi*, 1281-82 note a durative sense of "I love you" is also an appropriate English translation of the perfect of אהב.

50. Verhoef, *Haggai and Malachi*, 198.

51. E.g., Elizabeth Achtemeier, *Nahum-Malachi*, IBC (Atlanta: John Knox, 1986), 176; Verhoef, *Haggai and Malachi*, 198-99; Merrill, *Haggai*, 391; Hill, *Malachi*, 163; Taylor and Clendenen, *Haggai*, 244.

present faithfulness toward Israel. Likewise, God's *hate* (נאשׁ) toward Edom refers to *covenantal* disavowal.[52] It is also clear from 1:3b–5 that the reference to Israel and Edom's eponymous ancestors in 1:2b–3a is not genealogical but relates to God's contemporary stance toward the two "brother" nations.[53] Verse 3b graphically depicts God's covenantal hatred as "directed at the heart of the Edom tradition," Esau's special gift of Mount Seir (cf. Deut 2:4–5).[54] Verse 4 describes the permanence of Edom's ruin, with God (who is named as "Yhwh *Sabaoth*" against them) turning back on Edom the speech pattern of their plans for reconstruction (using the divine certification formula כה אמר יהוה):

כי־תאמר אדום	רשׁשׁנו /	ונשׁוב ונבנה חרבות /
כה אמר יהוה צבאות	המה יבנו /	ואני אהרוס /
וקראו להם	גבול רשׁעה /	והעם אשׁר־זעם יהוה עד־עולם /

Scholars note how Edom's downfall accords with their negative biblical characterization and OT prophecies foretelling their destruction.[55] In contrast to Israel's resettlement under the auspices of a superpower, Edom, who had "taken advantage of Judah's misfortunes … was far worse off," having been ignominiously eroded "at the hands of … Arab semi-nomadic group[s]."[56] God declares Edom will become a byword, called "wicked territory" and "the people with whom Yhwh is forever angry" (Mal 1:4), so that "the permanence of their demise would serve

---

52. This interpretation is almost universally argued by commentators. See e.g., Verhoef, *Haggai and Malachi*, 201; Tate, "Questions," 395; Stuart, *Malachi*, 1283–84; David L. Petersen, *Zechariah 9–14 and Malachi: A Commentary* (Louisville: Westminster John Knox, 1995), 165; Hill, *Malachi*, 166–67. See further Taylor and Clendenen, *Haggai*, 247n26 for a bibliography of the Deuteronomic tradition of God's covenant faithfulness in Malachi, especially in 1:2–3.

53. So Stuart, *Malachi*, 1284; Petersen, *Zechariah*, 196. etc. However, Sweeney, *The Twelve Prophets*, vol. 2, *Micah, Nahum, Habakkuk, Zephaniah, Haggai, Zechariah, Malachi* (Berit Olam; Collegeville, MN: Liturgical, 2000), 274 may be correct that vv. 2–3 rhetorically echo Gen 27:41 in order to "reiterate the role reversal and emotions of the Genesis narrative as preface to the contemporary experiences of both nations."

54. Petersen, *Zechariah*, 170.

55. For these as well as the historical background to Edom's destruction, see Achtemeier, *Nahum*-Malachi, 176–77; Verhoef, *Haggai and Malachi*, 202–4; Glazier-McDonald, *Malachi*, 34–41; Stuart, *Malachi*, 1287–89; Merrill, *Haggai*, 392–93; Hill, *Malachi*, 167–68; and Taylor and Clendenen, *Haggai*, 250–51.

56. Stuart, *Malachi*, 1284.

as a reminder of God's judgment against nations who oppose him."[57] Edom's devastation is thus an example (and warning?) to Israel, who in a reversal of their present attitude will proclaim, "'May Yhwh be called great beyond the territory of Israel!'" (1:5).

However, Malachi 1:2–5 does not portray this change as a result of a plaintive effort on God's part to persuade Israel of his love. Rather, he confronts them with the contrast between themselves and Edom. Even in the face of their rebellion that led to exile—and their current, postexilic rebellion—God restored Israel to the land where they have rebuilt Jerusalem and the temple. So when they complain of abandonment, his indignant retort, "I loved Jacob and Esau I hated," states that if Israel wants to know what covenantal hatred looks like then they should look at Edom—and then reconsider his treatment of them.

So in Malachi 1:2–5 God disputes Israel's unwarranted disregard for his covenantal love. Particularly, 1:2b–3a encapsulates both God's faithfulness and his indignation by contrasting his treatments of Israel and Edom. In context, the meaning of this tradition is this: to no credit of their own, and in fact in spite of both their historical and current rebellion, God has remained faithful to Israel and shown them mercy instead of the judgment he brought upon Edom.

Because of both the verbal similarity between this tradition and Genesis 25:23 and the fact that both traditions bespeak God's consistent choice of Israel at differing stages of their history, many early Jewish traditions cite Malachi 1:2–3 in connection with the negative characterization of Esau/Edom (again, frequently standing for Rome or Israel's enemies).[58] Other rabbinic traditions reference Malachi 1:2–3 in a decontextualized manner when discussing the various species of love that God shows Israel, among them covenantal love.[59] But many rabbinic traditions do exhibit a contextual awareness in their use of Malachi 1:2–3.

For instance, *Tanḥ Exod.* 7.7 reads Malachi 1:2 as a rebuke for Israel's exilic and postexilic sacrilege (and not having anything to do with Jacob's election in Gen 25). Or *Tanḥ Deut.* 3.4 uses Malachi 1:2–3 to explicate Deuteronomy 7:7–8 by identifying God's love there with his

---

57. Ibid.
58. *L.A.B.* 32.5; *Midr. Pss.* 9.14; 11.4; *S. Eli. Zut.* S29. In contrast, *Num. Rab.* 12.4 cites Mal 1:2 in reference to Israel's inherent righteousness.
59. E.g., *Tanḥ. Gen.* 7.22; *Gen. Rab.* 80.7; 86.1; *Midr. Pss.* 22.22. This means that for some of the rabbis, of course, Mal 1:2–3 is relevant to or even directly discusses election as such.

faithfulness to Israel in the Malachi setting, despite their unrighteousness and in contrast to the negative example of Edom. Similarly, in *Lev. Rab.* 7.1, possession of Torah is seen as a mercy, which is explained by God's adherence to Proverbs 10:12, "love covers all rebellion [פֶּשַׁע]," since postexilic rebellious Israel does not merit having Torah on their own. Israel's rebellion is then further characterized by the idolatry (see chapter 4 below) described in Ezekiel 20:7–9, despite which he loved them, citing (finally) Malachi 1:2.

So while no relevant Second Temple examples are extant, it is at least interesting how all rabbinic sources that are interested in the function of Malachi 1:2–3 in its original context agree on the reading given above. The passage never has to do with election per se (let alone so-called election to salvation or soteriology of any type) or with the episode recorded in Genesis 25, but rather with God's continued faithfulness amid and in the face of Israel's postexilic rebellion (which many of the rabbis considered to be an issue contemporary to themselves).[60] If this reflects an interpretive tradition contemporary with the first century, then it would not be unreasonable to expect that a contextually sensitive understanding like that above is what Paul is applying to his present circumstances with his quotation in Romans 9.

PAUL'S USE OF GENESIS 25:23 AND MALACHI 1:2–3 IN ROMANS

The possible objection that Isaac and Ishmael had different mothers affords Paul an opportunity to present in Romans 9:10–13 a second proof, highlighting in its introduction Rebekah as Jacob and Esau's common mother (9:10). In the first proof, not all of Abraham's physical descendants were his covenantal heirs since God only called through Isaac. Likewise, in 9:10–13, not all of national Israel are Abraham's covenantal heirs since he selected Jacob over Esau.[61]

However, it should not be presumed on the basis of οὐ μόνον δὲ ἀλλὰ καὶ (Rom 9:10) that the second proof is redundant. In verses 10–13, rather than the *fact* of God's selection of Jacob over Esau in Genesis 25:23,

---

60. See further *S. Eli. Rab.* [28]26; 68; *Exod. Rab.* 1.1; 49.1, also specifying Israel's rebellion as idolatry; *Song. Rab.* 8.6; *Num. Rab.* 17.3. This is not to say that the rabbis see a disjunction (let alone a non-relationship) between *love* and *election*, but that the numerous rabbinic sources named do not consider God's faithfulness in Mal 1:2–3 to be related to (or at least relevant to) the historical fact of Israel's election, even as regards Gen 25:23.

61. Verse 12b follows LXX Gen 25:23 verbatim, which faithfully reflects the Hebrew.

Paul focuses on the *circumstances* of God's choice. He qualifies Jacob's selection with the three conditions of shared parentage, lack of moral track record, and God's purpose, placing emphasis on the last of these. Paul cites Genesis 25:23 in Romans 9:12b to explain (γὰρ, 9:11) that because God selected Jacob before the twins were either born or had "done anything good or inconsequential," his calling is wholly dependent upon his own character instead of Jacob's intrinsic merit or moral effort. Moreover, with the occurrence of "Jacob" in 9:12b, Paul has invoked the examples of the patriarchs, thereby illustrating the fundamental relationship between Israel's covenantal identity and God's faithfulness to his covenantal purpose. The purpose of God's antepartum selection of Jacob was in order that (ἵνα) his "according-to-election purpose [κατ' ἐκλογὴν πρόθεσις]" might depend on nothing other than himself as "him who calls [ἐκ τοῦ καλοῦντος]" (9:11-12a, again reiterating that so-called election to salvation is not in view).

Paul's contrast of God as the one who calls with Torah observance (ἔργων, 9:12a) is significant, given that it was contrasted with trust in Christ (πίστις) when it last occurred in Romans 1-4.[62] In Romans 9:30-10:3, Paul will further discuss unbelieving Jews' devotion to Torah. But for now, when citing Genesis 25:23 he is presupposing how God is not "displacing" Torah and thereby excluding Jews from the covenant, because Torah was never basic to God's calling. That is, Paul is *not* weighing the options of whether God chose Jacob despite bad behavior versus apart from any behavior. Instead, Paul's point is an altogether different one regarding the foundation of Israel as an entity at all: he cites from Israel's narrative history the axiom that Israel's covenantal identity has always been and remains rooted solely in God and in his faithfulness to his covenantal purpose.

---

62. Many (though not all) scholars agree that ἔργον in Romans is generally a reference to Torah observance. Note also how Paul first characterizes the circumstance of Jacob's election (to carry forward the Abrahamic covenantal vocation) in Rom 9:11a as not "having done anything good or inconsequential," but then contextualizes this in 9:12a in terms of Torah observance. Such a move may initially seem anachronistic, in the sense that the fictive setting of Gen 25 is pre-Mosaic, but such retrojection is ubiquitous in the rabbis (and also postbiblical Jewish writings), especially as concerns Gen 25:23 specifically (and also in other discussions generally). As such, Paul exercises ordinary early-Jewish interpretation here, is not reductionistic, and is faithful to the Scripture's original context in transliterating God's extrinsically unconditioned choice of Jacob into a category familiar to a post-Mosaic audience.

Coming off of Paul's argument from Romans 9:6a (that the present occasion of national Israel's rejection of the gospel does not prove God unfaithful), the precedent of Genesis 25:23 thus means that God's choice of Israel is independent of their response to that choice: their rejecting the gospel does not entail their rejection by God. Paul is *not* arguing that God is faithful to "true" Israel in contradistinction to ethnic Israel because the former are "elect" and the latter are not (let alone referencing Esau's supposed rejection); both context and choice of Scripture entail that here Paul is not at all interested in election as such. Instead, Paul's point is one of theology proper vis-à-vis the historical people of Israel. Paul's use of Genesis 25 focuses not upon the nature of Jacob's election in light of its circumstances but rather upon God's character as the one who chooses Israel and how that is basic to their existence. So in Romans 9:11–12, Paul merely reminds his audience of the fundamental scriptural principle that, come what may, Israel has by definition always been God's people—God defines them in virtue of himself (and not themselves). This fundamental equation remains intact and independent of national Israel's present rejection of the gospel, which therefore casts no doubt upon God's character.

To this end, Paul quickly offers a coordinate point by citing Malachi 1:2b–3a in verse 13, which cannot (and should not) be reduced to an emphatic if redundant conflation with the Genesis tradition.[63]

MT Mal 1:2-3	Greek Mal 1:2-3	Rom 9:13
אהבתי אתכם אמר יהוה	Ἠγάπησα ὑμᾶς, λέγει κύριος	
ואמרתם במה אהבתנו	καὶ εἴπατε Ἐν τίνι ἠγάπησας ἡμᾶς	
הלוא־אח עשׂו ליעקב	οὐκ ἀδελφὸς ἦν Ησαυ τοῦ Ιακωβ	
נאם־יהוה	λέγει κύριος	
ואהב את־יעקב	καὶ <u>ἠγάπησα τὸν Ιακωβ</u>	καὶ <u>τὸν Ἰακὼβ ἠγάπησα</u>,
ואת־עשׂו שׂנאתי	τὸν δὲ Ησαυ ἐμίσησα	τὸν δὲ Ἠσαῦ ἐμίσησα

---

63. For Rom 9:13 as a coordinate point to 9:10–12, see Lenski, *Interpretation*, 604; Cranfield, *Romans*, 2:480; Dunn, *Romans 9–16*, 544. In 9:13 Paul alters the verb-object order in LXX Mal 1:2b (which preserves the MT syntax), but "the effect of change is more rhetorical than substantial" (Stanley, *Paul*, 105–6), perhaps slightly heightening the contrast between Israel and Edom.

Malachi 1:2–5 relates God's insistence that he is remaining faithful to postexilic Israel, despite their misperception and complaint that he has abandoned them. It is interpreted as such by all non-Pauline postbiblical witnesses (that are not discussing, e.g., Edom or Rome's inherent wickedness), none of which reduce the Malachi tradition into Genesis 25:23 despite their verbal resonance. It seems most likely that the καθὼς kicking off Romans 9:13 has the sense of a punctuating "moreover" that forcefully drives home the point of God's faithful record with Israel from beginning to in extremis. That is, just as with the patriarchs, in Malachi God remained faithful to Israel up to and following the exile, even continuing to pursue them after the exile despite their continued postexilic rebellion in comparison to Edom. Accordingly, Paul argues from Malachi 1:2–3 that, far from being unfaithful to national Israel, he has overlooked their failure to remain faithful to him.

Thus the note of indignation found in the original context of Malachi 1:2–3 also carries over into Paul's use in Romans 9:13: Why should unbelieving Jews' rejection of the gospel call into question God's faithfulness? For, Paul argues, not only has God's according-to-election purpose persisted independently from Israel's moral performance, but it has done so even *despite* their rebellion, particularly up to and during the postexilic period, which Paul as a Hellenistic Jew would have considered the first century to be. Therefore, since God has been loyal to Israel irrespective of *their* fidelity, national Israel's rejection of Christ and the gospel does not prove him unfaithful. To ascribe to Paul an understanding or usage of Malachi 1:2–3 in which it referenced Israel's election, explained the principle of election, or conflated with Genesis 25:23 would make him hold a view that is unattested in all early Judaism, that contradicts the original contextual meaning of Malachi 1:2–3, and that would make Paul's argument in Romans 9:6–13 incoherent. In the alternate reading offered here, 9:13 offers a new but complementary point to 9:10–12, all of which together constitutes the second proof in this pericope.

So then, Paul's proof here (Rom 9:10–13) offers his thesis (v. 6a) a twofold support: He cites Genesis 25:23 to demonstrate God's consistency in calling Abraham's covenantal heirs, presently as with the patriarchs, based on himself as the one who calls. (And because Israel's covenantal heritage is rooted in God's character, the apparent displacement of Torah observance does not undermine God's covenantal purpose, thereby proving him unfaithful.) Correspondingly, Paul quotes Malachi 1:2–3 to press home his point that both in Paul's past and at present, God's purpose and faithfulness persist not merely regardless of but *despite* national Israel's moral performance. Therefore, as with Romans 9:6b–9, in verses 10–13 God's constancy in relating to Israel now as he had in the past precludes an interpretation of unbelieving Jews' rejection of the gospel as the failure of God's promise.

SUMMARY OF ROMANS 9:6–13
IN LIGHT OF PAUL'S USE OF SCRIPTURE

As noted in the introduction to this study, traditional approaches to Romans 9:6–13 understand Paul as accepting the premise that God has rejected national Israel. Nevertheless, he tries to uphold God's faithfulness to "true" Israel by distinguishing the two entities from each other and explicating the election of so-called true Israel (or the nature of divine election generally). But when we take into account the occasional and literary setting, the shape of Paul's rhetoric, and his contextually faithful application of the Scriptures, we are led in another direction. Paul neither discusses nor employs the premise that God has rejected some part of Israel. Paul also does not expand upon either the nature or the objects of God's election. Instead, his point in 9:6–13 is much less complex. He is just pointing up how representative scriptural antecedents consistently recall 1) that Israel's existence has always been predicated upon God's character; 2) that there has been and is and Israel proves that God is irrefutably faithful; and 3) that this remains the case regardless of the fact that most of contemporary national Israel rejects Jesus as their resurrected Messiah.

Put more precisely: In this, the initial pericope of Romans 9:6–29, Paul is not seeking to explain why national Israel has rejected the gospel. Neither is he seeking to legitimate God's rejection of national Israel (whether before or after they rejected the gospel, although many interpreters assume the former). Instead, he explains how the fact that unbelieving Jews are rejecting the gospel does not prove God unfaithful, with the implication that he has never and is not now rejecting them at all. Paul argues this by way of two proofs.

First, he draws on Scripture to remind his readers how it is not now and never has been the case that all Abraham's physical descendants would participate in Israel's covenantal heritage. Second, none of Israel would have been Israel but for their identifying Abrahamic covenant, which is defined by God's faithful character. Based on this function of his quoted Scriptures in their original context, Paul's argument is that unbelieving Jews' separation from Israel's gospel (initially seen by his audience as an apparent exclusion) cannot mean the failure of God's promise (Rom 9:6-9). Accompanying this, Paul then relies on Scriptures that articulate how God's purpose for Israel depends wholly on his calling, both independently from and in spite of Israel's moral track record, to the point that now, as ever, their identity is secure so far as God's faithfulness is concerned. So, on this dimension as well, Paul argues, national Israel's rejection of the gospel neither entails nor can be equated with *God's* rejection of *them*, and therefore does not prove God unfaithful (9:10-13).

So Paul's initial move is not to defend God by discussing Israel's composition, initial impressions regarding 9:6b-7a notwithstanding. Instead, at this stage, Paul defends God's faithfulness by characterizing God vis-à-vis his role as the defining source of his people's identity, from their inception forward. Moreover, Paul's use of Malachi 1:2-3 also evokes the indignation present in its original context. This recollection of Israel's past unfaithfulness begins to hint that present circumstances might also involve unfaithfulness on national Israel's part, even in the process of defending the claim that God's covenantal faithfulness remains intact. Namely, a supporting point to Paul's main point in Romans 9:10-13 was that, up to now, God has shown mercy toward present (i.e., postexilic/Second Temple) national Israel. Thus, Paul elegantly achieves a second effect of juxtaposing national Israel's unfaithfulness with God's mercy by concluding the pericope with Malachi 1:2-3. In doing this, he sets the stage for his discussion of God's historical judgment upon Pharaoh and mercy toward Israel—and their relevance for present circumstances—in 9:14-18, the second pericope of Romans 9:6-29.

3

Paul's Use of Scripture
in Romans 9:14–18

¹⁴Then what shall we say? Is there not injustice on God's part? Certainly not! ¹⁵For to Moses he says, "I will show mercy to whom I show mercy and I will be compassionate to whom I might be compassionate."[1] ¹⁶So then, it depends neither on one's willing nor upon one's striving, but rather on God's showing mercy. ¹⁷For Scripture says to Pharaoh, "For this reason I raised you up: in order that I might show to you my power and that my name might be recounted in all the earth." ¹⁸So then, on whom he will he has mercy, but whom he will he hardens.

Romans 9:14–18

In Romans 9:14–18, Paul addresses the charge, "Why are the majority of national Israel estranged from God if he remains faithful and has not rejected them? And what has this to do with their rejection of Jesus as the Messiah?" The allegation is one of inconsistency on God's part, and Paul's answer points out God's consistency in how he has historically responded to idolatry and the fact that unbelieving Jews' present unbelief is itself a form of idolatry.

The more common interpretation of this pericope is that Paul is discussing the nature and scope of God's election, particularly in relation to human choice or response (largely on the working assumption that election had been the topic also of 9:6–13). Again, my positive thesis

---

1. Paul's language matches LXX Exod 33:19b, but it is interesting to note the conversion by the LXX of the first verb in each phrase from a perfect in the Hebrew (ורחמתי, וחנתי) to a future active indicative (ἐλεήσω, οἰκτιρήσω), and the second verb in each phrase from an imperfect (ארחם, אחן) to a present subjunctive (ἐλεῶ, οἰκτίρω). In contrast to the translation given, the two versions of the idiom if translated woodenly (i.e., improperly) would read, respectively, "I show mercy to whom I shall show mercy," and "I shall show mercy to whom I might show mercy." Cf. Paul's use of the present active indicative in the concluding Rom 9:18.

may imply that such traditional approaches are misguided in their understanding of Paul's focus. However, I am not undertaking a negative project against such approaches. Instead, the goal is the recognition that Paul recalls the history of God's various responses to Israel and Egypt's idolatry in the exodus event, and diagnoses that God is presently employing the same types of responses to instances of present-day idolatry, but that ironically unbelieving Jews now find themselves in the historical position of Pharaoh and Egypt.

INTRODUCTION TO ROMANS 9:14-18

In Romans 9:6-13, Paul argued that unbelieving Jews' rejection of the gospel does not prove God unfaithful. Rather, God remains faithful to his covenant just as he has in the past, regardless of and even despite Israel's rebellion and unfaithfulness.[2] Moreover, 9:13 (= Mal 1:2-3) seemed to bring up the question of national Israel's potential culpability. In Romans 9:14-18, the second pericope of 9:6-29, Paul is still addressing the question of God's apparent unfaithfulness (9:6a), but here he explains unbelieving Jews' apparent separation from Abraham's covenantal inheritance in terms of their idolatrous rejection of the gospel.

In Romans 9:14, Paul continues in diatribe fashion, rhetorically asking, "What should we say?" He employs this technique in Romans when an erroneous conclusion suggests itself. The potential charge that God exhibits *unrighteousness* or *injustice* (ἀδικία, 9:14) is not primarily forensic or concerned with unfair partiality, but continues the concern in verses 6-13 over whether God has violated his own character and promises.[3] Here as in 3:1-8 (in which chapters 9-11 are anticipated; cf. chap-

---

2. Regarding God's "according-to-election" purpose in Rom 9:11, many commentators rightly comment on the historical-redemptive purpose of Israel as a people as per Scripture (often with reflexive recourse to Gen 12:3). This does not need to be treated in this study, as this topic does not at all determine the structure or logic of Paul's argument. Likewise, the purpose of the covenant is not referenced even indirectly in Paul's defense of God's faithfulness to his covenant in Rom 9:14-18. The closest that Paul comes to explicating God's covenantal purposes in 9:6-29 will be the reference to his glory in v. 17, and in the latter half of the final pericope, in vv. 22-29, wherein Paul speaks of the purpose to which he puts his judgment upon national Israel in realizing certain eschatological expectations regarding the restoration of his people.

3. Lenski, *Interpretation*, 606; Moo, *Epistle*, 591; Wright, *Letter*, 638; cf. Byrne, *Romans*, 298, who claims that ἀδικία is more generally God's "acting contrary to what is right [δικαιοσύνη] or just in an absolute sense." Similarly, Jewett (*Romans*, 581) suggests that "injustice" is the more felicitous translation since it places the focus upon God's

ter 2 n. 18), God's righteousness is predicated upon his faithfulness. It follows, then, that Paul is not engaging the non-occasional and doctrinal question of how God's sovereignty relates to the fate of upright or even morally neutral people.

The question is, rather: What has changed in God's relationship with national Israel that he now seems to be negatively disposed toward them? This puzzle arises because of "God's covenanted obligation to bring salvation to the Gentiles through Israel, [and] his simultaneous obligation to deal with sin; both of these are brought into sharp focus by Israel's failure" (i.e., historically, to be faithful in the exilic and postexilic eras).[4] Paul hinted in Romans 9:13 that Israel is rebellious in their rejection of the gospel, but he also argued that God did not historically count Israel's sin against their covenantal inheritance; accordingly, in 9:14 Paul's interlocutor asks whether it is arbitrary for God to now do so. Would this not, once again, bring us around to unfaithfulness on God's part (9:6a)?

In answer, Paul turns to Exodus 33:19 (Rom 9:15) and 9:16 (Rom 9:17). Each scriptural citation is introduced by an explanatory γὰρ and followed by ἄρα οὖν that signals Paul's interpretation. The two couplets seem to be parallel, but, "On whom he will he has mercy, but whom he will he hardens," in 9:18 also seems to be Paul's conclusion for the entire pericope (and not just the interpretation of 9:17; cf. fig. 3).[5] Once again, then, it seems the key to Paul's argument in 9:14–18 lies in his use of Scripture.

EXODUS 9:16 AND 33:19 IN ROMANS 9:14–18

EXODUS 9:16 IN ITS ORIGINAL CONTEXT

Although Paul cites Exodus 33:19 before Exodus 9:16, in this case it is most clear to analyze them chronologically, due to the development

---

actions rather than leading into an abstract discussion of God's character. It needs noting, however, that this issue is not entirely settled. Some scholars do take ἀδικία in a primarily forensic sense, placing God on trial, as it were, for breaking his own laws with regard to his apparently arbitrary treatment of national Israel. The important point for our study is that—as demonstrated in 9:14–18—Paul is showing cause for God's actions (and not merely rooting them in his inscrutable sovereignty), regardless of English translations.

4. Wright, *Letter*, 638.

5. For this structure of 9:14–18, see also Lenski, *Interpretation*, 616; Cranfield, *Romans*, 2:485, 488; Käsemann, *Commentary*, 268; Piper, *Justification*, 139; Dunn, *Romans* 9–16, 554.

of narrative and theological patterns in the book of Exodus. Exodus 9:16 is one of several purpose statements in the plague cycle in Exodus 7:14-12:36, which is part of the larger exodus narrative in chapters 1-15.[6] As Moshe Greenberg helpfully summarizes,

> The plague narrative revolves around the theme: revelation by God of His name—his essence, his power, his authority—to Pharaoh, to the Egyptians, and to all men. ... [It is a] demonstration of God's essence to the arrogant pagan world and onlooking Israel. ... [It is] the decision of God to break into history on behalf of Israel.[7]

Regarding the plague narrative, the sovereign God's "intrusive action in Egypt" is akin to an ANE king's punishment and eventual removal of a rebellious subject.[8]

The plague narrative represents God's judgment (cf. שׁפט in Exod 6:6; 7:4) upon both Pharaoh and Egypt's pantheon of false deities. This also includes Pharaoh, since he believed himself a god, the son and incarnation of Amon Re (or Horus). At the conclusion of the exodus narrative God states his purpose in judging Pharaoh was "in order that I will be glorified [כבד; see below] over Pharaoh and all his armies and in order that the Egyptians might know [ידע; see below] that I am Yhwh" (Exod 14:4; cf. 14:17–18), thereby collocating his sovereign self-revelation with his judgment upon Egypt's gods as represented by Pharaoh.

However, in Exodus God also judges Pharaoh in relation to his hardness of heart (the cause and effect of this will be explored below). Although the judgment theme and hardening motif are only implicit in Exodus 9:16, Paul recognizes (cf. σκληρύνω, Rom 9:18) their interconnectedness. For a sound understanding of Paul's use of Exodus 9:16, then, it is necessary to understand the reason for Pharaoh's hardening and the function it serves within the larger narrative.

---

6. Cf. Exod 7:5, 17; 8:6; 9:14, 29; 10:1-2; 11:9; so also Piper, *Justification*, 144; and Beale, "Exegetical," 131.

7. "The Thematic Unity of Exodus 3–11," *WCJS* 1 (1967): 153.

8. Walter Brueggemann, "Pharaoh as Vassal: A Study of a Political Metaphor," *CBQ* 57 (1995): 31. However, Brueggemann overextends his analysis, asserting that God's "self-assertion" here is "prideful" and almost lustful for power (44).

THE HARDENING OF PHARAOH'S HEART

The hardening terms distributed throughout Exodus 3–14 are כבד, חזק, and קשה:

Context			חזק	כבד	קשה	Agent specified
1.	4:21	end of burning bush theophany (in 3:1–4:23)	X			God
2.	7:3	beginning of initial sign and introduction to plagues (in 7:1–13)			X	God
3.	7:13	end of initial sign and introduction to plagues (in 7:1–13)	X			none
4.	7:14	beginning of first plague		X		none
5.	7:22	end of first plague	X			none
6.	8:11	end of second plague			X	Pharaoh
7.	8:15	end of third plague	X			none
8.	8:28	end of fourth plague		X		Pharaoh
9.	9:7	end of fifth plague		X		none
10.	9:12	end of sixth plague	X			God
11.	9:34	end of seventh plague		X		Pharaoh
12.	9:35	end of seventh plague	X			none
13.	10:1	beginning of eighth plague		X		God
14.	10:20	end of eighth plague	X			God
15.	10:27	end of ninth plague	X			God
16.	11:10	beginning of tenth plague and summary of first nine plagues	X			God
17.	14:4	Pharaoh's final defeat (in ch. 14)	X			God
18.	14:8	Pharaoh's final defeat (in ch. 14)	X			God
19.	14:17	Pharaoh's final defeat (in ch. 14)	X			God

Fig. 3: Occurrence of Hardening Terminology in Exodus 3–14

G. K. Beale has demonstrated that in Exodus 3–14, these three verbs are "all related to Pharaoh's refusal to obey Yahweh's command to release Israel" and synonymously refer to Pharaoh's "intellectual-volitional power of refusal."⁹ It is significant that it is Pharaoh's *heart* that is hardened. In the biblical tradition, and to an even greater extent for the Egyptians, the heart was "an inner spiritual centrum and volitional, decision-maker."¹⁰ The use of כבד as one of the hardening terms is especially significant: in Egyptian mythology, after death a person's heart was weighed against a feather in the balance of truth, and "if the heart outweighed the feather," John Currid observes with wry understatement, "the deceased was in trouble."¹¹ Furthermore, since the king's heart was understood to be the all-controlling factor of Egyptian society and history, any judgment from God to do with *Pharaoh's* heart bespeaks God's judgment upon Egypt in terms that resonated with both Israelite and Egyptian tradition.

The question of the nature of God's relationship with and judgment upon Pharaoh within the exodus narrative is not an easy one. Scholars—and, historically, theologians and interpreters back to the rabbis and the fathers—have struggled with why Pharaoh is judged for a hardness that appears to have been at least partly caused by God.¹² Brevard Childs has

---

9. "Hardening," 132; 147; cf. Abasciano, *Romans 9.10–18*, 94. The terms are not wholly synonymous, however, such that subtle connotations may inform more detailed exegetical analysis and commentary of these traditions; cf. Meadors, *Idolatry*, 20–21.
10. Beale, "Exegetical," 133.
11. "Hardened Heart," 49: "If a person's heart was heavy-laden … the person would, in effect, be annihilated; if the heart was filled with integrity … the person would earn an escort to heavenly bliss" (ibid., 50).
12. E.g., U. Cassuto is somewhat unclear, but reasons that "Pharaoh sinned in that he imposed a hard bondage on the children of Israel, and decreed that their infant sons should be destroyed; for this he was hardened, not on account of his hardness of heart [?]. Had he immediately granted the request of Moses and Aaron, he would have gone forth free and suffered no penalty, which would not have been just. Thus his hard-heartedness serves as a means of inflicting upon him the punishment … he deserved for his earlier sins." *A Commentary on the Book of Exodus*, trans. Israel Abrahams (Jerusalem: Magnes, 1967), 57. Cf. Sarna, *Exploring*, 64–65. Also dissatisfying is William Propp, who in contrast to Cassuto concludes (without providing support) that God pours out justice on the wicked, some of whom he compels to wickedness, so that "God may be just, but he is not necessarily fair." *Exodus 1–18*, AB 2 (New York: Doubleday, 1999), 354. Cf. Lyle Eslinger, "Freedom or Knowledge? Perspective and Purpose in the Exodus Narrative (Exodus 1–15)," *JSOT* 52 (1991): 56–57; and Peter D. Miscall, "Biblical Narrative and the Categories of the Fantastic," *Semeia* 60 (1992): 44, wherein "Israel and Egypt are pawns in the hand of the divine player who plays both sides of the board" (Eslinger, "Freedom," 57). Although the reader knows of "God's educative intent, and of the historical contrivances he uses to teach his lessons," it is "difficult to applaud the divine pedagogy" since the narrative "raises questions about the morality of such teaching technique" (ibid., 58).

noted how J sources for the plague cycle (e.g., Exod 8:16–28; 9:1–7) place the hardening after the plague and include Pharaoh's request that God relents, with the effect that they explain why the plague failed to bring him to recognize Yhwh. By contrast, P sources (e.g., Exod 8:12–15; 9:8–12) state God's intent to harden before the plague episode unfolds and without demand of release or warning of the impending plague, in order that the plague be seen as an example of God's unilateral judgment.[13] Thus for the biblical authors and (reasonably) for the original audience, the portrayal of Pharaoh's hardening is not something to struggle with: "The motif has been consistently over-interpreted by supposing that it arose from a profoundly theological reflection and seeing it as a problem of free will and predestination."[14] In the final form of the text, where the whole is greater than the sum of the parts, the sources combine to relate God's appropriate and righteous judgment of Pharaoh and Egypt toward the end of achieving his purpose for Pharaoh. But Beale also correctly observes that the hardening in Exodus 7:13–14 occurs "*before* the signs [plagues] of this narrative were performed before him [Pharaoh]," so that its cause is located somewhere in the narrative prior to the plague cycle.[15] However, scholars differ as to what this cause may be, and the issue is convoluted enough that a brief survey is in order.

David Gunn cites a process of "narrational disclosure," wherein what had been in retrospect implicit beginning in Exodus 7 finally becomes explicit in 9:12. Immediately afterward, in 9:30, Pharaoh "is now so totally under Yahweh's control that he is unable to sustain any consistency in his responses."[16] However, Gunn still wants to conclude, "While in the early stages of the story we are invited to see Pharaoh as his own master ... as the narrative develops it becomes [clear] that God is ultimately the only agent of heart-hardening."[17]

Alternatively, Beale sees the pronouncement in Exodus 4:21 as interpretive for 5:1–5, where he thinks the hardening begins.[18] He then tries

---

13. *The Book of Exodus: A Critical Theological Commentary* (Philadelphia: Westminster, 1974), 171–74.
14. Ibid., 74; cf. McGinnis, "Hardening," 44–45.
15. "Hardening," 139, emphasis original. Perhaps the qualification in Abasciano, *Romans 9.10–18*, 96–97 can also be adopted: that the hardening also takes place partly because of Pharaoh's (re)actions during the plague cycle.
16. "Pharaoh's," 77, although it is ambiguous whether "now" refers to the culmination of the hardening process or of the narrational disclosure.
17. Ibid., 79.
18. "Hardening," 139–40.

to harmonize 4:21 with the obduracy texts in the first several plague episodes, and deduces (similar to Gunn) that in the obduracy texts up through 9:12, "*the subject of the hardening act was to be Yahweh himself.*"[19] Similar to Gunn, then, Beale correctly concludes Pharaoh is not "*independently*" the subject of the hardening and God is "*ultimately*" the cause of hardening (although he leaves the relationship between God's ultimate agency and Pharaoh's contributing agency a mystery).[20] However, Beale's reliance upon and interpretation of 5:2 is not wholly satisfactory.[21]

Charles Isbell focuses upon literary artistry like Gunn, but like Beale he argues that Exodus 4:21 and 7:3 "predict" the hardening and indicate "a conscious artistic effort by the narrator to shape the concept of hardening *from the beginning* as attributable to YHWH alone," in order to demonstrate that "the One who had made such a dire threat was the only One who was fully capable of carrying it out."[22] He convincingly demonstrates that there are exactly nineteen references in chapters 3–14, making God the explicit agent in the majority of instances (ten of nineteen).[23] He also concludes that, insofar as every obduracy text either has God as its subject or is predicated on his authority, "*all* references to hardening in the story agree on causality."[24]

---

19. Ibid., 141, emphasis original.
20. Ibid., 149, emphasis original. Or again, "even when Pharaoh is the subject of the hardening, or when the subject is unmentioned, [hardening] statements describe a resulting condition traceable to a previous hardening action caused by God" (ibid., 148–49).
21. Robert B. Chisolm, Jr., "Divine Hardening in the Old Testament," *Bibliotheca Sacra* 153 (1996): 416–17n20 defeats Beale's arguments ("Exegetical," 135–36) for hardening in Exod 5:1-2 and its relationship with 4:21. Instead, both Chisolm, "Divine," 417, esp. n21, and Brueggemann, "Pharaoh," 36, see Exod 5:1-2 as programmatic, with Chisolm drawing a connection to 3:19. David M. Gunn hesitates whether to interpret Exod 5:1-2 in light of 4:21 or to conclude this is "simply Pharaoh being 'Pharaoh' " (which on my reading also intersects with 3:19; see below). Gunn, "The 'Hardening of Pharaoh's Heart': Plot, Character, and Theology in Exodus 1-14," in *Art and Meaning: Rhetoric in Biblical Literature*, ed. David J. A. Clines, et al (Sheffield: JSOT, 1982), 74.
22. *The Function of Exodus Motifs in Biblical Narratives: Theological Didactic Drama*, Studies in the Bible and Early Christianity 52 (Lewiston, NY: Edwin Mellen, 2002), 29–30, emphasis original.
23. Ibid., 33–34 (cf. Chisolm, "Divine," 411–12), contra Sarna, *Exploring*, 64.
24. Ibid., 37, emphasis original. Chisolm ("Divine," 410–11)—who admits his commitment to avoid predestination, due to the presupposition that God is just yet loving—instead argues that Pharaoh's hardening is a process wherein he is offered "window[s] of opportunity" to repent before God actively performs the hardening. Application of this model proved difficult for Chisolm, since his verdict that it is not until Exod 9:12 that God hardens Pharaoh (i.e., confirms him in his choice) is

However, while these scholars correctly identify God as the principal agent in Pharaoh's hardening,[25] this does not necessarily explain either the reason behind the hardening or the function that it serves within the narrative.[26] The connection between God's hardening of Pharaoh and his reason for doing so resides in the biblical relationship between hardening and idolatry, especially in light of the biblical principle of humans created as God's image.

Hardening as a Judgment for Idolatry

Hardening by God in the Bible is always an act of judgment. According to Robert Chisolm, "objects of such judgment were never morally righteous or neutral, but were rebels against God's authority. Divine hardening ... was in response to rejection of God's authoritative word or standards."[27] In his discussion on Isaiah 6:9-10, another paradigmatic obduracy text, Beale points to the description of idols in Psalm 135:15-17 (cf. v. 14) and 115:5-6, which is similar to God's proscription of Israel in Isaiah 6:9-10. Psalm 135:18 (and 115:8) continues, "those who make [idols] and all who trust them shall become like them," entailing that idolaters will be judged by becoming like the idols they worship and subsequently sharing in their destruction.[28] Beale demonstrates that hardening lan-

---

inconsistent with his claim that "Yahweh was the first to harden him [prior to 9:12] in response to his *autonomous rejection* of Yahweh" (ibid., 429, emphasis added).

25. The work especially of Gunn, Beale, Chisolm, and Isbell facilitates analysis—for instance, in noting that while no agent is indicated in the obduracy text at Exod 7:13 and through the first five plagues, the force of the divine certification formula כאשר דבר יהוה(introduced in 7:13 and repeated in six of the first seven plagues; see below) is affirmed in its nature as an "attribution [to Yhwh] clause," and its use in Scripture to express exact fulfillment (Isbell, *Function*, 30; cf. Beale, "Exegetical," 140).

26. E.g., Beale ("Exegetical," 149-50) collapses the two when he states, "It is never stated in Exod 4-14 that Yahweh hardens Pharaoh's heart in judgment because of any prior reason or condition residing in him. Rather, as stated [in Exod 14:4, 17-18], the only *purpose or reason* given for the hardening is that it would glorify Yahweh" (emphasis added).

27. "Divine," 411.

28. "Isaiah VI 9-13: A Retributive Taunt Against Idolatry," VT 41 (1991): 258; cf. the narrator's evaluation of the northern kingdom in 2 Kgs 17:15: "they walked after worthless idols and so became worthless themselves." See also Rikki Watts, "The New Exodus/New Creational Restoration of the Image of God," in *What Does It Mean to Be Saved? Broadening Evangelical Horizons of Salvations*, ed. John G. Stackhouse, Jr. (Grand Rapids: Baker, 2002), 25, 27-28; Meador, *Idolatry*, 2-3 (whose study is by nature more synthetic than analytical), previewing the paradigm "The axiom [is] 'you become like that which you worship' ... '*Those who make them* (idols) *will become like them*" (emphasis original), where idolatry is contextually relevant even when

guage in Isaiah 6:9–10 is actually idolatry language that is employed "as a retributive taunt," convincingly identifying the judgment to which Chisolm refers as judgment for idolatry.[29]

Hardening as a judgment for idolatry also clarifies further obduracy texts—among others, Deuteronomy 2:30 and Joshua 11:18-20.[30] In Deuteronomy 2:30, the idolatrous Canaanites are hardened and defeated when they rebelliously resist God's will (cf. Num 21:21-23). Then, during the summary for Joshua 1–11 in 11:18-20, Israel is depicted as the executive arm of God's warfare against the idolatrous and hardened Canaanites (11:20).[31] If, then, in so many instances hardening is a judgment upon idolatry, what of the paradigmatic precedent in Exodus 3–14?

---

not always the only cause of hardening. The exception to this trend in interpretation is that of Donald E. Hartley, who does not so much refute or argue against the view that hardening is not punitive in Isa 6 as close off such a possibility by way of his admitted theological presuppositions and his philosophical commitments regarding what the text may coherently assert (*The Wisdom Background and Parabolic Implications of Isaiah 6:9–10 in the Synoptics*, Studies in Biblical Literature 100 [New York: Peter Lang, 2006]; see his chapter 2 on philosophical presuppositions). Partly in consequence to this, Hartley concludes that the hardening in Isa 6:9–10 is "deprivational," i.e., God's choosing to withhold or depriving salvation ("salvific wisdom") from those who are cosmically foolish on a *congenital* level, thereby causing their hearts to *remain* hard (his optimal translation of Isa 6:9–10; ad loc., 209).

29. Beale, "Isaiah," 277.

30. Cf. Chisolm, "Divine," 430-34. Beale ("Isaiah," 274-76) surveys numerous further references where idolatrous Israel is consequently judged as the idols they have worshiped and have thereby come to resemble: Deut 29:4, 17-20, 26; 30:17-18; 31:16-18, 20; 32:12, 15-18, 21, 37-39; Jer 5:21; 7:24, 26; 9:8; 25:4; 35:15; 44:5; Ezek 44:5, etc.; cf. also Hos 4:16-17; 8:5-6; 13:2. His conclusions are affirmed and extended for the remainder of Isaiah (patterned after Isa 6:9–10) in John L. McLaughlin, "Their Hearts *Were* Hardened: The Use of Isaiah 6,9–10 in the Book of Isaiah," *Bib* 75 (1994): 1-25; and Geoffrey D. Robinson, "The Motif of Deafness and Blindness in Isaiah 6:9–10: A Contextual, Literary, and Theological Analysis," *BBR* 8 (1998): 167-86.

31. There are other peripherally relevant traditions, for instance Deut 29:3, where Israel does not obtain from Yhwh a "heart to know (ולא־נתן יהוה לכם לב לדעת)" the significance of God's mighty deeds of deliverance in the exodus until their entrance into the land. Amid the curses portion of the covenantal blessings and curses (in the process of covenant renewal) in Deut 28-29, this verse separates the conquest generation from the exodus generation, who had been denied entrance into the land due to the rebellion of Num 13 (and who also committed idolatry in Exod 32). The reference to the previous generation's non-functioning heart is an evident instance of idolatry/hardening language, but it would be a leap to conclude that this is an instance of hardening by deprivation, as it were. This tradition gives no other context or explanation for its hardening(/hardened) language that allows for detailed analysis. It is also explicable in terms of the exodus generation's record (in locations such as Exod 32), even if it contains a particular nuance that would not affect

Following Beale's work in Isaiah 6:9–10, Dominic Rudman sees the language of idol fabrication of Isaiah 44:9–10 as being lifted from Genesis 1–3.[32] ANE idolaters believed they might achieve (semi-)divine status by making idols, yet biblical tradition views idol fabrication as an act of cosmic uncreation.[33] This observation is a clue that the biblical understanding of humans as God's image governs the dynamic of hardening as a judgment for idolatry, including that of Pharaoh in Exodus 3–14. In essence, from the biblical perspective, humans are what they worship. Failing to worship Israel's one, true, living God supplants one's livingness with the non-livingness of whatever non-living object one is worshiping instead.

This principle has to do with the biblical norm regarding the nature of humanity as made in God's image, which is presuppositional to the narrative in Exodus 3–14.[34] The fundamental statement for this seldom-articulated principle is preserved in the opening chapters of Genesis, and particularly Genesis 1:26–27, "Let us create humankind in our image [צלם], according to our likeness [דמות]" (v. 26). David Clines analyzes biblical occurrences of צלם and Semitic cognates, and is one of the first to argue that Genesis 1:26 defines humans as God's physical representations and/or representatives.[35] Moreover, several scholars com-

---

the understanding of idolatry/hard-heartedness presented by the biblical authors in the traditions just noted.

32. Many scholars agree that even if the final form of the creation accounts of Genesis 1–2 date to, e.g., the sixth century, they reflect and preserve a theological framework commonly held within Israel long before. And certainly so far as a precritical, first-century AD Hellenistic Jewish interpreter like Paul is concerned, Genesis 1–2(3) are simply the first words of received Scripture.

33. Rudman, "The Theology of the Idol Fabrication Passages in Second Isaiah," OTE 12 (1999): 117–18.

34. For a full account, see Aaron Sherwood, Paul and the Restoration of Humanity in Light of Ancient Jewish Traditions, AJEC 82 (Leiden: Brill, 2012), 135–47.

35. David J. A. Clines, "The Image of God in Man," TynBul 19 (1968): 73–80; Clines (ad loc., 56–63) surveys and rejects various other interpretations of צלם, such as its referring to either the same physical form of deity (so Günkel and von Rad) or to a "spiritual" image (mental faculty and/or "spiritual nature"; so Cassuto, Barth, and Bonhoeffer). Westermann's interpretation (Genesis 1–11: A Commentary, trans. J. J. Scullion [Minneapolis: Augsburg, 1984], 146)—that Gen 1:26 says nothing of the quality of humans but speaks only of them as ruling counterparts to God—is also unconvincing, especially in light of available ANE data (see below). The first-person plural of Gen 1:26 likely refers to a heavenly court (e.g., Gordon J. Wenham, Genesis 1–15, WBC 1 [Waco, TX: Word Books, 1987], 28; Waltke, Genesis, 64–65). Clines, "Image," 63–69, however, surveys several options, arguing that this issue is not determinative for the meaning of צל. Image and likeness are functionally synonymous,

pare the language of delegated sovereignty in Genesis 1:26-28 with that of texts like Psalm 8:4-8 to argue that in Genesis humankind is presented as the *royal* image of God.[36] By contrast, and to provide background, Mesopotamian and Egyptian sources describe the king as the image of deity, with some Egyptian sources further assigning to the king divine sovereignty or dominion over creation similar to that in Genesis.[37] For at least the Pharaoh—in contrast to Mesopotamian understanding—this anticipated a divine indwelling within the human image.[38] The degree of democratization is unique to the biblical tradition.

Furthermore, *image* in Genesis 1:26 is particularly provocative against an ANE background. There, the deity's palace was a temple, modeled as a microcosm of creation.[39] Both Mesopotamian and Egyptian social orders employed royal connotations of deity, wherein king and deity both hold back (on their respective planes) the agricultural chaos of "war, lawlessness, or flood."[40] After subduing his domain, the king

---

and are used together for specification and rhetorical emphasis; so, e.g., Clines, "Image," 90–92; Westermann, *Genesis 1–11*, 146; Wenham, *Genesis 1–15*, 29; Richard S. Hess, "Genesis 1–2 and Recent Studies of Ancient Texts," *Science and Christian Belief* 7 (1995): 145.

36. Jon D. Levenson, *Creation and the Persistence of Evil* (San Francisco: Harper, 1988), 113–14.

37. Levenson, *Creation*, 114, citing Hans Wildberger on both Mesopotamian and Egyptian sources (but cf. Watts, "New Creational Restoration," 21n17); James E. Atwell, "An Egyptian Source for Genesis 1," *JTS* 51 (2000): 463.

38. Atwell, "Egyptian," 463. Cf. some of the findings in A. L. Oppenheim, *Ancient Mesopotamia* (Chicago: University of Chicago Press, 1970), 184–86, which suggest echoes of this idea in Mesopotamian sources. Increasingly, scholars suggest Gen 1 may primarily reflect an Egyptian rather than a Mesopotamian background; besides Atwell, see James P. Allen, *Genesis in Egypt: The Philosophy of Ancient Egyptian Creation Accounts* (New Haven: Yale Egyptological Seminar, 1988), esp. pp. 56–63; James K. Hoffmeier, "Some Thoughts on Genesis 1 & 2 and Egyptian Cosmology," *JANES* 15 (1983): 3949; John D. Currid, *Ancient Egypt and the Old Testament* (Grand Rapids: Baker, 1997); Rikki Watts, "On the Edge of the Millennium: Making Sense of Genesis 1," in *Living in the LambLight*, ed. Hans Boersma (Vancouver: Regent College Publishing, 2001), 129–51. However, some admit significant disconnects between Genesis and Egyptian material (e.g., Currid, *Ancient*, 39; Watts, "Edge," 130). It is probably best to see Genesis as reflecting (possibly to varying degrees, and likely in part as a polemic) *both* Mesopotamian and Egyptian traditions; cf. George L. Klein, "Reading Genesis 1," *SwJT* 44 (2001): 32–33.

39. Watts, "Edge," 151–53. Especially in Egyptian traditions, pyramids were models of the primeval mountain of order, elevated out of the inundation of chaos (cf. Gen 1:9) and upon which were enthroned the god(s) (Currid, *Ancient*, 22–24).

40. Watts, "Edge," 146. For example, in the Ugaritic texts most closely resembling Genesis, cosmological creation is defined by the sequence of the ordering of chaos,

builds his palace; this is reflected on a cosmic level with the deity, who builds his palace-temple. Likewise, in the biblical tradition "creation is seen as Yahweh's palace-temple," which is mirrored in Israel's temple in Jerusalem, "itself [a] microcosm, a mini universe."[41] Then, the climactic moment in temple building is the placement of the deity's image. As Rikki Watts writes,

> First, the image would be formed, often in connection with sacred forests or gardens. Then there would be a series of ritual acts of animation in which the eyes, ears, and mouth of the image would be opened, its limbs enabled, and the spirit of the deity invoked to indwell the image. This indwelling of the image by the fiery spirit of the deity is perhaps the crucial event since it is only when this occurs that the idol truly functions as the deity's image. Finally, the "enlivened" image was installed in its temple so that the deity could dwell among his people and daily provision could be made for his or her sustenance.[42]

Such parallels give new dimension to the account in Genesis 1:26–27, wherein "on the last creative day, Yahweh fashions his own image and places it in his palace-temple."[43]

Thus, in the biblical understanding, humanity is God's image that he himself made and placed at the center of his palace-temple of creation. This explains the relationship between idolatry and hardening as previewed above: since God is the living God who breathes life into his images, separation from him leads to a distortion of that image and a

---

kingship, and temple building: Loren R. Fisher, "Creation at Ugarit and in the Old Testament," VT 15 (1965): 316. Here, the temple "is symbolic of the ordered cosmos and at the same time makes it possible to maintain order" (ibid., 320). And in Canaanite traditions, Baal's battle with Yam (and the lack thereof as a counterpoint in Genesis) is a creation battle, "creation" being the bringing of order or cosmos from chaos. Jakob H. Grønbæk, "Baal's Battle with Yam: A Canaanite Creation Fight," JSOT 33 (1985): 33.

41. Watts, "Edge," 147; cf. Psa 104:2–3; Isa 24:18; Job 38:4–39:30, data that Watts calls "overwhelming": "Given the rather widespread [ANE] notion linking creation, defeat-of-chaos, and temple-building, and the thorough-going architectural imagery which characterizes the biblical conceptualizing of creation, it would be very odd if Genesis 1 were not to be understood along the lines of cosmic palace-temple building" (ad loc.); cf. Fisher, "Creation," 319.

42. "New Creational Restoration," 19–20, citing Katherine Beckerleg and Christopher Walker. See also Gen 2:7, along with its parallels in some Egyptian and Mesopotamian human origins accounts (cf. Currid, Ancient, 37–38; Watts, "Edge," 145).

43. Watts, "Edge," 147.

distortion or loss of the life that he sustains. Furthermore, substituting an idol for God—in whose image humans are made and whom they are meant to worship—results in the idolater being re- or unmade in the image of the idol they worship.[44] Just as "we do not 'open' his [Yahweh's] eyes, ears, etc., instead he gives us sight, hearing, etc. and ultimately fills us with his 'breath,'"[45] so also idolatry leads to sharing the non-functioning organs of the idol.[46] Among those organs in question is the heart. Although previously unhardened, it becomes non-functioning and hardened along with the rest of the idolater when he is judged for his idolatry. In the biblical understanding, God's judgment for idolatry is his granting that the heart become like an idol's heart, as the idolater comes to share the idol's status as an object to be acted upon instead of a person with whom to relate—as with Pharaoh in Exodus 3–14.[47]

---

44. A colleague has suggested that the reason for all sin (including idolatry) is that humans do not inherently have God's presence within them (in Hebrew Bible settings, at least), being born "unregenerate." However, this contention would be off-topic, since the *why* of humanity's sin generally (and specifically in Gen 3) is not directly relevant to the fact that biblical traditions depict idolaters being unmade to resemble that which they worship. It is enough for this study to recognize that biblical authors evaluate idolatry as an anti-creational sin with concomitant consequences (regardless of how that fits into a larger doctrinal discussion on hamartiology).

45. Watts, "New Creational Restoration," 20.

46. There are few direct references to hardening in Second Temple tradition. At Qumran, 1QS 4.10–11 contrasts those who walk according to either a spirit of truth or of falsehood, the latter being identified as idolaters whose idolatry is manifested in "abominable deeds fashioned by whorish desire ... blind eyes, deaf ears, stiff neck and hard heart," and they will be punished by eternal suffering. Or again, 1QM 14.7 discusses the eschatological Day of the Lord, when Israel is victorious and their and God's enemies—the idolatrous nations—are defeated: "[God] has gathered a congregation of nations for annihilation without remnant in order to raise up in judgment. ... Among the poor in spirit [i.e., the nations] [...] a hard heart, and by [the righteous] shall all wicked nations come to an end." Finally, 1 *En.* 5:3–6 also identifies the "hard-hearted" as those who turn from God, whereby their destruction "shall be multiplied" and they "shall find no mercy."

47. Despite the foregoing, a colleague has asserted to me that nowhere do Hebrew Bible or New Testament traditions depict that hardening is ever a judgment, let alone for idolatry, and that logically hardening as a judgment could not be shown to be a form of judgment. His position is instead that hardening causes (rather than results in any way from) idolatry, and is an innate or "congenital" condition for all post-Adam humanity (or at least, as in the case of Pharaoh, is non-retributionally effected directly by God for no extrinsic reasons). He further points out how idolatry is not listed as a punishment in the Deuteronomic code, but I would point out how Deuteronomy presupposes the exodus narrative and the category of the exodus event as fundamental, even axiomatic (cf. further the interrelationship between Deut 29:3 and Isa 29:10 in Rom 11:8, in chapter 6 below). If correct, then his position

Idolatry as the Reason for Pharaoh's Hardening in Exodus 3–14

Beale observes that in Exodus 3–14, while 4:21 is the first explicit obduracy text, "the first hint of [Pharaoh's] hardening is found in Exod 3:18–20."[48] More properly, 3:18–20, and particularly verse 19, are the hermeneutical key for the obduracy motif throughout the entire narrative— namely, how Pharaoh's idolatry leads to his hardening. In 3:18–20, God commands Moses to confront Pharaoh (3:18), but warns, "I myself know that the king of Egypt will not allow you to go unless by a mighty hand. So I will send my hand and I will strike Egypt with all my wonders ... and after that, he will send you" (3:19–20). Regarding scope, 3:16–22 covers the larger narrative from 4:29–12:36.[49] This makes God's statement in 3:19–20 interpretive for the hardening motif throughout Exodus 3–14, even if the motif begins explicitly in 4:21.

The emphatic pronoun in Exodus 3:19 and its syntax as a disjunctive circumstantial clause qualifying 3:18 are both echoed in 4:21 and 7:3 (within 7:1–7, the proleptic summary for the plague narrative). All three texts describe Moses' duty to confront or perform signs before Pharaoh, but their emphases are on how God hardens Pharaoh's heart because of how intimately he *knows* him.[50] The occurrence of several plague narrative *Leitworten* in 3:19–20—including ידע, חזק, and שלח (which is used consistently regarding Israel's release; cf. 4:23; 5:1–2; 6:11; 7:2, 14–16, etc.)—also provides terminological links that strengthen the connection between 3:19–20 and the hardening motif. Particularly, ידע in 3:19 introduces another prominent motif of knowing intertwined with that

---

would also undercut my account of Pharaoh's idolatry as the reason for which God hardens him, confirming him in his idolatrous choice. Even though my colleague's theological commitment represents a well-developed doctrinal position (one certainly held by many others), care must be given to show that this position is based upon *a posteriori* support. So all things considered, I elect to stand on the above analysis of biblical traditions in forming and supporting my synthesis of the biblical view of idolatry.

48. "Hardening," 133.

49. Contrastively, Exod 4:21–23 merely expands upon 3:16–22 and only encompass events in 7:6–10:29, being finally fulfilled in 11:4–8; cf. Moshe Greenberg, *Understanding Exodus* (New York: Behrman House, 1969), 109–10; Chisolm, "Divine," 417 (cf. p. 415n19); Propp, *Exodus*, 252, who suggests the delay from 4:22–23 to 11:4–6 "frames the entire plague cycle."

50. This is even more pronounced in Exod 7:2–3 in the emphatic pronouns used for both God and Moses: "You yourself [אתה] will speak. ... But I myself will harden [ואני אקשה]."

of hardening throughout Exodus 3-14.[51] The narrator divides the characters into "those who ... do *not* know ... and the One who alone knows (YHWH)."[52] Then in 5:1 Pharaoh is confronted with his obligation to acknowledge God and "his own dependent role as a dependent vassal who rules by the leave of Yahweh."[53] Yet his refusal to do so (5:2, passim) reflects his (willful) ignorance of God (cf. 10:7) and his belief in his own divinity, which together define him as a biblical idolater.[54] God ironically sees Pharaoh just as Pharaoh sees himself, namely as the physical presence of Amon Re on earth. To Pharaoh, this means his own divinity; for God, it means Pharaoh is the idol of a false god.[55] In other words, given the biblical relationship between image formation and idolatry, in 3:19 — prior to the reciprocal in 5:1-2 — God preemptively announces that he knows Pharaoh for what he has chosen to become (as carried through in his rebellious actions): a detestable, lifeless object worthy of judgment.

This illuminates the final connection between Exodus 3:19-20, the hardening motif in 4:21, and the remainder of chapters 3-14 — namely, the paronomasia provided by חזק in *mighty hand* (cf. also 6:1).[56] Because

---

51. The conflict of Exodus is initially staged by the advent of a Pharaoh who did not "know" Joseph (Exod 1:8). In response, the first occurrence of ידע in Exod 3-14 is at 3:7, wherein God "knows" Israel's plight.

52. Isbell, *Function*, 40, emphasis original.

53. Brueggemann, "Pharaoh," 35. See especially Isbell, *Function*, 40-43, on the motif of knowing. In Exod 4-14, Israel must come to truly "know" God in what he does to the Egyptians in order to free them (Exod 10:1-2), and this knowledge is to be experiential rather than merely abstract (Brueggemann, "Pharaoh," 26).

54. There is something of a chicken-and-the-egg relationship between the creation accounts in Genesis and Israel's creation with Pharaoh's idolatry (and uncreation) in Exodus. Experientially, Israel's exodus predates the writing of the Genesis accounts; but at the same time, the presentation of the exodus narrative is tacitly framed in terms of the theological categories or framework normatively by the Genesis creation narratives in their final form.

55. Among others, Meador (*Idolatry*, 27) recounts Pharaoh's contribution to his own hardening in reference to Exod 5:1-2, in being a "living curse" over God's covenant people. Being king over enslaved, oppressed Israel, he "directly challenges ... Yahweh's exclusive kingship ... in confidence that he, his nation, and his gods, as dictating sovereignties, can authoritatively suppress and decisively defeat Israel and her Lord."

56. Although he does not make the connection regarding ביד חזקה in 3:19-20, Isbell (*Function*, 35) comments on יד בחזק in 13:14, 16: "יד and חזק in the passage cannot fail to remind readers of the twelve-fold use of חזקin the heart hardening references. The same power [יד] that now effects deliverance has been earlier seen controlling the Pharaoh. ... That the 'great power' (יד חזק) of YHWH is now given credit for all that has happened so far, is basic to the entire narrative."

of Pharaoh's idolatry and corresponding hardening, even as Amon
Re incarnate he has no control over his own heart. Instead, in 3:20 it
is Yahweh's mighty (חזק) hand that will compel Pharaoh's mighty (or
"hard"; cf. 4:21; 7:13, etc.) heart to release Israel.

Therefore, in Exodus 3–14 God hardens Pharaoh as a judgment upon
his idolatry. It is crucial to recognize that in hardening Pharaoh, God is
not dispensing judgment upon an innocent or neutral party, but is judging an idolater—specifically, one who is holding ransom the Hebrews.
Although idolatry is not uncommon in the Bible, God hardens Pharaoh
because Exodus is Israel's creational story.[57] Thus, Pharaoh's hardening
is intrinsic to Israel's self-identity: at the defining moment of Israel's
creation—in their deliverance and redemption from slavery—God
judges Pharaoh their oppressor, and his enemy, as the archetypal biblical idolater. Consequently, God's hardening of Pharaoh is both in continuity with and the prototypical pattern for subsequent instances of
judgment upon obduracy in biblical traditions. Having established the
reason for the hardening now enables an analysis of how Exodus 9:16
discloses the *function* served by Pharaoh's hardening in chapters 3–14.

EXODUS 9:16 AND THE FUNCTION OF PHARAOH'S HARDENING

Exodus 9:16 occupies a pivotal position within the structure of the
plague cycle, and comes at a turning point in the hardening motif there
and in the larger exodus narrative. The plague cycle in particular is
"nothing less than architectural," being divided by several features into
three sets of three plagues and a final, overflowing tenth plague (a 3 + 3 +
3 + 1 structure).[58] The first two plagues in each set begin with an ultimatum marked by כה־אמר יהוה (cf. 5:1) and a forewarning of God's response
to Pharaoh's continued refusal to release the Israelites, while the final

---

57. For greater detail, see Aaron Sherwood, "The Mixed Multitude in Exodus 12:38:
Glorification, Creation, and Yhwh's Plunder of Israel and the Nations," *HBT* 34 (2012):
149–52. Further, God's treatment of Pharaoh invites exploration into the nature of
humanity's fallenness for the biblical authors generally. Do all people post-Genesis 3
fundamentally share Pharaoh's status as idolaters? If so, why does God not deal with
all idolaters thus (starting with Adam and Eve)? However, that conversation is not
relevant to analysis of Exod 9:16 either in context or in Paul's use and understanding
of it, except insofar as it relates to how God chooses to relate to Pharaoh *cum* object
with judgment and the appropriateness of doing so.
58. Greenberg, *Understanding*, 170. For much of the following, see Sarna, *Exploring*,
76–78; Chisolm, "Divine," 419–26; Greenberg, *Understanding*, 171–73.

plague in each set has neither.[59] The tenth plague is offset in that it begins with a drastic forewarning (11:4–8) but lacks any ultimatum. It is as
if God requires nothing of Pharaoh; his fate is already decided. Again, in
the first plague of each set, God commands Moses to stand (יצב) before
Pharaoh early in the morning, and the second plague of each set begins
with the instruction to go to Pharaoh. Finally, while no pattern emerges
in the second set, the first and third sets of plagues are enacted through
the agencies of Aaron and Moses, respectively; the final plague is again
offset with God as the agent. The narrator also increases the relative
lengths of each successive set, so that the third set is longer than the
prior two (both on the whole and in comparing parallel episodes).

A further pattern within the plague narrative is that of Pharaoh's responses to God and Moses. The first four plagues conclude with a report
that Pharaoh would not listen (לא־שמע אלהם) and the divine certification formula (כאשר דבר יהוה). In the second and fourth plagues Pharaoh
requests Moses' help and tries to bargain with him, but then recants
the promised release. The seventh plague, the first episode in the third
set, contains the final occurrence of the certification formula, and the
phrase לא־שמע אלהם disappears. And at first in this third set, Pharaoh
initially repents of his sinfulness but recants a final time. But then by
contrast, when the judgment of hardening has been decisively imposed,
in the two remaining plagues of the final set Pharaoh attempts to repent
but God hardens his heart and prevents him from releasing the Israelites.
Similarly, following the tenth plague, God actively dictates Pharaoh's actions, keeping him from submitting to him even if Pharaoh had chosen
to do so (Exod 14:4, 8). The data can be diagrammed as follows:[60]

---

59. The forewarnings usually come with a conditional statement (e.g., Exod 7:27;
8:17; 9:2). However, it is significant that Exod 9:14–16 has a purposive statement in
place of the conditional (see further below).
60. Cf. Sarna, *Exploring*, 76; Chisolm, "Divine," 426–28.

Plague	Set	Name	Exodus source	Forewarning and ultimatum	Time of warning	Instruction formula	Agent	States Pharaoh "does not listen"	Certification formula	Pharaoh's response
1.	1st Set	Blood	7:14–24	yes	"early in the morning"	none	Aaron	yes	yes	—
2.	1st Set	Frogs	7:25–8:11 [ET 8:15, etc.]	yes	none	"go in to Pharaoh"	Aaron	yes	yes	requests aid, but recants
3.	1st Set	Gnats	8:12–15	no	—	none	Aaron	yes	yes	—
4.	2nd Set	Insects	8:16–28	yes	"early in the morning"	"stand yourself"	God	yes	yes	bargains, but recants
5.	2nd Set	Pestilence	9:1–7	yes	none	"go in to Pharaoh"	God	no	yes	repents, but prevented
6.	2nd Set	Boils	9:8–12	no	—	none	Moses	yes	yes	—
7.	3rd Set	Hail	9:13–35	yes	"early in the morning"	"stand yourself"	Moses	no	yes	repents, but recants
8.	3rd Set	Locusts	10:1–20	yes	none	"go in to Pharaoh"	Moses	no	no	repents, but prevented
9.	3rd Set	Darkness	10:21–29	no	—	none	Moses	no	no	relents, but prevented
10.	Climax	Death of Firstborn	11:1–8; 12:29–36	forewarning; no ultimatum	none	none	God	no	no	submits, but prevented

Fig. 4: Structure of the Plague Narrative

The divine speech via Moses in Exodus 9:14-16 opens the seventh plague episode (and the third set), which marks the turning point in the cycle. Immediately prior, the hardening reference in 9:12 (to close the sixth plague episode and second set) is both the medial obduracy text in Exodus 3-14—the tipping point of the hardening motif within the larger narrative—and the first plague narrative text explicitly identifying God as the agent.[61] Then the final set begins with one of the longest episodes in the cycle, marking "the buildup with the narrative leading to the final judgment."[62] At the outset of the seventh plague, the sense of כל in 9:14 is "all the remaining," hyperbolically conveying the idea that "the Lord's incomparability will now be shown in blows of unprecedented severity."[63] The effect of this is that the final set is the weightiest, and is characterized by the inevitability of God's judgment.[64] Reports that Pharaoh did not listen are dispensed with as if no longer a factor. Likewise, the subsequent cessation of the certification formula (following two consecutive obduracy texts in Exod 9:34-35) suggest that hereafter the events themselves are God's final word. Perhaps most dramatic is that following the combination of 9:12, God's speech in 9:14-16, and the final unrepentance, Pharaoh is no longer in control of himself. In the remaining plagues of the final set, he tries to repent (Exod 10:16-17, 24) but is prevented by God (Exod 10:20, 27), and in the tenth plague his

---

61. One colleague privately declared that God is the ontological and theological agent of the hardening verbs in every obduracy text in Exod 3-14, regardless of the actual subject of the verb. But that the author elects to specify God as the subject only at the halfway point of the obduracy texts in the narrative is a datum that needs accounting for. Such a claim is therefore a bald assertion, and naïve given the absence of evidence toward such a point and also in the face of the evidence to the contrary.

62. Brevard Childs, *The Book of Exodus: A Critical Theological Commentary* (Philadelphia: Westminster, 1974), 158.

63. Greenberg, *Understanding*, 160-61. On the significance of כל in Exod 3-14, see Propp, *Exodus*, 347.

64. Greenberg (*Understanding*, 161) remarks, "The third triplet is thus *expressly* depicted as the most prodigious" (emphasis added). Correspondingly, Pharaoh's repentance in Exod 9:28-29 is the most extensive in and his recantation (Exod 9:34, modified by ויסף לחטא) is all the more definitive. Beale's ("Exegetical," 145) suggestion that "continued to sin" entails that Pharaoh's obduracy earlier in the plague narrative was also sin(ful) may indicate another instance of the narrator exploiting Egyptian tradition, since "in striking contrast to the Egyptian belief in the perfection of Pharaoh," he "was simply judged to be a sinner and worthy of condemnation." Currid, "Why Did God Harden Pharaoh's Heart?" *BR* 9 (November/December, 1993): 51.

attempt to submit (Exod 12:31–32) is prevented by God to his ultimate destruction (Exod 14:4, 8).[65]

Exodus 9:14–16 is the hinge about which this shift takes place. In 9:15, God states his intention to "'now … send my hand in order to strike you and your people with pestilence, with the result that you will be swept from the earth.'"[66] However, God puts in abeyance Pharaoh's destruction "for one particular reason: in order that I might make you see my strength and thereby proclaim my name throughout all the earth" (9:16). The piel ספר—which here means to declare continuously and repeatedly—and the treble refrain "from/throughout (all) the earth" together confirm that God "[prolonged] the series of judgments by hardening Pharaoh's heart" because "the Lord's agenda [in hardening Pharaoh] included more than just saving His people."[67]

Specifically, the delay of God's final destruction is not a form of mercy but an amplification of his judgment that serves his larger purpose of glorifying his name (which is foundational to but also facilitates even his redemptive designs for Israel). As the recurrence of the ידע motif in Exodus 9:14 demonstrates, God hardens Pharaoh in order to bring him to a firsthand familiarity of his own incomparability, power, and sovereignty. Whereas Pharaoh boasted in Exodus 5:2 that he did not know and/or refused to recognize (ידע) the name "Yhwh," in 9:16 God turned Pharaoh's rebellion to his own ends, establishing him as an historical example of infamy for the sake of his own great name.[68]

---

65. If the foregoing analysis is sound, then the resultant interpretation stands even if it is philosophically or theologically difficult (or distasteful). One may object that, post-hardening, Pharaoh is interpreted to be a literal automaton. The response to this is, yes, exactly, that is just the biblical author's point: the nature of idolatry and its consequences in biblical understanding is such that one who undergoes a judgment of being (un)made like idols she worships is nothing but a mere object, having in that sense been stripped of her humanity and creatureliness. This result may be unpalatable, but it is theologically coherent, consistent with the data, and entirely comprehensible.

66. Cf. John I. Durham, *Exodus*, WBC 3 (Dallas: Word Books, 1987), 125, 127; Propp, *Exodus*, 333; and the LXX (νῦν γὰρ ἀποστείλας τὴν χεῖρα πατάξω) for taking עתה שלחתי in Exod 9:15 in the future sense.

67. Chisolm, "Divine," 415; cf. Cassuto, *Exodus*, 116. In Exod 9:14–16 and throughout the plague narrative, it is ambiguous whether ארץ—even in מצרים ארץ—refers to Egypt or to the whole world. It may be a case of both/and, since for Pharaoh Egypt is the whole world (cf. Childs, *Exodus*, 125; Isbell, *Function*, 43).

68. Ford (*God*, 10–11) considers that previous work by those such as Beale and Gunn "share the tendency to abstract the 'hardening' as a theological issue which needs to be solved." "Instead of considering the 'hardening as a separate issue," he examines

Therefore, nothing in the immediate or relevant wider context can make Exodus 9:16 to be about a dogmatic consideration of God's sovereignty, its role in salvation, or its nature in comparison to (or tension with) human free will. Instead, to sum up, Exodus 9:16 *in situ* articulates that since the *reason* God hardened Pharaoh was in judgment for his idolatry, specifically at the paradigmatic moment of Israel's creation and redemption from slavery, consequently Pharaoh's hardening served the *function* of glorifying God as he brought deliverance to Israel. As a result, all who hear of his great power and reputation will seek to share in Israel's deliverance from Pharaoh, the archetypal biblical idolater and opponent of God's creational purposes. The purpose statement in Exodus 9:16 therefore subsumes and encapsulates the others in Exodus 10:1-2; 14:4, 17-18, since by the end of the narrative Pharaoh's hardening results in both Israel and Egypt knowing and revering God (cf. Exod 14:30-31; 15:1-18): "The *kvd* (honor or glory) was Yahweh's, while the *kvd* (the sinfulness of a heavy heart [e.g., 7:14]) was Pharaoh's ... the whole point of the Exodus story."[69]

It is difficult to establish early Jewish theologies regarding Pharaoh's hardening or the narrative significance of Exodus 9:16 specifically. Rabbinic references to Pharaoh's hardening are ubiquitous, but for the most part neither Second Temple nor rabbinic sources discuss Exodus 9:16 specifically.[70] The standouts may be *Tanḥ. Exod.* 2.14 and 2.19 (although cf. 1QM 14.7) and the rather late *Exod. Rab.* 3:9 and 10.6, which consider Exodus 9:16 to be the definitive plague-narrative statement of God's purpose in hardening Pharaoh. Besides these, even the rabbis

---

it in context of the wider theological issues involved in the exodus narrative. Ford finds that the conversation between God and Pharaoh in Exod 9:13-19 marks a turning point in which Pharaoh's ultimate failure to respond to God's warnings and commands results in his self-hardening being taken over by God for the purpose of making known his glory to Israel and Egypt alike, the shift in agency facilitating a shift in the audience's perception (ad loc., 63-75, 82, 123-24, 214-15).

69. Currid, "Why," 51; cf. Greenberg, "Thematic," 153; Isbell, *Function*, 38-39: "Clearly the reader is expected to understand that the one who had 'kavodded' the Pharaoh would now 'kavod' himself" (emphasis original). Sarna (*Exploring*, 65) comments that because "God deprives 'god' of his freedom of action ... his so-called divinity is mocked."

70. Abasciano (*Romans 9.10-18*) is able to list, e.g., *Jub.* 43:14, which relates Pharaoh's obduracy to his deserved destruction, and specifies that it was according to God's purposes that Mastema carried out the hardening. But in this and other examples he attempts to force irrelevant traditions into the analysis of Exod 9:16 even while admitting, e.g., that "*Jubilees* does not quote Exod. 9.16 or even allude to it" (ad loc., 143).

resort to Exodus 9:16 only because it is understood to attribute Pharaoh's hardening to God in response to Pharaoh's pride[71] and/or wickedness.[72] Given the attention received by Pharaoh's example from at least the rabbis, it is reasonable to suspect that their lack of discussion specifically on the relationship between God's hardening and Pharaoh's free will reflects a lack of concern for this issue, a common presuppositional understanding akin to the interpretation offered above, or both. But if such traditions are indicative of an understanding of Exodus 9:16 that was contemporary with Paul—and there is no record of competing understandings—then it is likewise reasonable to suspect that Paul held a common Jewish understanding of Exodus 9:16 within its original context.[73] To what use he puts this understanding in Romans 9 can be considered after an examination of his other (first) Exodus citation, of Exodus 33:19.

EXODUS 33:19 IN ITS ORIGINAL CONTEXT

Exodus 33:19 belongs to the narrative unit of Exodus 32–34, which is positioned between the instructions regarding the tabernacle in chapters 25–31 and their implementation in chapters 35–40. The narrative begins with the Israelites' commission of idolatry at the foot of Sinai (Exod 32:1–6), in antithesis to their immediately prior theophanic encounter.[74] The golden calf incident was either simultaneous with or even preceded the giving of instructions in chapters 25–31, which indicates that "the present arrangement of material must have been deliberate to argue a theological point."[75] Martin Hauge, arguing that the three theophanic episodes of 19:3–24:2; 24:3–34:5; and 35:1–40:38 form the structure for chapters 19–40, comments on the gravity of chapters 32–34 as a disruption in the narrative. Because these chapters follow the second theophanic episode, they threaten to usurp the position of the climactic third

---

71. E.g., *Tanḥ. Exod.* 4.2, 4.8; *Lev. Rab.* 12.5; *Pesiq. Rab Kah.* 11.1; *Exod. Rab.* 11.6; *Midr. Pss.* 33.1; *b. Sanh.* 94b; *Eccl. Rab.* 5.2; *Exod. Rab.* 18.5; *Num. Rab.* 13.3.
72. E.g., *Tanḥ. Exod.* 4.2; *Midr. Pss.* 2.1; *S. Eli. Rab.* 13.3; *Exod. Rab.* 3.9; 10.6; 5.2.
73. I am familiar with the objection that even though both the exodus narrative and Exod 9:14–16 are not about eternal salvation, it does not mean that it is not possible for Paul to employ this material in a discussion of salvation. However, as seen so far (and further below), that is not in fact Paul's interest in Romans 9. Besides this, his doing so would be exceptional among all early Jewish witnesses.
74. See Martin Randal Hauge, *The Descent from the Mountain: Narrative Patterns in Exodus 19–40*, JSOTSup 323 (Sheffield: Sheffield Academic, 2001), 66.
75. Isbell, *Function*, 63; cf. Childs, *Exodus*, 562–63.

theophany as a false episode, a "nonevent ... distorting and threatening the proper succession of events," but for Moses' intercession.[76] This gravity is also present in the repetition in chapters 32–34 of plague cycle elements, including an assertion of Yhwh as the only God in Israel, affirmation of Moses' authority, and the occurrence of death.[77] As such, the two pieces of Exodus revolve around the issues of idolatry and its consequences, although chapters 32–34 progress not toward destruction but covenant restoration.[78] This movement occurs through a series of dialogues between God and Moses (Exod 32:7–14; 32:30–33:5; 33:12–19; and 34:8–27), wherein 33:19 is situated at a critical point in the negotiations.

During the golden calf episode—as with Pharaoh—God initially means to judge and destroy Israel for their idolatry (Exod 32:9–10).[79] And while Moses' intercession results in God retracting his decree of destruction, it leaves unresolved the issue of judgment (32:11–14). In 32:34, God hints at his judgment, in that henceforth Israel will merely have his angel going before them (הנה מלאכי ילך לפניך, 32:34) for guidance.[80] Then the narrator suddenly shifts attention to a plague(!), which is not God's judgment but does underscore the impending reckoning (32:35). Unforgiven Israel's fate is revealed in 33:1–5, wherein they will still be granted Canaan, but their idolatry has destroyed the basis for their relationship with God. Consequently, he will no longer remain in their midst (33:3). Worse than destruction, worse than purging by death, and worse than a plague, Israel's judgment for their idolatry is their existence without God, "a punishment ... that negates every announcement, every expectation, every instruction" so far in Exodus.[81]

---

76. *Descent*, 156; cf. p. 65.

77. Cf. Isbell, *Function*, 63.

78. Exodus 32–34 also follows the form of the other Exodus theophanies, including the introductory encounter, mediation and response, human movement toward God, and God's self-revelation. Here, however, the elements describe a restoration of God's presence rather than theophany (Hauge, *Descent*, 78).

79. It may also be that the Israelites—like Pharaoh—have started to become hard as a result of their idolatry. Although he does not make the idolatry connection, Isbell (*Function*, 68–69) cites further hardened body parts that signify rebellion or disobedience in Deut 2:30; Ezek 3:7; Prov 21:29; Jer 5:3; 2 Chr 36:13. He argues the Israelites' stiffness/hardness of neck (32:9 קשה-ערף; cf. קשח in Exod 4–14) is equivalent to Pharaoh's hardness of heart in the plague narrative. Thus, whether Egypt or Israel, "if they become [God's] enemy by denying His sovereignty, by seeking another deity, He will treat them all the same" (ad loc., 69).

80. Durham, *Exodus*, 432.

81. Ibid., 437; cf. Nahum Sarna, *Exodus: The Traditional Hebrew Text with the New JPS Translation* (Philadelphia: Jewish Publication Society, 1991), 211. See Hauge, *Descent*,

An interposed description of God's removal (Exod 33:7-11) rhetorically stages Moses' intercession for God's presence on Israel's behalf (Exod 33:12-16). The latter portion of chapter 33 in which our text occurs "serves to climax the intercession of Moses for Israel on account of her sin, and forms the bridge to the restoration of the covenant in the succeeding chapter."[82] Finally, Exodus 34 recounts God's paradigmatic OT self-revelation (34:5-7) and his concomitant restoration of the covenant (34:10-27). Thus, as the narrative builds toward covenant restoration, the entire narrative pivots upon the dialogue of 33:17-19.[83]

Exodus 33:19 concludes Moses' penultimate interaction with God in these chapters. Remarkably, this is one of only two instances in the Pentateuch where Moses initiates conversation with God (33:12; cf. Num 11:11). Moses' exchange with God is highly diplomatic, as possession of Israel seems to be up in the air. Paraphrasing God's language from Exodus 32:7, Moses first asks whether "this" people may be accepted by their association with himself (33:12-13). After God concedes to remain with Moses alone (second-person singular "you," 33:14), Moses insists on referring to the people along with himself for the remainder of the discussion (first-person plural "us," 33:15-16).[84] Finally in 33:17, God grants Moses' request (33:15-16) that his distinguishing presence would go among his people. As surety, Moses further requests in 33:18 a direct vision of God's glory (כבד). At this Donald Gowan remarks,

> having understood the reference to "glory" as a request for direct vision, [most interpreters] then are puzzled over the apparent discontinuity with what had just ensued. ... Why would Moses

---

71-72, for a description of how the poetics of Exod 32:30-33:6 underscore the significance of God's absence. It might be suggested that God's absence is not judgment, but rather a comment on his holiness, since, "If for one instant I went up in your midst, then I would finish you off" (Exod 33:5). However, whereas fear/reverence in God's presence was positive earlier in Exodus (e.g., Exod 20:20), since it kept the people from sinning and thereby brought sanctification, in Exod 33:3, 5, following Israel's idolatry, "rather than sanctification, God's presence in the midst of his people now means judgment for the people. ... While earlier the people feared YHWH because of their mortality, now they must fear him because of their sinful condition." Scott J. Hafemann, "The Glory and the Veil of Moses in 2 Cor 3:7-14: An Example of Paul's Contextual Exegesis - A Proposal," *HBT* 14 (1992), 34-35.

82. Childs, *Exodus*, 597; cf. Durham, *Exodus*, 426.

83. Eep Talstra, "'I and Your People': Syntax and Dialogue in Exod 33." *JNSL* 33 (2007): 91-92.

84. Ibid., 94-95.

now be asking for ... a personal, mystical experience [when his request for God's presence had just been granted]?[85]

But the reason for Moses' further request is that 33:17 leaves unresolved the issue of Israel's idolatry. It is only because of Moses' second request in 33:18 and God's agreeing to appear before him that the narrative does not end with Israel's rejection. Moreover, it concludes not only in with the restoration of God's presence (33:17; cf. 34:9) but also with the restoration of the covenant, which provides that presence with meaning (34:10-27). In the subsequent Exodus 34 theophany, God defines his glory in terms of his goodness (טובי)—which in the Bible often refers to Israel's experience of his blessing—and his name, Yhwh (33:19a). Yet God further amplifies his name in the following couplet, which exhibits synonymous parallelism, "I show mercy [or 'favor'; חנן] to whomever I will show mercy, and I show compassion [רחם] to whomever I will show compassion" (33:19b). God's positive statement of his character in terms of mercy and compassion (רחום וחנון, 34:6) enables Moses to request a full pardon and repeat his request for the restoration of God's presence (34:9), to which God responds with full covenant renewal (34:10-27).

However, going back to Exodus 33:19, the couplet in the latter half of the verse twice employs the Hebrew *idem per idem* formula, which idiomatically preserves the manner of performing an action at the agent's discretion.[86] It is the same formula used in Exodus 3:14, when God described his name according to his sovereignty, or self-definition (during

---

85. *Theology in Exodus: Biblical Theology in the Form of a Commentary* (Louisville: Westminster John Knox, 1994), 232; e.g., the misinterpretation in Piper, *Justification*, 60 ("the magnitude of Moses' request [in vv. 12-16] drives Moses to probe into the very heart of God, as it were, to assure himself that God is in his deepest nature the kind of God who could 'pardon our iniquity...(34:9de)'"); cf. Durham, *Exodus*, 452; Hauge, 171. Gowan's own solution is to argue that 'glory' in v. 18 is shorthand for 'God's presence' elsewhere in Exodus (ad loc., 233).

86. So *TDOT*, s.v. חנן, D. N. Freedman and J. R. Lundbom, 5:30; H. Simian-Yofre and U. Dahmen, *TDOT*, s.v. רחם, 13:440; Childs, *Book*, 596; Piper, *Justification*, 61-62; Durham, *Exodus*, 452. Cassuto, *Exodus*, 436 captures this meaning of v. 19 in his free translation, "You may know that I am compassionate and gracious, but...I shall be gracious and compassionate if it pleases Me, when it pleases Me, and for the reasons that please Me" (in order that God's justice should not be manipulated through predictability). For his interpretation, Abasciano, *Romans 9.1-9*, 66-69 wants the *idem per idem* formula generally to be applicable to arbitrary or conditioned usage, and for all biblical occurrences to be partly externally influenced. Additionally, because v. 19 mentions "compassion," Abasciano jumps to the conclusion that it refers to God's essentially merciful character and at the same time (somewhat inconsistently) his prerogative regarding whether or not to withhold mercy.

the same pericope that outlines the hardening and knowing motifs for the exodus narrative). God's response is therefore somewhat gnomic, as the couplet in 33:19b emphasizes God's discretion in choosing how to respond to Israel's idolatry. Here, God's response is as yet hidden, so that 33:18–19 represent the climax of the dramatic tension in the narrative, and therefore the hinge upon which it turns.

As with Pharaoh in Exodus 3–14, in dealing with Israel in chapters 32–34 God is dealing with idolaters. Although by the end of the narrative he responds to their idolatry with mercy for his name's sake, as of Exodus 33:19 Israel sits on a knife's edge. By committing idolatry they consigned themselves to God's judgment. Given the precedent of the plague cycle and the thoroughgoing biblical pattern of God's response to idolatry patterned after that in the exodus narrative, it is to be expected that Israel's stiff neck from Exodus 32:9 should and will metamorphose via judgment into a fully hardened heart (see n. 70, above), and for Israel's history (and Scriptures) to abruptly end in destruction in Exodus 34. As Wright comments, "The surprise, in other words, is not that some were allowed to fall by the wayside [cf. 32:25–28], but that any were allowed to continue as God's covenant people."[87]

In this instance, it is God's grace alone that the covenant is renewed, since God has absolute discretion in choosing whether to respond to idolatry with judgment or mercy.[88] So, similar to Exodus 9:16 above, there are no indications in the episode of 33:12–19 or the context of chapters 32–34 that allow 33:19 to be read in terms of a discussion of God's merciful character, the doctrine of election, the salvation of groups or individuals, or the like. Instead, the contextual meaning and function of Exodus 33:19 is to explicate God's discretion in dispensing either judgment or mercy in response to idolatry in the case of Israel his people. Particularly, as a pivotal text within the narrative of chapters 32–34, Exodus 33:19 is crafted in the way that it is in order to highlight the precariousness of Israel's future caused by their idolatry.

---

87. *Romans*, 638.

88. This, of course, is not what election (to salvation or otherwise) is about, as it were, but that is unproblematic since that is not the interest (let alone topic of discussion) for either the author of Exod 33 or Paul in Rom 9 (let alone what they are discussing). As noted previously (n. 44), traditions like Exod 33:19 are perhaps of interest in another discussion regarding the post-Genesis 3 sinfulness and/or idolatry of all humanity. However, this particular presentation of the exodus generation as idolatrous stands alone within this narrative context, and functions in a manner that obviates the topic of hamartiology occupying the primary level of the narrative.

Paul's reference to Exodus 33:19 is the only one in Second Temple Judaism, such that no contemporary points of comparison are available in establishing his understanding in Romans 9.[89] Potentially relevant references are plentiful in rabbinic sources, directly drawing upon or arguing for Exodus 33:19 as an instance in which dispensing mercy specifically in response to idolatry is at God's discretion (e.g., *Tanḥ. Exod.* 9.16; *Tanḥ. Deut.* 2.3; *Pesiq. Rab Kah.* 17.1; *b. Ber.* 7a; *Midr. Pss.* 25.6; *Exod. Rab.* 45.6). Other sources acknowledge the severity of Israel's idolatry in Exodus 32–34 and its deserved consequences of either hardening, destruction, or both (*Tg. Onq.*; *Sifre Deut.* 43; *Tanḥ. Exod.* 9.13).[90] Furthermore, regarding both Pauline and rabbinic usage, it is worth noting that there is no appeal to the theophany in Exodus 34:5–9 in explaining 33:19 (whose own relative context is the contained scene of 33:12–23). This is in striking contrast with the presumption of many modern Romans scholars.[91]

With the exception of the Targumim (and perhaps *Tanḥ. Exod.* 9.13), relevant rabbinic traditions recognize the wickedness of Israel's idolatry but shy away from discussing the nature of God's mercy together with its implications for Israel's idolatry. This means that Paul's usage (assuming it aligns with the above analysis) is of another level of magnitude: Whereas the rabbis extrapolate concerning God's mercy, Paul takes these elements to their logical conclusion and *characterizes* Israel as idolatrous, focusing upon them and their wickedness in relation to God's sovereignty.

PAUL'S USE OF EXODUS 33:19 AND 9:16 IN ROMANS

In Romans 9:15, Paul continues his defense of God's faithfulness (9:6a) and begins his response to the charge of injustice (9:14) by drawing

---

89. Confirmed by Abasciano, *Romans 9.10–18*, 141–42. It may be noted that while dealing with the issue of idolatry, neither Exod 33:19, Paul in Rom 9:15–16, nor any of the following rabbinic sources reference the judgment of hardening.

90. Of more peripheral interest are references wherein Exod 33:19 is understood to reflect a positive view of God's mercy in 33:19 (*Midr. Pss.* 119.21; *Lam. Rab.* 1.2; *Exod. Rab.* 2.1), or to explain how God's mercy is conditioned on the merit of those receiving it (*Tg. Neof.*; *Tg. Ps.-J.*; *Midr. Prov.* 63).

91. There is a limit (on an *ad hoc* basis) to the amount of context that should be considered relevant in an early Jewish citation of a given tradition. A method of intertextual reading needs compelling reasons (additional contemporary usage/ applications, the intrinsic structure of the biblical tradition in question, etc.) to conclude that, e.g., Exod 33:19 is somehow "about" 34:5–10, none of which are present here (barring other presumptions regarding Paul's theological interest in Rom 9:14–18).

upon Israel's idolatry at the base of Sinai. While God there responded with mercy, Exodus 33:19 makes clear that he was not obligated to do so. Just as in its original context, Paul's citation of Exodus 33:19 emphasizes that God is sovereign (even if gracious) such that his response to idolatry is wholly at his discretion. With this, Paul is not theorizing about God's mercy or sovereignty (let alone their relationship with human free will)—such discussion would be a non sequitur—and is he also not engaging in midrash, technically understood. Instead, he is applying Israel's situation in Exodus 32–34 to present-day circumstances in order to interpret unbelieving Jews' rejection of Christ and the gospel, identifying that rejection as idolatrous.[92] Like Israel in Exodus 33:19, contemporary national Israel stands at a precipice—will they receive mercy or judgment? Paul accordingly extrapolates in Romans 9:16 that presently their fate is beyond their own means and depends now upon God's potential mercy.[93]

Although Paul cites only Exodus 33:19b, the first half of the verse establishes the glory of God's name as its context (cf. Exod 33:16). In Romans 9:17, Paul carries this echo of God's name forward when quoting Exodus 9:16, which in its original context states that God's purpose (the glorification of his name) is served by his judgment upon idolatrous Pharaoh.[94] As another atypical citation formula, ἡ γραφὴ in Romans 9:17 may be meant to directly invoke God's authority (instead of that

---

92. In Rom 9:30–10:4 the issue is the character and consequences of ethnic Israel's idolatry, whereas the issue in Rom 9:14–18 is how God's response to it may be wrongly taken as objectionable.

93. Beginning with Sanday and Headlam (*Epistle*, 2:254), most commentators agree that the implicit subject of Rom 9:16 is God's showing mercy or his response to sin generally. Scholars who think the subject is something else, such as [the mercy of] salvation (e.g., Piper, *Justification*, 160), often do so because they impose their own interests upon Paul. Similarly, Abasciano (*Romans 9.1–9*, 66–69) takes the subject to be the gift of covenantal election and partnership. But at best it would be correct to say that the subject is *indirectly* the *potential* mercy of *restoration* of covenant depending upon God's forthcoming response, as Exod 33:19 addresses the question of how God will respond to Israel's idolatrous covenant breaking.

On a separate point, the substantive τρέχοντος captures "a more intense expression of the biblical idea of 'walking'" (Byrne, *Romans*, 298; e.g., Psa 1:1; 119:1), and "willing and striving" together "sum up the total of man's capacity" (Dunn, *Romans 9–16*, 562). Here, then, Paul echoes himself from Rom 9:10–13: just as God's faithfulness to Israel was independent from Torah observance, Torah observance cannot merit God's mercy in response to idolatry.

94. Cf. Dunn, *Romans 9–16*, 563.

of Moses as an intermediary), indicating that for Paul it "represents a statement of the divine intent."[95]

MT Exod 9:16	LXX Exod 9:16	Rom 9:17
וְאוּלָ֗ם בַּעֲב֥וּר זֹאת֙	καὶ <u>ἕνεκεν τούτου</u>	<u>εἰς αὐτὸ τοῦτο</u>
הֶעֱמַדְתִּ֔יךָ	<u>διετηρήθης</u>	<u>ἐξήγειρά σε</u>
בַּעֲב֖וּר	<u>ἵνα</u>	ὅπως
הַרְאֹתְךָ֣ אֶת־כֹּחִ֑י	ἐνδείξωμαι ἐν σοὶ τὴν	ἐνδείξωμαι ἐν σοὶ τὴν
	ἰσχύν μου	<u>δύναμίν</u> μου
וּלְמַ֛עַן סַפֵּ֥ר שְׁמִ֖י	καὶ ὅπως διαγγελῇ τὸ	καὶ ὅπως διαγγελῇ τὸ
	ὄνομά μου	ὄνομά μου
בְּכָל־הָאָֽרֶץ	ἐν πάσῃ τῇ γῇ	ἐν πάσῃ τῇ γῇ

Likewise, while the quotation resembles the Hebrew more closely than the LXX, its differences from both accentuate the sense of God's purposefulness from the original context.[96]

---

95. Byrne, Romans, 299.

96. The change of the LXX ἕνεκεν τούτου to εἰς αὐτὸ τοῦτο places "greater stress upon the precise intention of God" (ibid., 299; cf. Cranfield, Romans, 2:485–86). It is likewise for Paul's substitution of ἐνδείξωμαι for the passive διετηρήθης, where the former is used throughout the LXX "in the sense of raising up on the scene of history for a particular purpose" (Murray, Epistle, 2:27, citing Num 24:19; 2 Sam 12:11; Job 5:11; Hab 1:6; Zech 11:16; cf. Cranfield, Romans, 2:485–86). Finally, the change of ἵνα to ὅπως may be to make parallel or even coordinate the two purpose clauses, thereby unifying them as two halves of a single purpose (Cranfield, Romans, 2:485–86; Dunn, Romans 9–16, 563; Wagner, Heralds, 55; cf. Tg. Neof.). Stanley (Paul, 107–9), whose textual analysis is the most thorough, alternatively speculates that Paul used an unattested Vorlage or possibly "a Greek text that had already been 'corrected' toward the Hebrew" (ad loc., 108). His argument is supported in that LXX mss of Exod 9:16 are equally divided between δύναμίν and ἰσχύν, whereas NT mss unanimously testify to Paul's use of δύναμίν, and ἰσχύν never occurs in the undisputed Pauline letters (ad loc., 109). However, we might instead suggest Paul's awareness of the nuances in the MT, in which case his selection (if not modification) of Stanley's hypothetical Vorlage carries a rhetorical purpose. It is also worrisome that Stanley's theory requires speculative multiplication of entities.

   Generally speaking, whether Paul knew or ever worked from a proto-Masoretic text or other Hebrew recension is debated by scholars. The interpretation given here is not conditional upon settling this issue, but in principle I know of no good reasons to conclude that a Hellenistic Pharisee trained in Tarsus and exported to Palestine would not have known the Scriptures in Hebrew. As this citation has raised the question for Rom 9:6–29, in relation to Rom 9:17//Exod 9:16 Abasciano (Romans 9.10–18, 158–59) provides a compelling argument that Paul indeed knew and in this instance worked from a Hebrew Vorlage.

So the two couplets of Romans 9:15–16 and 9:17–18 imply the conceptual parallel that God responds to idolatry with either mercy or hardening judgment for his name's sake.[97] However, for Paul the couplets are complementary, since 9:17 answers the question posed in 9:15–16. While later Jewish traditions agree with Paul about Pharaoh's deserved judgment (e.g., *Tanḥ. Exod.* 2.14; *Midr. Pss.* 106.5; *Exod. Rab.* 11.6; 13.3), Paul's present application of this precedent (so understood) removes unbelieving Jews from Israel's position in Exodus 34 (which resolves their idolatry in Exod 32), and in an unprecedented and surprising reversal places them instead in the position of Pharaoh in Exodus 4–14. This application and evaluation never would have been made by Second Temple Jewish interpreters who did not identify themselves relative to Jesus of Nazareth.[98]

Therefore, as in the case of the archetypical biblical idolater Pharaoh—a "Gentile"—God is presently dispensing judgment upon national Israel. They first rebelled and hardened themselves in their rejection of Christ and the gospel, and so as a judgment God hardened them in confirmation of their idolatry. And as Paul will elaborate in his next pericope (see chapter 5), just as God used Pharaoh's idolatrous rebellion to bring deliverance to Israel, he is now using unbelieving Jews' idolatry to redeem the equally sinful and idolatrous nations (cf. Rom 1:18–29; 3:9–18). Paul, then, sees God's judgment upon national Israel as an ironic fulfillment of his promise to Abraham that Israel would bring blessing to the nations. They are being held up in display of God's glorious redemption as they now fill "Pharaoh's antithetical role ... in relation to God's calling of Gentile as well as Jew through the gospel."[99] Like Pharaoh, God has "allowed Israel ... to stand—that is, he has withheld instant judgment, in order that mercy may spread into the world."[100] And conversely, idolatrous Gentiles have now received the position of mercy occupied by the Israelites in Exodus 34 (see chapter 5). Thus, in Romans 9:14–18, on the basis of the historical precedents of God's

---

97. Since Paul is not here expounding—or even referencing—his view of God's mercy as such (related to his sovereignty or otherwise), it is not reductionistic of Paul's view of God's mercy to interpret him as discussing God's mercy or lack thereof with regard to idolatry (and particularly national Israel's present idolatry).

98. Cf. Cranfield, *Romans*, 2:485; Dunn, *Romans 9–16*, 563; Wright, *Letter*, 638, although none of these scholars either explores the significance of idolatry or understands the relationship between the couplets in this way.

99. Dunn, *Romans 9–16*, 563.

100. Wright, *Letter*, 638; cf. Rom 2:4–6, where God's kindness is meant to lead to repentance.

dealing with two instances of idolatry in the formative event of Israel's exodus, Paul argues that God is acting consistently (if unexpectedly) in the present circumstances. Appearances could be interpreted as God's unfaithfulness toward national Israel, but the truth is that he is passing judgment on their idolatry.

SUMMARY OF ROMANS 9:14–18
IN LIGHT OF PAUL'S USE OF SCRIPTURE

In Romans 9:14–18, Paul references God's response to both Pharaoh's and Israel's idolatry during the course of the exodus. Though different, each case had in common the purpose of glorifying God and advancing his purposes for human history. For the bulk of the pericope Paul spends some time explicating the implications of the exodus precedent: God's showing mercy to idolaters is conditional on God alone (Rom 9:16) since they have surrendered their humanity. In at least some instances, God's judgment upon them is to refrain from restoring their humanity to them and to secure them in less-than-human state, allowing it then to persist in order that he may make use of it (Rom 9:17). Romans 9:18, then, brings to the fore Paul's application of this to the present situation: God chooses to have mercy upon some idolaters, as with Israel in the exodus, while "on whom he will" God judges in confirming their hardening, as with Pharaoh and Egypt—and now national Israel in their opposition to God in the Christ event.[101]

In this fashion, Paul answers to the primary concern of this pericope, namely, the charge of injustice in Romans 9:14. Regarding the structure, then, 9:18 in a sense concludes 9:17 just as 9:16 concluded 9:15, both couplets stating that God may respond to idolatry with either mercy or, as

---

101. Curiously, Alexander A. Di Lella argues that he has identified a lacuna in Romans scholarship in a connection between Rom 9:18 and Tob 4:19 in certain Greek mss. These are the only two traditions in which ὅν θέλω / ὅν ἄν θέλῃ (respectively) occurs. He reckons this linguistic similarity to be a parallel especially on his assumption that both texts are concerned with God's free choice in Israel's election, with the Tobit tradition particularly affirming "that God has total freedom of choice in granting good counsel only to Israel" due to his sovereign power. Di Lella, "Tobit 4,19 and Romans 9,18: An Intertextual Study," *Bib* 90 (2009): 262.

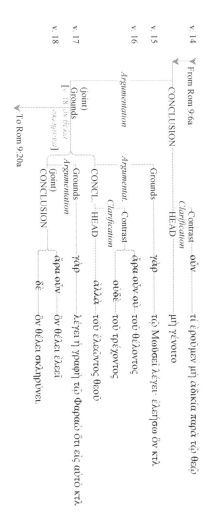

Fig. 5: Structural Analysis of Romans 9:14–18

in Pharaoh's case, hardening.[102] But 9:18 also incorporates a reiteration of 9:16 and is thereby the conclusion for the argument in 9:15–18:[103]

---

102. This structure at least is agreed upon by also Piper, *Justification*, 158–59; and Abasciano, *Romans 9.10–18*, 193–94.

103. The CONCLUSION of "Certainly not!" (Rom 9:14b) is the main independent clause for the pericope, *Argued* for on the basis of the (joint) Grounds that God hardens whom he will in an idolatry context (9:18b). This (joint) Grounds captures the

Justice is receiving from God what is merited, whereas mercy is the reception of what is unmeritable. Thus, God's justice and mercy remain independent factors specifically regarding his disposition toward unbelieving Jews, for when it comes to idolatry the absence of mercy cannot be equated with the absence of either faithfulness or justice.

Accordingly, for Paul the rhetorical question in Romans 9:14 incorrectly supposes God's justice and mercy are two extremes of a single spectrum. Hypothetically, God would then be obligated to continue to show favor to sinful national Israel as he had done historically (as Paul just finished arguing in 9:13). But Paul's conclusion in 9:18 is that because national Israel has assumed for themselves Pharaoh's position by their idolatry (9:17), God's sovereign choice (9:15) to harden them is not injustice (9:14) but, tragically, a faithful although unmerciful execution of justice.

The next stage of the argument, Romans 9:19-29, supports this refutation of the charge of injustice against God. Paul delves further into the connection between idolatry and its judgment of hardening, and the role served in God's redemptive purposes by national Israel's hardening. Whereas 9:14-18 did not specify how God's judgment upon national Israel has caused his name "to be recounted in all the earth" (9:17), Romans 9:19-29 explains that his refraining from showing mercy to unbelieving Jews has shown mercy to the nations, and thereby transformed them into God's people Israel.

---

two possible precedents, each *Argued* that God's showing mercy in response to idolatry depends upon presenting a theology of mercy.

4

Paul's Use of Scripture in Romans 9:19–29

[19]Then you will say to me, "Why does he still find fault? For who resists his intent?" [20]O man, on the contrary! Who are you, who answers back to God? "Will what is formed say to one who forms, 'Why did you make me this way?'" [21]Or, does not the potter have authority over the clay, to make from the same lump on the one hand an object relegated to an honorable use but on the other hand an object relegated to a dishonorable use? [22]Moreover, what if God, because he willed to display his wrath and to make known his power, endured with much long suffering objects of wrath prepared for destruction [23]and did so in order that he might make known the riches of his glory toward objects of mercy whom he prepared ahead of time for glory? [24]Namely, we whom he called, not only from the Jews but also from the nations, [25]even as it says in Hosea, "I will call that which is not my people 'my people' and that which was not beloved 'Beloved,'" [26]and, "It will be that in the place where it was said to them, 'You are Not My People,' there they will be called, 'Sons of the living God.'" [27]But Isaiah cries out concerning Israel, "Although the sons of Israel were as the sand on the seashore, only the remnant will be saved, [28]for the Lord will make a comprehensive and decisive work throughout the earth," [29]and accordingly Isaiah spoke beforehand, "Except that the Lord *Sabaoth* left us a seed, we would have become as Sodom, and we would have come to resemble Gomorrah."

Romans 9:19–21

Having covered the first two pericopes of Romans 9:6–29, this chapter analyzes the final pericope of 9:19–29. Most interpreters see here—building upon a standard understanding in which Paul discussed in 9:6–18 the nature and scope of election and/or salvation—Paul's insistence that God's election of "true" Israel over national Israel is legitimate even if unpalatable, and this truth must be taken on authority (9:19-21).[1] Then interpreters take Paul to be expanding (9:22-29) upon how God's salvation of the Gentiles (and perhaps the "remnant" of believing Jews) in Christ is a scriptural fulfillment of his vision for "true" Israel—or perhaps upon how God is using his judgment upon the hardened non-elect (wherein hardening is not itself understood as a judgment, for idolatry or otherwise) in glorifying himself with respect to the elect, that is, "true Israel."

While Paul might be capable of saying such things given another context (since I do not presume to offer a conclusion on Paul's theology of election here), this would not seem to be his focus in Romans 9:19-29, given that we have seen how election as such has not been under direct discussion to this point. Rather, in continuity with what has been seen of Paul's discussion and communicative strategy in 9:6-18, I shall show here that Paul begins the pericope by redressing in 9:19-21 any potential misunderstanding of his evaluation in 9:14-18, that God is unfair to judge national Israel for his hardening of them. Paul's answer is that God's current response parallels that in preexilic Israel, when it is their antecedent idolatrous rebellion that precipitates his bringing hardening as judgment, and that, theologically, it is his prerogative to do so in such circumstances. Second to this, Paul evaluates in 9:22-29 God's response to equally idolatrous Gentile and Jewish nonbelievers in terms of scriptural eschatological expectations in order to clarify how God is ironically using his judgment upon national Israel in fulfilling his redemptive promises for his people as a whole.

INTRODUCTION TO ROMANS 9:19-21

In Romans 9:14-18, Paul responded to a supposed inconsistency (from 9:6-13) between God's former faithfulness to Israel and his present apparent rejection of unbelieving Jews. He identified their rejection of Christ and the gospel as idolatrous rebellion, arguing that God has *not* rejected national Israel but rather hardened them as judgment for *their* idolatrous rejection of Christ. In so doing, God removed national Israel from the place of Israel in Exodus 34 and assigned them instead the place of Pharaoh in the plague cycle, whose judgment God used in his deliverance and formation of his people. Now in Romans 9:19-29, Paul details further the nature and consequences of idolatry, and then specifies how

---

1. Recall N. T. Wright's quip, noted above (p. 10n33).

God is using his judgment on national Israel (like Pharaoh) in his redemptive purposes.[2]

Paul begins in Romans 9:19 by addressing the charge that national Israel is being forced into poor company, since they are not, any more than Pharaoh, able to act contrary to the purposes of a sovereign God. Therefore, they should not be held liable for their so-called rebellion. It is generally agreed that in the challenge, "Why does he still find fault? For who resists [ἀνθέστηκεν] his will?" the imaginary interlocutor supposes Paul has just committed himself (in 9:14–18) to the position that, even when apparently sinning, Pharaoh and present national Israel did not actually rebel against God, since their actions have been according to his purposes.[3] Thus, the objection goes, no one—present national Israel included—should be punished for apparent rebellion.[4] But Paul decries this misinterpretation in 9:20–21. The intensity of his response is marked by the rare combination of the interjection ὦ and the vocative ἄνθρωπε (directed against his interlocutor), and also by his use of ἀνταποκρίνομαι, which "denotes disputation and resistance, not merely an attempt to procure an answer to a difficult question."[5]

In Romans 9:20b, Paul clarifies and defends his position by an appeal to the potter/clay metaphor of Isaiah 29:16. Many agree with Hays' assessment that

> the potter/clay image must not be read simply as a rebuke to silence impertinent questions, nor is the effect of the allusion … limited to … establishing God's absolute power; … it also resonates deeply with Paul's wider argument about God's [present] dealings with Israel. … The reader who recognizes the allusion will not slip

---

2. Despite its length, Rom 9:19–29 holds together as a single pericope and thus needs to be treated as a single literary sub-unit; so both the NA and UBS. As argued below, 9:19–21 and 23–29 are directly related, as the first piece answers the interlocutor's objection and the second piece turns back on the interlocutor his own point. The bulk of the pericope is due mainly to the length of the catena of 9:25–29, but for which dividing the pericope would not be tempting.

3. Most interpreters go further, reading the accusation that *no one* has ever *actually* rebelled against God, since by definition every human action is according to his purposes. Separately, Paul's diatribe style is intensified by his alternation between the second-person singular and the vocative in Rom 9:19–20.

4. E.g., Sanday and Headlam, *Epistle*, 2:259; Murray, *Epistle*, 2:31; Cranfield, *Romans*, 2:490; Dunn, *Romans 9–16*, 556, all contra the unwarranted NRSV translation of ἀνθέστηκεν in Rom 9:19.

5. Schreiner, *Romans*, 515; cf. Käsemann, 269; and Piper, *Justification*, 166, who likewise note ἀνταποκρίνομαι indicates an indignant declaration of what *ought* to be.

into the error of such a reading … because the prophetic subtexts keep the concern [of] the fate of Israel … sharply in focus.[6]

That is, to this point in Romans 9:6-29 the issue under discussion has been national Israel's rejection of the gospel and its implications for God's faithfulness. Likewise, the interlocutor's objection in 9:19 is in response to Paul's foregoing discussion of national Israel's rejection of the gospel. Therefore, given the absence of indications to the contrary, it appears that in 9:20-21 Paul is appealing to the potter/clay metaphor of Isaiah 29:16 to further explain how God is not unfair to hold national Israel liable for their idolatry.

ISAIAH 29:16 IN ROMANS 9:19-21

Establishing Paul's Scriptural Reference

Textually, μὴ ἐρεῖ τὸ πλάσμα τῷ πλάσαντι in Romans 9:20 reproduces verbatim part of Greek Isaiah 29:16. But Paul changes Isaiah's denial (οὐ σύ με ἔπλασας) to a recrimination (τί με ἐποίησας οὕτως) that is more suited to his diatribe style.[7] As Christopher Stanley has demonstrated, such freedom is wholly within the standards for citation technique in late antiquity, which were less restrictive than modern standards.[8] Accordingly, most scholars agree that in 9:20b Paul quotes (or alludes to) Isaiah 29:16.[9] But despite this, the lack of introductory formula, the changes made to Isaiah 29:16, and varying resemblance to other texts lead scholars to consider that Romans 9:20(-21) additionally—or alternatively—allude(s) to one or more of Isaiah 45:9; Jeremiah 18:5-11; or Wisdom of Solomon 15:7.

Dunn suggests that τί με ἐποίησας in Romans 9:20b is a "conscious allusion" to τί ποιεῖς in Greek Isaiah 45:9.[10] But this would be the only verbal

---

6. *Echoes*, 65-66; cf. Dunn, *Romans 9-16*, 564; Fitzmyer, *Romans*, 568-69; Wright, *Letter*, 641.

7. So Dunn, *Romans 9-16*, 556.

8. See chapter 3 n. 30.

9. E.g., Piper, *Justification*, 175-76; Dunn, *Romans 9-16*, 556; Fitzmyer, *Romans*, 568; Moo, *Epistle*, 601-2. Shum (*Paul's*, 204-6) suggests the explicit citation of Isa 29:10 in Rom 11:8 further strengthens the likelihood of Paul's awareness and use of Isa 29 in 9:20b. However, Shum thinks that Paul only alludes to Isa 29:16—and avoids citation—to allow himself greater latitude in usage. I would disagree with his conclusion that Paul's use of Isa 29:16 is merely "some sort of linguistic borrowing" (ad loc., 206).

10. *Romans 9-16*, 556. Wagner's argument (*Heralds*, 59-62) is the most ardent for Paul's use of Isa 45:9. Based on *Tg. Isa.* 29:16 and 45:9 (each of which incorporates

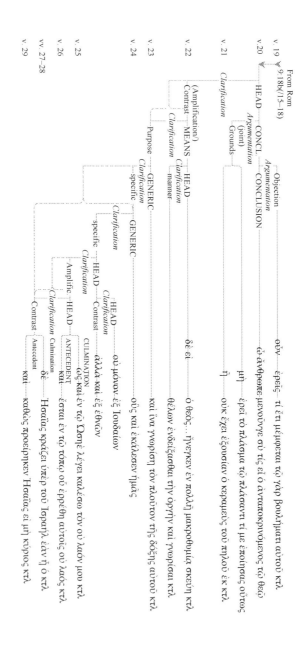

Fig. 6: Structural Analysis of Romans 9:19–29

connection between the two, and even this requires also a manipulation of the meaning of τί to be "Why?" instead of the original "What?" without which verse 20b and Isaiah 45:9 more linguistically dissimilar than similar.[11] More importantly, the shared contexts of Romans 9:19-21 and Isaiah 29:16—that of God's judgment upon Israel (see chapter 4, and on Isa 29:16 below)—is divergent from the context of Isaiah 45:9-17, namely, God's defense of his use of Cyrus (and *not* judgment upon Israel for their resistance). The only common factor between the two Isaianic texts is the underlying principle that God is not answerable to human expectations, but this principle is applied quite differently in the two separate contexts. It therefore seems that Isaiah 29:16 and 45:9 are two distinct uses of similar prophetic imagery (the latter potentially alluding to the tradition of the former). This, together with the verbal dissimilarity between Isaiah 45:9 and Romans 9:20, militates against the view that Paul is alluding to Isaiah 45:9 in addition to Isaiah 29:16.

The suggested use by Paul of Greek Jeremiah 18:5-11 presents a similar case. It shares no verbal overlap with Romans 9:20-21 (although there is limited shared vocabulary), and does not reference, describe, or interpret God's judgment upon Israel, let alone a particular instance of judgment (nor does it question God's faithfulness or Israel's unfaithfulness, as in Isa 29 and Rom 9). Rather, Jeremiah 18:5-11 employs the potter/clay metaphor to spell out in principle God's *right* to judge Israel as a motivation for them to repent and avoid judgment in that particular circumstance. And the prophet uses the potter/clay metaphor not in reference to judgment but to describes God's creative intentions for Israel, while warning that if the only type of creation they are willing to undergo is reconstruction following their destruction, then he will judge them with destruction. Consequently, the only shared element between Romans 9:20-21 and Jeremiah 18:5-11 is the use of a versatile, common metaphor (see below) for unrelated purposes.[12] Therefore, giv-

---

elements of the other to create two similar texts), he thinks Paul either depended on the *Targum* or shared its interpretive impulse, and thus invokes both Isa 29:16 and 45:9 simultaneously.

11. Greek Isa 45:9 would then read, "What is this that you doing?" in reference to God's choice of Cyrus, while Rom 9:20 would incongruously read, "Why are you making me in this way?" in reference to God's judgment of shaping the speaker; cf. Wagner, *Heralds*, 59-62.

12. Piper, 174; cf. Wagner, *Heralds*, 70; contra Meadors (*Idolatry*, 130-33), who without critical support operates with the view that Paul is citing Jer 18:1-6/15 (as well as Isa 45:9) in that the motif there of God's mercy that is conditioned upon repentance

en the verbal and contextual dissimilarity between the two texts, it is also unlikely that Paul is alluding to Jeremiah 18:5-11 in Romans 9:20-21.[13]

Finally, Wisdom of Solomon 15:7 likewise bears at best only superficial resemblance to Romans 9:21. Again, verbal overlap (κερανεὺς, πηλός, σκεῦος) is due to independent, mutual use of the potter/clay metaphor. And whereas Romans 9:20-21; Isaiah 29:16; 45:9; and Jeremiah 18:5-11 all cast God in the role of potter, Wisdom of Solomon 15:7 takes the opposite approach, identifying the potter with idolaters. The context of 15:7 entails it "has *almost nothing in common* with Paul's meaning"; its point is the absurdity of idol worship since idol makers are supposedly "better than the objects they worship" (Wis 15:17).[14] Additionally, a strong case can be made for a relatively late date for the Wisdom of Solomon, in which case "there seems almost no chance that Paul ... would have known about this work—or given it the time of day had he known of it."[15]

All told, given in addition the much greater degree of verbal similarity between the two, it seems best to investigate Romans 9:20-21 primarily in terms of Isaiah 29:16.

ISAIAH 29:16 IN ITS ORIGINAL CONTEXT

Isaiah 29:16 belongs to a woe oracle (29:15-24), one of a series in Isaiah 28-31 that together constitute the longest continuous polemic against Jerusalem's leadership in chapters 1-39.[16] These oracles also lie in the trajectory of the so-called wisdom debate, which scholars recognize is initiated during the opening chapters of the book and runs throughout

---

is an "authoritative, biblical background" with which "Paul's portrayal [in Rom 9:22] is consistent."

13. Given the evidence against Isa 45:9 and Jer 18:5-11, a main reason for insisting on their occurrence in Rom 9:20 is the assumption that Paul's focus is to legitimate his position regarding God's sovereignty in forming at least nonbelieving Jews (if not all humans), which almost entirely misses his concern regarding the specific case of national Israel's idolatry (see below).

14. Piper, *Justification*, 176, emphasis original; cf. Byrne, *Romans*, 300; Wright, *Letter*, 640.

15. Fee, "Wisdom Christology in Paul: A Dissenting View," in *To What End Exegesis?: Essays Textual, Exegetical, and Theological* (Grand Rapids: Eerdmans, 2001), 371n56, citing David Winston, *The Wisdom of Solomon*, AB 43 (Garden City, NY: Doubleday, 1979). Fee presents a devastating argument against Paul's use of the Wisdom of Solomon in his Christology, which may call into question its use in other circumstances such as Rom 9:20-21.

16. Sweeney, *Isaiah 1-4 and the Post-Exilic Understanding of the Isaianic Tradition* (Berlin: Walter de Gruyter, 1988), 54-57.

chapters 1-39.[17] Sound analysis of 29:16, therefore, must take into account the opening chapters of the Isaianic corpus.

Idolatry and the Wisdom Debate in Isaiah 1-39
The introduction of Isaiah is a trial or disputation convened by God against his people Israel, who are full of iniquity, rebellious, and neither know (ידע) him nor understand (בין) his wise rule (Isa 1:2-4).[18] Because they have responded with superficial cultic observance (Isa 1:10-17), God threatens to close his eyes and ears to their prayers (Isa 1:15) and passes judgment: for Jerusalem's infidelity, God will turn against Israel as an enemy (Isa 1:24-28). Chapters 1-4 identify the problem as the entwined themes of idolatry/corrupt cultus (e.g., Isa 2:6-8, 18-20; 3:3) and the leadership's rejection of God's wisdom in favor of their own autonomous, foolish "wisdom" (e.g., Isa 1:10, 23-26; 3:12b-15; 5:18-24).[19] Then, in the so-called Song of the Vineyard (Isa 5:1-7), God invites Judah to ironically pass judgment upon themselves as God's lovingly cultivated but unfruitful vineyard, giving way to a series of woe oracles (Isa 5:8-23) wherein God declares that his people do not "see [ראה] the work of his hands" (Isa 5:12b), call "darkness 'light,' and light 'darkness'" (Isa 5:20), and are "wise in their own eyes [חכמים בעיניהם] and understanding [נבנים] in their own sight" (Isa 5:21; cf. 1:3).

These six woes, which echo the six days of creation in Genesis 1, are followed by a profound scene of uncreation (Isa 5:30, presenting a 3 + 3 + 1 structure—although the final woe comes in 10:1-4; see below). For Israel, creation has reverted to darkness and the roaring sea (cf. Gen 1:2).[20] In the subsequent *Denkschrift*—whether a call or commissioning[21]—Isaiah

17. William McKane, *Prophets and Wise Men* (London: SCM, 1965), 65; Joseph Jensen, *The Use of tôrâ by Isaiah: His Debate with the Wisdom Tradition*, CBQM 3 (Washington: Catholic Biblical Association of America, 1973), 51; Evans, "On Isaiah's Use of Israel's Sacred Tradition," BZ 30 (1986): 99, stating "Isaiah understood Israel's sacred traditions in a way diametrically opposed to the understanding of his professional rivals" (e.g., Jerusalem's presumed inviolability vis-à-vis the Davidic covenant, God's only being permitted to bring Israel out of exile, etc.).
18. Sweeney, *Isaiah 1-39: With an Introduction to Prophetic Literature*, FOTL XVI (Grand Rapids: Eerdmans, 1996), 66 for a description of the "trial" genre.
19. Jensen, *Use*, 65-104; Sweeney, *Isaiah 1-4*, 38-39. Throughout Isa 1-39 God's condemnation is interspersed with invitations to repent or descriptions of future deliverance, which nevertheless do not mitigate the judgmental implications of the wisdom debate in these chapters.
20. Cf. Watts, "New Creational Restoration," 28.
21. Cf. Childs, *Isaiah* (Louisville: Westminster John Knox, 2001), 53.

is charged with bringing God's pronouncement of uncreation to Israel (Isa 6:1–13).[22] In this scene, God (twice named as Yhwh *Sabaoth* against Israel) engages in judgment with his royal council as divine king-judge, on a royal throne that is also a judgment seat.[23] The judgment of Isaiah 6:9–10 is hardening in response to Israel's idolatry, whereby God confirms them in their choice by remaking them in the image of their blind, deaf, and uncomprehending idols, so that they will neither "see [ראה] with their eyes [עין], nor hear with their ears, nor understand [בין] with their hearts" to "turn and be healed" (Isa 6:10; cf. 1:3; 5:21).[24]

Much if not all of the remainder of Isaiah 1–39 may be viewed as the outworking of 6:9–10. Next comes the historical narrative of Isaiah 7:1–8:18, wherein Ahaz rejects God's wisdom under the guise of false piety. He rebelliously refuses God's provision and instead seeks Assyria as a suzerain, resulting in God's removal of his counsel from those who refuse to listen.[25] The historical narrative is succeeded by a series of

---

22. Robinson ("Motif," 177) draws out the connection between God's initial disputation with Israel in Isa 1:2–5 and Isaiah's *Denkschrift*, whereby "6:9–10 focuses on the fact *that* the people suffer deafness and blindness," while 1:3–5 make clear *what* they fail to see, hear, and understand (emphasis original). He compares Isa 1:3//6:9 (a failure to understand/know), 1:4//6:10 (turning from God), 1:5//6:10 (sick and in need of healing, and also rebellion/refusal to repent and be healed), and 1:7–8//6:11 (destruction).

23. Rolf P. Knierim, "The Vocation of Isaiah," VT 18 (1968): 55.

24. Cf. the discussion in chapter 4 on hardening as a judgment for idolatry. Recall the analysis of Beale ("Isaiah," 277) that God's judgment in Isa 6:9–10 employs idolatry language as a "retributive taunt," as per Psa 115:5–8; 135:14–18 ("those who make [idols] and all who trust them shall become like them"; cf. Psa 135:18). Robinson ("Motif," 181) concurs, similarly concluding that God confirms the people's chosen state of willing continued blindness and deafness.

Greek Isaiah changes the causative hiphils of Isa 6:10a in the Hebrew to a causal clause: "For the heart of this people has grown dull [ἐπαχύνθη γὰρ ἡ καρδία τοῦ λαοῦ τούτου]," etc. (and the imperatives of 6:9 to future indicative), making 6:10b a result clause instead of a purpose clause. However, the two traditions are not in conflict: the Hebrew emphasizes the consequences of Israel's idolatry, whereby they are to be confirmed in their idolatrous uncreation and judged as the idols they worship. The Greek recognizes that Israel has become hard because they are idolatrous, and will therefore unhearingly reject Isaiah's message since it comes from God.

25. Isaiah's prophecy in conjunction with the sign child *Shear-yashub* (Isa 7:3–9) "is designed to force Ahaz to trust solely in Yahweh" (Kirsten Nielsen, "Is 6:1–8:18 as Dramatic Writing," ST 40 [1986]: 12). When Ahaz refuses this word (Isa 7:12; cf. 2 Kgs 16:7)—and Ahaz's court indeed recognized "their own '*etsâ* must yield to Yahweh's if the latter could be known" (Jensen, *Use*, 58)—Isaiah produces *Immanuel*, signifying God's presence among Israel in judgment. Before *Immanuel* comes of age, God's destruction of the Syro-Ephraimite coalition will prove his word true and his coming

oracles in Isaiah 8:19–12:9, beginning with a judgment oracle (8:19–22) describing the cataclysmic future consequences of 6:9–10: Those idolatrously trusting in their own wisdom "will look to the earth, but will see only distress and darkness, the gloom of anguish; and they will be thrust into thick darkness" (8:22; cf. 5:30).

The first indication that Isaiah 28–31 continues the wisdom debate and the outworking of 6:9–10 lies in the structure of chapters 28–39, which unfolds after the pattern of chapters 7–12. In correspondence to 8:19–12:6, chapters 28–35 relate a series of oracles that pertain to Isaiah 6, but now in direct response to contemporary events.[26] Finally, in correspondence to 7:1–8:18, chapters 36–39 comprise the historical narrative of Hezekiah's crisis with Assyria:

Isaiah 6 – COMMISSION NARRATIVE

Isaiah 7–39 – COMMISSION IN ACTION:

Historical Narrative: Ahaz and the Syro-Ephraimite Crisis (Isa 7:1–8:18)

---

judgment certain (Isa 7:16–17). The telescoping timeline is seen in the final sign child *Maher-shalal-hash-baz*. Before he is even weaned Assyria will bring a flood of destruction to Jerusalem (Isa 8:4–8; cf. 6:11–13; 8:5–22), resulting in "a contrast of staggering proportions" given the nearly Davidic prosperity of Judah under Uzziah. William J. Dumbrell, "Worship in Isaiah 6," *RTR* 43 (1984): 1–2.

26. With slight variations, scholars generally see Isa 28–35 as a literary unit. See, e.g., John N. Oswalt, *The Book of Isaiah Chapters 1–39*, NICOT (Grand Rapids: Eerdmans, 1986), 504–5; Sweeney, *Isaiah 1–4*, 55, 60–61 (although Sweeney later emends his view, distinguishing Isa 34–35 as a sub-unit [idem, *Isaiah*, 353]); Gary Stansell, "Isaiah 28–33: Blest Be the Tie that Binds (Isaiah Together)," in *New Visions of Isaiah*, JSOTSup 214, ed. Roy F. Melugin and Marvin A. Sweeney (Sheffield: Sheffield Academic, 1996), 85–87; Joseph Blenkinsopp, *Isaiah 1–39: A New Translation with Introduction and Commentary*, AB 19 (New York: Doubleday, 2000), 380; Childs, *Isaiah*, 200. The oracles against Israel in Isa 28–31 precede oracles concerning God's rule (but still containing judgment) in Isa 32–33, and a contrast between the desert resulting from trusting the nations and the garden resulting from trusting God in Isa 34 and 35, respectively (cf. Oswalt, *Isaiah 1–39*, 505; Blenkinsopp, *Isaiah*, 380). The connection between Isa 8:19–12:6 and the oracles in Isa 28–31, especially, is seen in their thematic overlap and linguistic borrowing from God's judgment in Isa 8:11–18, just prior to the oracles beginning in 8:19 (cf. Isa 8:14–15 and 28:7–8; 8:16–17 and 29:11; 8:16–17 and 29:15).

Oracles: Future judgment mixed with future hope and deliverance (Isa 8:19–12:6)

Oracles: against nations (with hope of Jerusalem *cum* Zion) (Isa 13–23)

"Isaianic apocalypse": **Oracles** against nations and Jerusalem together (hope moved to future eschatological hope) (Isa 24–27)

Oracles: Judgment mixed with future hope and deliverance (Isa 28–35)

Historical Narrative: Hezekiah and the Assyrian Crisis (Isa 36–39)

Fig. 7: Literary Structure of Isaiah 1–39

From Isaiah 7:1–8:18 to chapters 28–35, the situation has moved from Jerusalem's reliance upon Assyria for defense against the Syro-Ephraimite coalition to their collusion with Egypt for defense against Assyria. Some players have changed but the issues remain the same.[27] Beginning in Isaiah 28:1, chapters 28–33 employ the six-woe pattern of chapter 5 (Isa 28:1; 29:1, 15; 30:1; 31:1; 33:1). They continue the prophet's polemic against the leadership's foolish wisdom of trusting the nations rather than God.[28] Although the parallelism is only approximate, since the material in chapters 28–33 is somewhat "formally and thematically heterogeneous," these chapters—especially Isaiah 28–29—enhance and complete the trajectory of chapters 1–12 by describing the outworking of Isaiah 6:9–10.[29]

---

27. Cf. W. A. M. Beuken, "Perversion Reverted," in *Scriptures and the Scrolls: Studies in Honour of A. S. van Der Woude on the Occasion of his 65th Birthday*, ed. F. Garcia Martinez, A. Hilhorst, and C. J. Labuschagne; trans. B. Doyle (Leiden: Brill, 1992), 63–64.

28. Oswalt, *Isaiah 1–39*, 504.

29. Blenkinsopp, *Isaiah*, 382. McLaughlin ("Hearts," 9–17) further argues the divine hardening in these chapters is patterned after Isa 6:9–10, such as in Isa 29:9–10 where the sensory malfunction and prophetic imperative to "engage in unproductive

God's Judgment in Isaiah 29:16

In the oracles in Isaiah 28-31, Isaiah "railed against the willful obtuseness of his hearers [the Jerusalem leadership]" for their reliance upon a policy of *realpolitik* (in seeking aid from Egypt in dealing with the Assyrian threat).[30] In the opening oracle (Isa 28), Israel is depicted as corrupt and foolish, and their rejection of God's wisdom is evident in their drunken senselessness (28:7-8), their inability to see (ראה, 28:7), hear (שמע, 28:12) or learn (ידע, 28:12), and their understanding of God's word likened to that of infants (Isa 28:9-13; cf. 1:2; 6:9-10; 30:1, 9-10). The dominant theme here of confusion versus clarity reverberates throughout the oracles in 29:1-14 and 29:15-24 (and following oracles) as the background for God's judgment against Jerusalem's leadership in 29:16.[31]

The woe oracle beginning in Isaiah 29:15 continues Isaiah's polemic against Israel's leadership for not only their lack of reliance on God but also for their foolishness in supposing to hide from him their cloak-and-dagger diplomacy.[32] They pursue their own counsel (29:15) despite the prophet's clear message that "the only legitimate *ēṣâ* [plan] was that of Yahweh," thereby refusing to "accept [God's wisdom through Isaiah] or give it a place in their council."[33] The leadership merely intends secrecy, but Isaiah characterizes their scheming with OT underworld imagery (hiphil עמק; חשך; cf. Psa 88:7) whereby "their 'deeds' thus take place within the region where death rules."[34] Furthermore, in 29:15b, by placing in their mouths the words of the wicked from Psalm 94, "Isaiah describes the leaders of Judah in the same way the godless enemies … are described in the individual and communal [biblical] songs of lament."[35]

---

activity" are explicitly paired with God's actively confirming the idolater's stupor (ad loc., 10).

30. Blenkinsopp, *Isaiah*, 383.

31. J. C. Exum, "Isaiah 28-32: A Literary Approach," *SBLSP* 2 (1979):145.

32. McKane, *Prophets*, 70; Sweeney, *Isaiah 1-39*, 375. Ironically, since the leadership's autonomy is predicated on their reliance upon Egypt, it is absurdly a non-autonomous autonomy (Blenkinsopp, *Isaiah*, 408).

33. Jensen, *Use*, 55-56. Since 29:9-10 in the previous oracle sarcastically recalls 6:9-10 as an attack on Israel's religious leadership (Evans, "Isaiah's," 98), the occurrences there of חכמה and בין (v. 14) and of עצה at the outset of this oracle (v. 15) are subverted: "The ambitious vocabulary of wisdom belongs to [God] alone and the ['wise'] are deluded in their use of it" (McKane, *Prophets*, 70).

34. Hans Wildberger, *Isaiah: A Commentary* (trans. Thomas H. Trapp; Minneapolis: Fortress Press, 1990), 3:98. In *Pesiq. Rab Kah.* 9.1 God's righteousness—as visible as mountains (citing Psa 72:5)—is contrasted with the leadership's hidden deeds which, by implication, are wicked; cf. *Tanḥ.* Gen 2.8.

35. Wildberger, *Isaiah*, 3:98.

Isaiah 29:16 opens with the declaration, "Your perversion [הפככם]!" which identifies the leadership's foolish wisdom as "a turning upside down of the counsel and wisdom of God."[36] Accordingly, Isaiah once again describes the outworking of God's judgment on Israel's idolatry (cf. Isa 6:9–10), this time using the potter/clay metaphor. Here, Isaiah is not providing a sustained reflection on God as creator, but is instead straightforwardly directing everyday imagery against the Jerusalem leadership.[37] In their idolatry, they would dare to reduce the living God to an object to be manipulated or ignored; thus Isaiah's indignant demand, "As *clay* should the potter be reckoned?"

Therefore, in Isaiah 29:16 within its original context, the prophet is applying to the Jerusalem leadership the object language of the potter/clay metaphor. This is fitting in that their rebellion against him is idolatrous: as a result of God's hardening judgment in Isaiah 6:9–10, the leadership's reversal (הפככם) is now reversed back on *them*, as God will now relate to them as inanimate things. According to the prophet's evaluation, in this context at least, they are not clay in God's hands because God is God, but precisely due to idolatry. Their idolatrous suppositions, "He did not make me," and "He is not discerning," ironically identify them as "a made object [מעשה]" and "a formed thing [יצר]," highlighting God as the potter.[38] Having thus forfeited their relationship to God as his images, they are now clay in his hands for him to do what he wills.

Accordingly, in Isaiah 29:17–21, God extends his reversing judgment by announcing

> his intention to grant knowledge to those who would not normally have it ... and deny it to [Judah's leaders]. ... Since those who are wise have reversed their roles in their own minds, thus reversing justice, YHWH will reverse His gift of knowledge and grant it to those who did not have it before.[39]

The leadership's object status will be underscored by the restoration of the deaf and blind who will hear the scroll (cf. Isa 8:16; 29:11–12) and

---

36. Christopher R. Seitz, *Isaiah 1–39* (IBC; Louisville: John Knox, 1993), 215.

37. Blenkinsopp, *Isaiah*, 408.

38. 1QIsᵃ substitutes חמר for אמר in ויצר אמר ליוצרו. The form in the received text may seem unexpected—even extraneous—and does not follow that in the previous line (יאמר; Blenkinsopp, *Isaiah*, 407), but is supported by Greek Isaiah and the Targum (Oswalt, *Isaiah 1–39*, 388). Likely the Qumran text represents an intentional alteration for favorable effect, and the MT should be regarded as original (ibid.).

39. Sweeney, *Isaiah 1–4*, 57.

emerge from darkness (cf. Isa 5:30; 8:22), and by the ultimate result of their judgment (Isa 29:24): to their exclusion, Israel will be populated by an unspecified group of those who formerly erred in spirit (תעי־רוח), and who, in contrast to the rejected idolaters, will have understanding (בינה) and accept instruction (ילמדו־לקח).

Therefore, Isaiah 29:16 does *not* employ the potter/clay metaphor to describe God's judgment of Israel prior to and irrespective of their actions. Rather, the context of Isaiah 29:16 is one of Israel's sin and idolatry, which is manifested in their attempt to supplant God's wisdom with their own. The potter/clay metaphor describes God's response to Israel's antecedent rebellion. Isaiah 29:16 responds to rebellious Israel by diagnosing the idolatry of the Jerusalem leadership, thereby identifying God's judgment with the outworking of their hardening in Isaiah 6:9-10: as a result of their foolish wisdom, God now views them as objects to be judged for their idolatry.

Despite Wagner's argument, there are no Jewish references to Isaiah 29:16 contemporaneous to Paul that would confirm (or refute) that his understanding is in line with what was said above.[40] The potter/clay metaphor is common in both the Bible and in ancient Judaism, but this is of little value in that it was polyvalent and lent itself to a variety of unrelated uses (as indicated above, by its occurrence also in Isa 45:9; Jer 18:5-11; and Wis 15:7).[41] In every occurrence of the potter/clay metaphor in a context of judgment or where judgment is an element, God's judgment is conditioned upon prior sin, rebellion, and/or idolatry (Isa 29:16; 45:9; 64:7 [8]; Jer 18:5-11; 1QS 11:22). However, references to Isaiah 29:16 in particular are rare and late. Relevant rabbinic traditions almost universally recognize Israel's rebellion and wickedness in substituting God's wisdom for their own foolish wisdom (*Mek. Isa.* 29:15; *Tanḥ.*

---

40. Wagner (*Heralds*, 68-71) analyzes what he considers to be a parallel usage in 1QS 11.22, but his account is built upon the mistaken position that Paul has conflated Isa 29:16 and 45:9, and that Isa 29:16 is concerned with the relationship between God's righteousness and his wisdom. 1QS 11.22 asks a rhetorical question not dissimilar from that in Rom 9:20, but for the purpose of emphasizing God's power and desire to save his faithful people.

41. Such usages besides those already listed include creation (of God's people) (Gen 2:7; see LXX πλάσσω and Greek Isa 29:16; Sir 33:7-13); the consequences of wickedness (Isa 64:5); recognition of human mortality (Job 10:9; 1QH 1:21; 3:20-21, 23-24, etc.); and God's wisdom (*T. Naph.* 2:2-4). Notably, with the possible exception of Sir 33:12-13, none of these texts speaks of humans—"innocent" or otherwise—being shaped against their will and subsequently judged.

Gen. 2.8; Num 2.6; *Pesiq. Rab Kah.* 9.1; *Midr. Pss.* 14.1; cf. *Pesiq. Rab Kah.* 9.1). Additionally, the Targum on Isaiah 29:16 draws out a direct causal relationship between Israel's sin and God's subsequent response of considering them as helpless objects that are worthy of judgment.

So although the evidence is sparse, it appears when employing Isaiah 29:16 early Jewish interpreters held an understanding of it that was essentially similar to that presented above in light of the original Isaianic context. But once again, whereas early Jewish traditions interpret or use Isaiah 29:16 to discuss the nature of God, Paul uniquely draws upon parallels between Jerusalem's idolatrous leadership and present national Israel and applies Isaiah 29:16 to the occasion of Romans.

PAUL'S USE OF ISAIAH 29:16 IN ROMANS

In Romans 9:14–18, Paul worked from the biblical understanding of idolatry vis-à-vis humans as God's image to explain that God is hardening unbelieving Jews as a judgment in response to their idolatry (i.e., their rejection of the Christ event). But the objection in 9:19 arises from the misunderstanding that 9:14–18 argue for God's freedom to harden (read: condemn or reject) *regardless* of human actions. So in answer to the interlocutor's objection in 9:19, Paul fleshes out in greater detail the nature and implications of unbelieving Jews' idolatry by quoting Isaiah 29:16.[42]

MT Isa 29:16	Greek Isa 29:16	Rom 9:20b
הפככם אם־כחמר היצר יחשב כי־יאמר מעשה לעשהו לא עשני ויצר אמר ליוצרו לא הבין	οὐχ ὡς ὁ πηλὸς τοῦ κεραμέως λογισθήσεσθε μὴ ἐρεῖ τὸ πλάσμα τῷ πλάσαντι <u>οὐ σύ με ἔπλασας</u> ἢ τὸ ποίημα τῷ ποιήσαντι οὐ συνετῶς με ἐποίησας	μὴ ἐρεῖ τὸ πλάσμα τῷ πλάσαντι <u>τί με ἐποίησας οὕτως</u>

---

42. Since the differences between the Hebrew and Greek Isa 29:16 are negligible, it is unclear whether Paul quotes the Greek (to which Romans is slightly closer than the MT) or an unattested Hebrew *Vorlage* (see Shum, *Paul's*, 204).

As Wright aptly states:

> The setting, again, is not Israel as tabula rasa, but Israel as the sinful, rebellious, idolatrous people to whom God, after years of pleading, threatening, promising, and cajoling, could in the end only respond with devastating judgment. Paul here stands on the same ground as Isaiah, Jeremiah, Daniel, and the rest of the prophets who interpreted the exile as God's necessary action not only to punish Israel for its long-term infidelity but strangely ... to set forward the ultimate covenant purpose.[43]

Paul charges in Romans 9:20-21 that, like Israel in the wisdom debate of Isaiah 1-39, God's own people are now inverting (or "perverting"; cf. הפככם, Isa 29:16) his wisdom by rejecting Christ and the gospel. In choosing to rebel and follow the idol of their own foolish wisdom, present national Israel—like preexilic Israel—have forfeited their humanity and been uncreated into mere objects.[44] According to Paul, they have committed themselves as lumps of clay into God the potter's hand, and he may judge them as is appropriate for those made in the image of detestable idols.[45] Paul's use of Isaiah 29:16 in Romans 9:20b, then, further enables him to explicate in 9:21 God's latitude in responding to idolatry: he may either recreate the clay of national Israel into an object earmarked for honor or allow it to remain unmade as an object consigned to a dishonorable fate.

The slight similarities between Romans 9:21 and the Wisdom of Solomon 15:7 thus likely reflect a common first-century understanding

---

43. Wright, *Letter*, 640; cf. Murray, *Epistle*, 2:32.

44. In another discussion, this could be one step in extrapolating to the idea that Paul understands *all* people who reject Christ to be tautologically idolatrous. This is as may be, but in this context at least Paul limits the scope of his discussion to first-century nonbelieving Jews and is at pains to clarify God's response to them in particular. Thus, caution must be exercised in applying his clarification to a larger, more abstract position, especially since such a synthesis is unnecessary to the meaning of (or for interpreting) Paul's discussion in context.

45. Glancing ahead to Rom 9:22, this reading is affirmed in Paul's identification of the "object relegated to a dishonorable use" in 9:21 with "objects of wrath [ὀργὴν] prepared for destruction [ἀπώλειαν]," since in Paul, "Both ὀργή (Rom. 2:5, 8; 5:9 ...) and ἀπώλεια (Phil. 1:28; 3:19; 2 Thess. 2:3; 1 Tim. 6:9; cf. ... 1 Cor. 1:18, 19; 8:11; 10:9, 10; 15:18; 2 Cor. 2:15; 4:3; 2 Thess. 2:10) refer frequently to eschatological judgment" (Schreiner, *Romans*, 518); cf. Sanday and Headlam, *Epistle*, 2:261; Piper, *Justification*, 200. In contrast, Cranfield (*Romans*, 2:492n2) insists ἀτιμία in Rom 9:21 merely means "menial," while similarly Dunn (*Romans 9-16*, 557), followed by Fitzmyer (*Romans*, 569), think it refers to a low historical role, although such interpretations do not fit the context.

whereby those who idolatrously revert to being clay deliver all control over their fate into the potter's hands. However, whereas Wisdom 15:7 uses the potter/clay metaphor to ironically highlight that an idolater and his clay have more in common with each other than either does with God, Paul uses the same metaphor to tragically identify national Israel's hardening as a holy God's just judgment for idolatry. Accordingly, his use of Isaiah 29:16 also remains faithful to its original context in applying object language (σκεῦος, Rom 9:21) to idolaters, whether those who subsequently receive judgment or mercy (cf. 9:22–23).

So for Paul, God does not "find fault" with national Israel (as the interlocutor thinks in Rom 9:19) because of some sin to which he sovereignly compelled them via hardening. Rather, in response to their *prior* sin and chosen hardening, he is subsequently judging them by confirming that hardening and then (potentially) subjecting them to wrath. So Wright's impulse is correct insofar as he notices that Romans 9:6–29 tells "the story of Israel's patriarchal foundation ... then of the exodus ... and then of God's judgment that led to exile."[46] But more precisely, the theme of idolatry reveals that 9:6–29 recounts the story not just of Israel but, in particular, the story of *Israel's idolatry.* Paul alleges that this idolatry-history from the patriarchs to exile is perpetuating itself in the activity of present national Israel. He does this by evaluating them to be just like Jerusalem's idolatrous leadership with their autonomous, foolish wisdom in Isaiah 29:16.[47]

Further, Paul's position in Romans 9:19–21—coupled with his comparison in 9:14–18 of national Israel with Pharaoh, whom God "raised up" for his purposes—prompts the question, "What does God's response to idolatrous national Israel means for his people, that is, those who submit to the Christ event?" Here, Paul's quotation of Isaiah 29:16 may also echo its wider context, where following 29:16, in 29:17–25, idolatrous Israel's judgment coincided with their healing, restoration, and

<hr>

46. *Romans*, 635.
47. This reading is additionally in harmony with Paul's rebuke in Rom 9:20a, wherein the interlocutor is not just challenging God, but is doing so while misunderstanding the nature and implications of idolatry. Given that Paul earlier established the wickedness of the nations and Jews' transgressions against Torah (Rom 1:18–3:23), the interlocutor and Paul's entire audience—whether Jew or Greek—share in the idolatry-induced predicament of national Israel described by Paul's use of Isa 29:16. Therefore, the interlocutor is either an unbelieving Jew who has surrendered his humanity or is wrongly speaking on behalf of such offenders, and has no right to "answer back" to God (Rom 9:20a).

inheritance being passed on to those who were formerly wicked but now accept God's wisdom. So too, Paul's answer to his interlocutor's challenge returns to him the initiative, giving him the stage to discuss how God uses his judgment upon national Israel in the redemption of believers even from among the nations in the remainder of the pericope, in Romans 9:22-29.

So to this point in the pericope, after likening unbelieving Jews to Pharaoh in Romans 9:14-18, Paul quotes Isaiah 29:16 in Romans 9:19-21 in order to clarify the nature of God's response toward national Israel's idolatrous rebellion. His answer to the interlocutor is *not* that the interlocutor and/or unbelieving Jews do not have the right to second guess God because God is sovereign. Rather, Paul's stance is at once theologically deeper and less complex. By way of the applied exemplar of Isaiah 29:16, because mere *things* are unable to do anything a living image of God can do, such as speak, those who have become things due to their rebellion now cannot and have no right to question God. And secondarily, Paul has clarified the nature of God's response toward national Israel's rebellion in order to direct the discussion toward God's use of his judgment upon national Israel as "an object relegated to a dishonorable use"/"objects of wrath" (Rom 9:21-22).

INTRODUCTION TO ROMANS 9:22-29

Paul, after he has proven in Romans 9:19-21 that God is not judging unbelieving Jews for their behavior for which he is responsible, continues in Romans 9:22-29 by turning toward the use to which God puts his hardening of national Israel. In 9:22, Paul expands on his identification of unbelieving Jews with Pharaoh by now calling them "objects of wrath." God is not hardening national Israel just for hardening's sake, Paul explains, but (see the adversative δὲ beginning 9:22) because (with a causal θέλων)[48] he has a use for their hardening, as he did with that of Pharaoh.

---

48. Cranfield, *Romans*, 2:494; Dunn, *Romans 9-16*, 558; Moo, *Epistle*, 604-6; Schreiner, *Romans*, 520; Wright, *Letter*, 641-42. The grammar here is awkward, since Rom 9:22-23 are a conjunctive protasis for a real conditional (one that Paul clearly believes is the case) for which there is no apodosis; the anacoluthic conditional instead gives way to a relative clause in 9:24. Scholars have argued for several readings and punctuations: 1) "what if, because he desired to display his wrath ... God endured ... in order that he might make known his riches," making the causal clause the dominant idea of the sentence. But this contorts the syntax and produces a strong theological statement that does not fit with the topic of the pericope (God's desire to display his riches rather than wrath). Then, 2) "what if, *despite* desiring to display his wrath ...

Thus Romans 9:22b (the dominant clause of 9:22-23) explains why, if unbelieving Jews are under judgment, God has delayed his destruction of them: as with Pharaoh, he has indeed dispensed wrath in the form of a hardening judgment that confirms them in their idolatry, but he has also deferred a judgment of instant destruction for the sake of a long-term fulfillment of his wider purposes.[49] It pays to reflect here on Paul's analogy between Pharaoh and present national Israel. It would be facile to suggest that Jews' rejection of the gospel turned Paul to the Gentiles; this is not what Paul presents in Romans 9. The eschatological context of God's present ingathering of his people, even from the nations (as per Hos 2 in Rom 9:25-26, below) is one of cosmic momentousness: given that Jesus is David's true son and God's Messiah (Rom 1:2-6), rejecting the Christ event as national Israel have done is tantamount to cosmic rebellion during this final age of the consummation of history.

The designation of national Israel as objects need not be permanent (see on Rom 11:25-32 in chapter 6); indeed (as with Pharaoh), God is not immediately visiting destruction upon them. They serve as an example to the watching peoples and nations (as did Pharaoh) regarding how important it is now to place allegiance and trust in God through Christ, upon which their Israelification and redemption from object status is conditional. As such, the same gospel that national Israel has rejected is the means by which Gentile believers are being saved (cf. Rom 1:16-17), which makes use of the parallel pairing of Pharaoh and the Israelites

---

God *nevertheless* endured ... in order that he might make known his riches," takes the participle as concessive and strongly subordinates the circumstances while placing the emphasis upon God's ostensibly merciful activity. However, this arguably bends the language too far and is only motivated out of the difficulty in finding a logical connection between desiring to show wrath to one group in order to show mercy to another (see below). Finally, 3) "what if, desiring to display his wrath ..., God endured ... in order that he might make known his riches," offers little clarity, placing the two pieces in apposition and ambiguating God's first desire as an attendant circumstance of his second (i.e., to make known his riches). Instead, the causal reading makes most sense in context (the epexegetical infinitives in 9:22a belong to the subordinate causal clause of θέλων, and 9:23 is a purpose clause subordinate to the dominant ἤνεγκεν in 9:22; cf. Dunn, *Romans 9-16*, 560), since 9:24 doubtlessly builds on 9:22-23 in that God simultaneously dispenses wrath as instrumental in dispensing mercy; see below.

49. Soteriologically, "had God simply condemned Israel at once, following its decisive rejection of Jesus as Messiah, there would have been no space either for Jews to repent (beginning, one may suppose, with the disciples themselves!), or for Gentiles to be brought in" (Wright, *Letter*, 642).

in Exodus as two idolatrous parties that received variable responses to their need for God's mercy.

Given this, the relative clause in Romans 9:24 rhetorically narrows "objects of mercy" (9:23) to "we whom he called" (9:24), including reference to Gentile believers (the principal element of the contrastive clause in 9:24b).[50] As shown in fig. 6, in 9:22-29 Paul's emphasis is on the fact that God is and has patiently endured the rebellion of national Israel—human creatures *cum* objects of wrath. The reciprocal is God's purpose to make known his glory to objects of mercy *cum* rehumanized creatures (9:23). To a degree, these elements are presented as a parallel, conjoined pair of emphases (the dashed line grouping 9:22 and 23 in fig. 6). So it can be said that Paul's communicative strategy is delicately balanced, which is further seen in 9:24-29 (subordinate to 9:23 γνωρίσῃ), where the emphasis is on the fact that the "we whom he called" includes even those from the nations, but the counterpoint is that this is in contrast to substantial representation of national Israel as per 9:22. That is, to a degree the elements of the nations' ingathering and national Israel's winnowing are at the same time an additional parallel, conjoined pair of emphases (the dashed lines grouping 9:24 and 27-29, and again grouping 9:25-26 and 27-29 in fig. 6). So in order to *clarify* the dynamic of God's present relationship with both *goyim* believers and unbelieving Jews, by way of a catena of scriptural citations Paul discloses (γνωρίζω, 9:23) God's surprising use and realization of Israel's promised covenantal blessings, in part facilitated by the negative example being made of national Israel.

---

50. This is reinforced by the aural quality of the text, on which Dunn (*Romans 9-16*, 570) remarks: "The awkwardness of the phrasing ... almost certainly meant that in being read aloud the words would have to be taken slowly and with emphasis. ... The careful reader (to the congregation) was intended to leave the incomplete vv. 22-23 hanging, pause, catch fresh attention with the unexpected οὕς ... and reinforce the impact with the identifying ἡμᾶς. Obviously encouraged thereby is the 'double-take' corollary indicating the implied identity of the other 'vessels' ['we' in v. 24]."

The subordinate clause ἃ προητοίμασεν εἰς δόξαν is not logically operative for Paul's argument (see fig. 8), regardless of how scintillating its theological derivatives may be. A neutral and grammatically acceptable reading could be that God decided in advance what his purposes would be for "objects of mercy," whomever they may have turned out to be. Brian Abasciano privately suggested that my analysis could be strengthened by engaging Calvinistic readings such as those of Piper, Moo, and Schreiner. But besides such engagement going beyond the scope of this study, doing so would be difficult since—according to the analysis thus far—their interpretations depend upon false premises regarding the scope of Paul's argument and the biblical theological themes upon which he is drawing.

THE USE OF HOSEA AND ISAIAH IN ROMANS 9:22–29

HOSEA 2:1 AND 2:25 IN THEIR ORIGINAL CONTEXT(S)

Paul takes his first two citations (Rom 9:25-26) from Hosea 2:25 [2:23 ET] and 2:1 [1:10 ET]. Although he cites these texts in reverse order, it is best to analyze them chronologically due to the thematic development of Hosea 1–3.

Hosea 2:1 in Its Original Context
Hosea addresses the northern kingdom in its twilight, near the end of Jeroboam II's reign (Hos 1:1; cf. 2 Kgs 14:22-29).[51] Israel's relative military might during Jeroboam's reign (2 Kgs 14:25, 28) led to prosperity, and in turn a cosmopolitan Samaria.[52] This prosperity was taken for granted (cf. the agricultural motif in Hos 2:5, 7-8, 11, 14, 23-24) and produced a rise in syncretistic polytheism. Hosea prophesied that it would be "only a few years before [Assyria] changed Israel's attitudes from complacency to desperation."[53]

Most scholars agree that the literary unit of Hosea 1–3 was produced by a single author, and that it addresses issues in Israel contemporaneous to Hosea.[54] The portions of chapters 1–3 that depict restoration (Hos 2:1-3, 16-25; 3:5) are bound by an overall negative context, and the remainder of the book (Hos 4–14) foresees an era when the curses outlined in Deuteronomy 4:20-31 would be executed. Despite moments of hope, Hosea's primary task was not to announce the mitigation of judgment but its onset. Douglas Stuart offers a summary of Hosea 1:2–2:3:

---

51. Yielding a date of ca. 750-724 BC for the prophet's oracular ministry; cf. Francis I. Andersen and David Noel Freedman, *Hosea*, AB 24 (New York: Doubleday, 1980), 58; Stuart, *Hosea-Jonah*, WBC 31 (Waco, TX: Word Books, 1987), 9; Gale A. Yee, "'She Is Not My Wife and I Am Not Her Husband': A Materialist Analysis of Hosea 1-2," *BibInterp* 9 (2001): 346.

52. See Yee, "She," 346-67, for the political and socioeconomic conditions of Israel during the time of Hosea.

53. Stuart, *Hosea*, 9.

54. E.g., Andersen and Freedman, *Hosea*, 58; Stuart, *Hosea*, 8; Thomas McComiskey, "Hosea" in *The Minor Prophets: An Exegetical and Expository Commentary*, vol. 1, *Hosea, Joel, and Amos* (Grand Rapids: Baker, 1992), 4; Yvonne Sherwood, *The Prostitute and the Prophet: Hosea's Marriage in Literary-Theoretical Perspective*, JSOTSup 212 (Sheffield: Sheffield Academic, 1996), 16; Yee, "She," 345; contra Sweeney, "Hosea," in *The Twelve Prophets*, vol. 1, *Hosea, Joel, Amos, Obadiah, Jonah*, Berit Olam, ed. David W. Cotter, Jerome T. Walsh, and Chris Franke (Collegeville, MN: Liturgical, 2000), 11-13, 24, who groups Hos 2:3-3:5 with Hos 4-14.

[Hosea] 1:2-9 functions as a summarizing preface to the entire book. It represents an overview, in stark and moving terms, of the prophet's proportionately dominant message: God has given up on his people. The theme of restoration *after* this judgment then follows immediately in 2:1-3.[55]

In Hosea 1:2, God commands Hosea to marry a promiscuous woman.[56] Chapters 1-3 relate the narrative of Hosea's marriage as a metaphor for God's relationship with Israel. In 1:3-9, God metes out judgment upon Israel according to the names of the three sign children produced by Hosea's marriage. The first sign child's name, *Jezreel*, captures both God's provision and the apostasy of Israel's kings (1:4-5).[57] *Lo-ruhamah* (לא רחמה) signifies that God will "never again" (לא אוסיף עוד) have compassion on Israel; because of their apostasy they have been "expelled from a relationship of love" (1:6).[58] Finally, *Lo-ammi* (לא עמי, 1:9) negates God's most "intimate and honorable" title for Israel, first given in Exodus 3:12.[59] Just as God had identified himself as אהיה in Exodus 3:14, here he designates himself אהיה-לא to them.[60]

Abruptly, the oracle of judgment shifts to one of eschatological restoration, reflecting "the chronological presupposition: ... in the short run there will be woe, but later there will come a time of weal."[61] In 2:1, Hosea describes Israel's restoration in terms of Genesis 22:17, which in light of Assyria's expansionism "was almost laughable in Hosea's day."[62]

---

55. Stuart, *Hosea*, 35, emphasis original; cf. McComiskey, *Hosea*, 4.
56. Translating אשת זנונים (Hos 1:2) as "harlot" or "whore" incorrectly identifies Hosea's wife with either an ordinary or cult prostitute (Andersen and Freedman, *Hosea*, 116; A. A. Macintosh, *Hosea*, ICC [Edinburgh: T&T Clark, 1997], 8; Yee, "She," 371). A promiscuous woman may have been the more effective image, since a prostitute was at least "tolerated" in ANE culture (cf. Phyllis A. Bird, "The Harlot as Heroine: Narrative Art and Social Presupposition in Three Old Testament Texts," *Semeia* 46 [1989]: 119), whereas an adulterous wife was not (Yee, "She," 371).
57. Andersen and Freedman, *Hosea*, 173.
58. Ibid., 188.
59. Ibid., 197.
60. Cf. Stuart, *Hosea*, 33.
61. Ibid., 7 (cf. p. 18), who continues, "The blessings portions of the book are therefore *eschatological* in their orientation, while the curses are more immediate. There is no hint in Hosea that Israel can actually escape from the wrath of Yahweh expressed in destruction and exile" (emphasis original). Cf. the period of post-punishment restoration prescribed in Lev 26:41-42; Deut 4:30; 30:2-3.
62. Duane A. Garrett, *Hosea*, NAC 19A (Nashville: Broadman and Holman, 1997), 71. Hos 2:1 in the MT (1:10 ET) begins והיה, which the LXX translates with an imperfect καὶ ἦν. This either requires that the MT originally read ויהי, or reflects an

Those included within Israel will shed the brand "Not-my-people" to be called "sons of the living God," a phrase unique to Hosea. Furthermore, if מקום אשר־יאמר (Hos 2:1) can be identified as the desert,[63] then the very "place" of renunciation becomes the place of reinstatement, and Israel's restoration in Hosea 2:1–3 takes on overtones of a New Exodus theme. In this New Exodus restoration, "Israel's population will be immeasurably expanded, partly by the inclusion of people not originally Israelite."[64]

That the restoration in Hosea 2:1–3 is eschatological in its original context is seen in its contrast with the judgment in Hosea 1:2–9, since these texts together follow "the covenant juxtaposition of pre-exilic curses and post-exilic restoration promises" of both Hosea and the Pentateuch.[65] The depiction of "one leader" (ראש אחד, 2:2 [1:11 ET]) over a reunited Judah and Israel appeals to the past unification under David and Solomon, thereby implying Davidic rule.[66] Finally, Hosea 2:3 (Eng 2:1) anticipates 2:16–25 by naming the renewed Israel עמי and רחמה in contrast to Hosea's sign children.[67]

Therefore, Hosea 2:1 introduces God's eschatological restoration of Israel. It overturns his judgment by repopulating Israel (under a Davidic ruler) with those who did not originally participate in the covenant community, in a fulfillment of Genesis 22:17. This restoration trajectory then culminates in Hosea 2:23–25.

Hosea 2:25 in Its Original Context

Hosea 2:4–25 (2:2–23 ET) metaphorically applies the narrative of 1:2–9 to God's relationship with Israel.[68] The judgment/restoration pattern of 1:2–2:3 is recapitulated, but in a more unified manner due to the

---

interpretation wherein 2:1–3 is so closely related to the preceding as to require the past tense. However, context seems to support the MT, which is supported by α' and σ› (Stuart, *Hosea*, 35).

63. Cf. *Tg. Hos.* 2:1; and Andersen and Freedman, *Hosea*, 203.

64. Stuart, *Hosea*, 37, understanding מקום to imply locations and/or contexts to which Israel did not contemporaneously extend; cf. ad loc., 35.

65. Ibid.

66. Sweeney, *Hosea*, 24; ראש is used to contrast Israel's apostate מלכים in Hosea's day (Stuart, *Hosea*, 39).

67. Because it is the *lectio difficilior* and due to the context of Hos 2:1, the plural of the MT is preferable to the singular in Greek Hosea; cf. ibid., 35–36.

68. Cf. Clines, "Hosea 2: Structure and Interpretation," in *Studia Biblica 1978. I. Old Testament and Related Themes. Sixth International Congress on Biblical Studies, Oxford, 3–7 April, 1978*, ed. E. A. Livingstone (JSOTSup 11; Sheffield: JSOT, 1979), 83–103; Andersen and Freedman, *Hosea*, 218; Walter Brueggemann, "Crisis-Evoked, Crisis-Resolving Speech," *BTB* 24 (1994): 96.

consistent use of the marriage metaphor. However, the restoration depicted is still eschatological, since in Hosea 2:16-25 as in verses 1-3, "the
doom and destruction guaranteed in 1:4-9 and 2:4-15 ... will have come
to pass, yielding to a future in which such harsh judgment never again
need be feared."[69]

The disputation (ריב) beginning in 2:4 describes God's divorce of
Israel in terms of exile, using uncreational (i.e., reversal of cosmogony)
and anti-exodus imagery to reinsert Israel into the chaotic wilderness.[70]
God responds to the evidence of Israel's harlotry in 2:4-5 with three
judgments, each introduced by לכן (2:8-9, 11-15, 16-17), wherein God "re-
verses the images of Israel's [Exodus] creation to deprive God's people
of their very identity, separating them from all they consider theirs."[71]
From the finality of 2:15, "it is not known whether there is any more future, indeed, whether there is any more poem."[72] But the climactic third
judgment in 2:16-17 instead reveals the "surprise verdict" of God's se-
duction and restoration of his wife Israel.[73]

Hosea 2:18-25 explicate the "judgment" of 2:16-17. Whereas 2:4-5
suggested that Israel's punishments are conditioned on a lack of reform,
the promises in 2:16-25 are unconditional; although Israel implemented
none of the exhorted changes, their punishments will be eschatologically undone (cf. 2:5//2:16; 2:14//2:20; 2:11//2:24).[74] God's transformation
from enraged husband into wounded lover is marked by Israel's restored
purity (2:18-19) and is declared in creational terms (2:20; cf. Genesis 1).[75]
Then, the use of the same fidelity language from Exodus 34:6-7 (חסד,
רחמים, אמונה) is remarkably intensified in the wedding vow of 2:21-22,
leading to a concrete restoration of prosperity in 2:23-25a. In answer to
the curse of Leviticus 26:16, God exercises verbal *fiat* in answering the

---

69. Stuart, *Hosea*, 61.
70. Mary Joan Winn Leith, "Verse and Reverse: The Transformation of the Woman,
Israel, in Hosea 1-3," in *Gender and Difference in Ancient Israel*, ed. Peggy L. Day
(Minneapolis, Fortress: 1989), 96.
71. Winn Leith, "Verse," 96, further stating, "Hosea goes so far as to depict a nulli-
fication of Israel's identity" and describes exile as "a wilderness...fraught with the
terrors of chaos" (ad loc., 102).
72. Brueggemann, "Crisis," 97.
73. Stuart, *Hosea*, 53; cf. Sweeney, *Hosea*, 33.
74. Andersen and Freedman, *Hosea*, 263.
75. Cf. the paronomasia evident in איש and בעל/הבעלים.

heavens that send rain, producing a bountiful harvest and meeting the needs of Israel who had been reduced to a wilderness.[76]

The restoration in this literary sub-unit climaxes in Hosea 2:25. God declares, "I will sow the land of Israel for myself" (2:25a),[77] employing an agricultural metaphor to describe God's restoration of a vastly repopulated Israel in fulfillment of 2:1. Then the judgments of 1:2–9 are completely undone when God has compassion upon "Those-without-compassion," and when God repatriates Israel with "Not-my-people" by verbal fiat, that is, simply by saying to them, "'You are my people'" (2:25b). Finally, God's relationship with Israel is fully restored with the reversal of לא-אהיה, the final word of judgment from 1:9, as God's people once again turn to him and say, "'You are my God'" (2:25b). Thus, in culmination of 2:1–3, Hosea 2:25 depicts an eschatological restoration that undoes God's judgment, and even results in far more blessing than Israel had prior to chastisement. And in accordance with 2:1, these blessings are extended to those of God's choosing, regardless of Israel's previous boundaries.

Early Jewish references to Hosea 2:1 and 25 are rare and late, being found only in the rabbis.[78] The meager data do not support any firm external understanding as to whether Paul—or any other Second Temple interpreter—must have held the above or another reading of the Hosea traditions that he cites. Generally, though, whereas other early Jewish interpreters merely speculate upon the character of Israel's eschatological restoration, Paul sees its fulfillment in the nations' present identification with God's people.

---

76. ענה in Hos 2:23–24 portrays "a positive answer to a call for help" (Garrett, *Hosea*, 94–95).

77. The implicit subject of the first-person singular pronominal suffix in וזרעתיה is ישׂראל ארץ. Sweeney (*Hosea*, 37) notes this view is further supported by the aural paronomasia of Jezreel (*yizreʿel*) and Israel (*yiśrāʾēl*). The land's fertility is an "obvious polemic against the Baal cult," since Yahweh rather than Baal will restore Israel, their land, and prosperity (cf. Hos 2:7, where idolatry led to the perspective that provision came from Baal; McComiskey, *Hosea*, 48).

78. Perhaps most interesting is the expectation that the eschatological restoration of Israel described in the opening chapters of Hosea somehow includes the Gentiles in *b. Pesaḥ.* 87b. But also, the rabbis do consistently recognize in these traditions the dominant theme of God's compassion on a wayward Israel (esp. *b. Pesaḥ.* 87b; and *S. Eli. Zut.* 178), and largely that the mercy received by Israel in Hosea is wholly dependent on God's compassions (*b. Pesaḥ.* 87b; *S. Eli. Zut.* 178; *Pesiq. Rab.* 44.2; *Num. Rab.* 2.15).

ISAIAH 1:9 AND 10:22-23 IN THEIR ORIGINAL CONTEXTS

Paul takes his next set of citations (Rom 9:27-29) from Isaiah 10:22-23 and 1:9. Again, as with the Hosea texts, it is best to analyze these texts chronologically, due to their location within the thematic development of Isaiah 1-12.

Isaiah 1:9 in Its Original Context

As mentioned above in connection with Isaiah 29:16, the book of Isaiah begins with God's indictment of Israel for their rebellion. Isaiah 1 is the introduction for the book as a whole and 2:1-4(5) is the introduction to chapters 2-12. However, the skillful integration of 2:1-4(5) creates a consistent thematic development to Isaiah 1-12, upon which Paul plausibly drew. Similarly, Paul likely would have focused on Isaiah's theological evaluation rather than historical referents, since the dehistoricized presentation of the oracles in Isaiah 1 grants them "a new function within [the] literary context."[79]

The introduction(s) to Isaiah 1-12 and the book as a whole set forth Isaiah's message as God's judgment upon Israel (Isa 1:2-31), conjoined with a future restoration that includes the nations (Isa 2:2-4).[80] The bright eschatological moments in Isaiah 1-4 (2:2-4; 4:2-6; cf. 8:23-9:6 [9:1-7 ET]; ch. 11) form a chiaroscuro with the darkness of Israel's present failure and doom.[81] Specifically, Israel's present condition and situation is summarized at the outset, in 1:2-9.

God begins his indictment in Isaiah 1:2-3 by enjoining all creation to bear witness against his children, Israel: they have rebelled and neither know nor understand him. The inwardly telescopic language of 1:4 (גוי, עם, זרע, בנים) identifies relationally distant Israel as God's household, those who are meant to be most intimate with him. Isaiah 1:4 also begins a woe oracle (הוי) describing Israel's self-inflicted, pitiable state (1:5-6). The context equates Israel's sin (משחיתים, מרעים, עון, התא, 1:4) with rebellion (הם פשעו בי, 1:2; cf. סרה, 1:5). Since rebellious Israel is thereby characterized by the weight (כבד, 1:4) of their sin, "the holiness of God

---

79. Childs, *Isaiah*, 16 (who condemns Sweeney's attempt at formal refinement); cf. Seitz, *Isaiah*, 23; Sweeney, *Isaiah 1-39*, 77; Blenkinsopp, *Isaiah*, 183.
80. Cf. Peter R. Ackroyd, "Isaia I-XII: Presentation of a Prophet," in *Congress Volume: Göttingen, 1977*, ed. Walther Zimmerli, VTSup 29 (Leiden: Brill, 1977), passim; and Sherwood, *Paul*, 38-42, on the structure of Isa 1-12, as well regarding Isa 10:22-23, below.
81. Ackroyd, "Isaia," 45.

is thus repudiated by a people whose entire life now reflects the exact opposite character [from his own]."[82] Isaiah 1:7–8 explicates the metaphorical sickness of 1:5–6 by describing Jerusalem's isolation and decline (a description apt to the SyroEphriamite crisis of Isa 2–12 and the Assyrian crisis of Isa 36–39). Fittingly, the title "daughter Zion" in 1:8, which recalls all that is good and hopeful regarding Jerusalem and Israel, is starkly juxtaposed by its description as a "besieged city."[83]

The judgment of Isaiah 1:4–9 climaxes when, in 1:9, Israel is warned that their rebellion will lead to their being all but annihilated. While the brief appearance of the remnant motif (which is often positive in Isaiah—as well as in later Hellenistic Judaism) entails God's mercy in Israel's token preservation,[84] the emphasis is on their tragic reduction as the result of God's judgment when they should have grown innumerable and uncountable (Gen 15:5; 22:17; cf. Hos 1:10 above). Thus, despite beginning with a concessive clause (לולי), Isaiah 1:9 is plainly a judgment text.

Therefore, at least in Isaiah 1:9, the remnant motif (ironically?) underscores the severity of both God's judgment and Israel's rebellion, and is not a portrayal of God's mercy. Indeed, up through verse 9, it appears that "the question of Israel's continued existence is an open one for [Isaiah]."[85] Isaiah 1:2–9 signals that chapters 1–12 and the book as a whole will portray an Israel under God's judgment, as a result of which they will lose nearly all visibility as his people among the nations.

Moreover, the remnant-as-judgment motif in Isaiah 1:9 of the introductory woe oracle of Isaiah launches a trajectory that follows the arc of God's judgment upon Israel in chapters 1–12. This motif recurs and its trajectory culminates in Isaiah 10:22–23 (much in the same way the trajectory of eschatological restoration in Hosea 1–3 was launched in Hosea 2:1 and culminated in Hosea 2:25).

---

82. Childs, *Isaiah*, 18–19.
83. Oswalt, *Isaiah 1–39*, 92.
84. The כמעט of MT Isa 1:9 is lacking in the Greek but retained by the Targum; it is followed by Wildberger, *Isaiah*, 1:20; and Blenkinsopp, *Isaiah*, 180. John D. W. Watts, *Isaiah 1–33*, WBC 24 (Waco, TX: Word Books, 1985), 14, tries to read כמעט as modifying כסדם *metri causa*, but Wildberger, ad loc., rightly denounces this tactic.
85. Wildberger, *Isaiah*, 1:32. Moreover, if Ronald Bergey, "The Song of Moses (Deuteronomy 32.1–43) and Isaianic Prophecies: A Case of Early Intertextuality?" *JSOT* 28 (2003): 33–54 is correct, then just as God's judgment in Deut 32:19–27 was in response to Israel's idolatry and rebellion in Deut 32:15–18, all of Isa 1:2–9 may be understood as God's judgment in response to Israel's rebellion.

Isaiah 10:22-23 in Its Original Context

Isaiah 10:1 begins a woe oracle (Isa 10:1-4) that comes after the six woe oracles of 5:8-23 and the narrative interpolation of 6:1-8:18 (forming another 3 + 3 + 1 pattern that overlaps with that noted above in 5:8-30). Despite the eschatological hope offered by 8:23-9:6 [9:1-7 ET], Ahaz's faithlessness during the narrative of Isaiah 7-8 instigates the seventh climactic woe,[86] whereupon Israel merits the judgment prescribed in the first chapter. Isaiah 10:5 shifts attention away from Jerusalem and its leadership by introducing a new woe oracle (10:5-19), this time directed against Assyria for their arrogance regarding their role in God's judgment.[87] But subsequently, in 10:20-27, the focus reverts back to Israel. So talk of Israel's "remnant" (שאר) in 10:20 is triggered by Assyria's insubstantial remnant in 10:19:[88] Assyria is under God's authority and therefore subject to his purposes, ensuring they will not of their own accord bring complete destruction to Israel.

Accordingly, Isaiah 10:22-23 is framed by the basically positive verses 20-21 and verses 24-27. First, verses 20-21 describe the return of a remnant of Jacob (10:21), who will lean on God "in trust."[89] Then, verses 24-27 likewise describe the immanence of God's deliverance, as a result of which the "burden [of God's chastisement] will be removed from [their] shoulders" (10:27; cf. עם כבד עון, 1:4).[90] However, inside this frame sits the central warning of verses 22-23. The explanatory כי beginning 10:22 jarringly introduces a concessive clause that juxtaposes Israel's reduced status with their deliverance spoken of in verses 20-21 (and

---

86. Cf. the recurrence in 10:4 of בכל־זאת לא־שׁב אפו ועוד ידו נטויה from 5:25. Childs, *Isaiah*, 90 notes that the "negative" interpolation of 9:7-10:35 within 8:23-11:16 matches the Isaianic dialectic wherein "the promise of eschatological salvation" is offset by "the present reality of Israel's persistent obedience."

87. Michael Chan, "Rhetorical Reversal and Usurpation: Isaiah 10:5-34 and the Use of Neo-Assyrian Royal Idiom in the Construction of an Anti-Assyrian Theology" [sic], *JBL* 128 (2009): 717-733 proposes that the oracles in Isa 10 subversively recontextualize an Assyrian royal idiom in order to condemn Assyrian royal policies.

88. Oswalt (*Isaiah 1-39*, 270) notes how Isa 10:19 subverts Assyrian texts that express the efficacy of their conquests by using the remnant motif negatively in reference to their enemies.

89. In contrast to Ahaz in Isa 7:9, who was warned, "If you do not stand in *faith* [in God], then you will not stand at all" (emphasis added).

90. Walter Brueggemann suggests עוד מעט מזער in Isa 10:25 refers not to a time scale but the sincerity of God's invitation to trust him: Assyrian power is "dependent only upon Yahweh's inclination" and therefore ends when God's wrath ends. Brueggemann, *Isaiah 1-39*, Westminster Bible Companion (Louisville: Westminster John Knox, 1998), 95-96.

10:24–27). Despite their expected deliverance from the Assyrians, it is of central importance that Israel remembers they were "like the sand of the sea" (again, as with 1:9 above, cf. Gen 15:5; 22:17; Hos 1:10), but now merely "a remnant will return [שְׁאָר יָשׁוּב]" (Isa 10:22).

Because of Ahaz's rebellion, Isaiah's sign child שְׁאָר יָשׁוּב (Isa 7:3)—originally meant to demonstrate the Syro-Ephriamite coalition's defeat had he trusted God rather than allying with Assyria—is now turned against Israel, with Assyria as God's instrument of judgment. Isaiah's promise of a frightfully small remnant does not negate God's plan, and "there is nothing glorious about it from this point of view" (despite what some Romans scholars may suppose).[91] That the promise of a remnant is double-edged is seen in the hyperbolic continuation (woodenly translated), "decisive annihilation, overflowing with righteousness, for annihilation and decisively the Lord Yhwh *Sabaoth* will do throughout all the earth" (Isa 10:22b–23). Turned against his people as יהוה צבאות (cf. Isa 1:9, 6:3, 5), God reduces them to a remnant, so that the divine promise in Genesis 22:17 is "now restricted by … divine judgment."[92]

Therefore, in its original context, Isaiah 10:22–23 is a judgment tradition that interpolates and thereby overshadows the frame of 10:20–27, through its invocation of the remnant-as-judgment motif from Isaiah 1:2–9. In this manner, the trajectory initiated within chapters 1–12 by 1:9 culminates here in 10:22–23: despite God's saving preservation, Isaiah 10:22–23 depicts an Israel who remains under the judgment warned of in 1:2–9 as a result of their and Ahaz's faithlessness (e.g., Isa 5) and rebellion (e.g., Isa 6–8).

Direct references to Isaiah 1:9 and 10:22–23 generally concern little more than evaluation of the remnant motif in those traditions. Philo likens the remnant in Isaiah 1:9 to the olive branch brought to Noah in Genesis 8:11, calling the remnant a small mercy (as a memorial) in the midst of cataclysmic judgment (*QG* 2:43). Similarly, the Isaiah pesher at Qumran interprets Isaiah 10:22–23 as a reference to the

---

91. Watts, *Isaiah*, 154.

92. Childs, *Isaiah*, 95; similarly, Oswalt (*Isaiah 1–39*, 271) states the remnant is merely a small hope in the midst of a vast judgment. Greek Isaiah here basically reflects the Hebrew, and may be seen as carrying the same negative overtones: "And though the people of Israel were like the sand of the sea, the remnant of them will be saved, for a comprehensive and decisive work with righteousness, since a decisive work God will do throughout the whole world." The most distinctive feature, the translation of σωθήσεται for יָשׁוּב in Isa 10:22, need not have soteriological connotations here (or in Paul), but can simply refer to return *qua* deliverance, as in the Hebrew context.

remnant-as-judgment motif ("how few shall return" because "an anni-hilation is being decided. … For a complete destruction is determined … in the midst of all the land," 4Q163 f4 VII 2.17–19). The Targum, on the other hand, offers a positive interpretation of the remnant motif in its gloss of both Isaiah 1:9 and 10:22–23, in the latter case harmonizing vers-es 22–23 with its frame in verses 20–21, 24–27: "A remnant *that have not sinned and that have repented from sin,* for them there are done prodigies which are mightily wrought and carried out with virtue. For YHWH God of hosts is accomplishing the expiration and destruction of *all the wicked* of the earth."[93]

So while there does not appear to be a consensus on the connota-tion or purpose of the remnant in Isaiah 1:9 or 10:22–23 (the latter cited hardly at all), the available pre-rabbinic witnesses (dating to at least the first century BC) attest to readings substantially the same as those ar-gued above, making it plausible and even likely that Paul would have operated within the same interpretive framework just a few years later. The contrast between Paul and his contemporaries is, once again, that other Jewish interpreters reference these Isaianic sources for the pur-pose of theological reflection (besides 4Q163 f4 VII 2.17–19, which *antic-ipates* an eschatological fulfillment of Israel's winnowing), while Paul takes an attested understanding and applies it to the present circum-stances, the judgment of a remnant once again coming upon national Israel as they repeat the rebellion of their past.

Paul's Use of Hosea and Isaiah in Romans 9:22-29

Coming to the catena in Romans 9:25–29 means coming to the end of the first stage of Paul's argument in chapters 9–11. Immediately after rhe-torically narrowing his discussion of the "objects of mercy" to Gentile believers (9:23–24), Paul expands on their inclusion by citing together Hosea 2:25 [2:23 ET] and 2:1 [1:10 ET] (Rom 9:25–26; see fig. 8).

---

93. Emphasis added. Further rabbinic sources are divided; e.g., *Sifre Deut.* 322 reads the remnant in Isa 1:9 as a slight mitigation of God's judgment, in order to preserve his reputation as he invokes the covenantal curses of Deut 32 (cf. Deut 32:26); while *Song. Rab.* 8.9.3 offers a positive interpretation of 1:9, understanding the remnant as a substitution for the destroyed second temple. Despite the data, especially as it re-lates to the specific Isaianic traditions, Wagner, *Heralds,* 108; Gadenz, "Lord," 84 and others focus generally on the trend in Second Temple Judaism(s) of taking the rem-nant motif positively, supposing that Paul's particular references would fall in line.

In the original Hosean context, in both wording and eschatological tone, there is open-endedness to the future restoration of God's people, "Israel." That is, the emphasis lies less on the identity of those who repopulate Israel than on the quality of Israel's restoration. Paul's use of these joint traditions to explain non-Jewish believers' identification with Israel as objects of mercy is a logical extension of Romans 9:6–13, wherein God's people were constituted by his calling.[94]

Moreover, given that Hosea 2:25 completes a trajectory begun in 2:1, Paul's inverted arrangement of the Hosean traditions adds to their rhetorical power without distorting their meaning. Israel's eschatological restoration and expansion takes the shape of those formerly not participating in the covenant relationship now identifying as Israel (Rom 9:25 = Hos 2:25), in accordance with the antecedent promise that those formerly identified as οὐ λαός μου would receive sonship (Rom 9:26 = Hos 2:1, echoing the blessing of υἱοθεσία in Rom 9:4) under the auspices of a Davidic ruler (Hos 2:2; cf. Rom 1:3).[95] This is further accentuated by Paul's stylistic adaptations of Greek Hosea 2:25 in Romans 9:25.[96]

---

94. Moo, *Epistle*, 610.

95. W. Edward Glenny argues that in Rom 9:25 "Paul used Hosea [2:25] to show that Gentiles who previously had no covenant relationship with God are now, through faith, His elect, covenant people." Glenny, "The 'People of God' in Romans 9:25–26," *BSac* 152 (1995): 53.

96. Rom 9:26 follows Greek Hos 2:1 verbatim, which is a transparent rendering of the Hebrew except for the addition of ἐκεῖ. The explanation given by Schreiner (*Romans*, 528) is that this difference "should not be pressed for a geographical reference [in Romans]. Not every single word of the OT citation should be forced to yield the Pauline intention." But recall also Stuart's suggestion (discussed above) that "in the place where" (Hos 2:1) extends to contexts beyond the ethno-political boundaries of Israel's original identity. Similarly, Greek Hos 2:25 reflects the Hebrew, only adding κύριος and making explicit εἶ σύ.

MT Hos 2:25	Greek Hos 2:25	Rom 9:25
וזרעתיה לי בארץ ורחמתי את־לא רחמה	καὶ σπερῶ αὐτὴν ἐμαυτῷ ἐπὶ τῆς γῆς <u>καὶ ἐλεήσω τὴν οὐκ -ἠλεημένην</u>	
ואמרתי ללא־עמי עמי־אתה	<u>καὶ ἐρῶ τῷ οὐ -λαῷ -μου λαός μου εἶ σύ</u>	<u>καλέσω τὸν οὐ λαόν μου λαόν μου</u> <u>καὶ τὴν οὐκ ἠγαπημένην ἠγαπημένην</u>
והוא יאמר אלהי	καὶ αὐτὸς ἐρεῖ Κύριος ὁ θεός μου εἶ σύ	

For instance, the substitution of καλέσω for ἐρῶ echoes καλέω in Romans 9:24, which brings Paul's citation into closer alignment with its new context.[97] Likewise, Paul's inversion of the Hosean clauses emphasizes the critical element by its new forward placement. Finally, by changing οὐκ -ἠλεημένην to οὐκ ἠγαπημένην, Paul adds power to his picture of Gentile inclusion by bringing the (now) second clause under the new main verb (which accounts for the omission of ἐρῶ) without distorting the original sense of the citation.[98]

Accordingly, scholars are nearly unanimous that, in W. Edward Glenny's words, the Hosean citations in Romans 9:25-26

> argue that God's receiving Gentiles as His covenant people is consistent with what the Old Testament prophesied concerning His dealings with the northern kingdom of Israel. ... [Just as] He could call Israel who had broken her covenant relations with Him to be His people once again, He could call into covenant relationship Gentiles who never had been His people before.[99]

---

97. In this instance, this typical Pauline strategy also accounts for the grammatical shift of dative and nominative in the Greek to the accusative and the omission of the second person in Romans (cf. Stanley, *Paul*, 110).

98. Stanley, *Paul*, 110-12. Regarding the substitution of "beloved" for "mercied," Stanley reckons that since Paul would likely have seized upon the opportunity to use ἐλεέω given its thematic and frequent occurrence in Rom 9:6-29, it is likely the text reflects his own *Vorlage*, to which several important Greek mss are witness (B V 407, etc.). Alternatively, Paul may have purposefully used ἠγαπημένην because of covenantal connotations it may have, which is still faithful to the original context and only strengthens this reading.

99. Glenny, "'People,'" 55.

Moreover, since "what God promised through Hosea ... has for Paul become a historical fact," Romans 9:25-26 also support Paul's thesis for Romans 9:6-29 in verse 6a as "evidence that God's word has not been terminated."[100] Therefore, Paul's citations of Hosea 2:1 and 25 in Romans 9:25-26 explain why God tarried in punishing national Israel without obfuscating that they are under his judgment for their idolatry. Gentile believers in Paul's gospel, which includes the breadth of God's authoritative creator-kingship claim over all creation, have accepted that reconciliation with their Creator takes place through trust in Christ his son, while rejection of the gospel (even for adherence to the narrative of God's pre-Christ-event relationship with his people) invites the judgment due to idolaters (so 9:22-24).

Accordingly, in Romans 9:27-29 Paul likewise contrastively underscores Gentile believers' new status with a characterization of national Israel's situation as the "objects of wrath" (9:22) by citing Isaiah 10:22-23 and 1:9 (see fig. 8).[101] In so doing, Paul completes his discussion of God's judgment upon national Israel's idolatry in Romans 9:6-21 by answering his question of verses 22-23:

Objects of wrath (9:22)
 Objects of mercy (9:23)
  We, both Jewish and Gentile believers (9:24)
 The nations' identifying with Israel (9:25-26)
Judgment upon national Israel (9:27-29)

Fig. 8: Thematic Structure of Romans 9:22-29

The atypical citation formula of the Isaianic citations in Romans 9:27 introduces them with a sense of intensity and urgency (cf. κράζω, 9:27).[102]

---

100. Leander E. Keck, *Romans*, ANTC (Nashville: Abingdon, 2005), 239.

101. Cf. the contrastive δὲ opening 9:27; so, e.g., Schreiner, *Romans*, 528.

102. Dunn, *Romans 9-16*, 572. Although context is ultimately determinative, it should be noted that in the other eleven Romans occurrences where it refers to people, ὑπὲρ means "on behalf of" instead of "concerning" as in 9:27 (John Paul Heil, "From Remnant to Seed of Hope for Israel: Romans 9:27-29," *CBQ* 64 [2002]: 707). But in context, the meaning of Isa 10:22-23 in context along with the δὲ opening 9:27 are determinative.

Also, Paul's several adaptations of Isaiah 10:22–23 rhetorically enhance its function in Romans 9:27–28.[103]

MT Isa 10:22-23	Greek Isa 10:22-23	Rom 9:27-28
כי אם־יהיה עמך ישׂראל	καὶ ἐὰν <u>γένηται ὁ λαὸς</u> Ἰσραηλ	ἐὰν <u>ᾖ ὁ ἀριθμὸς τῶν υἱῶν</u> Ἰσραὴλ
כחול הים	ὡς ἡ ἄμμος τῆς θαλάσσης	ὡς ἡ ἄμμος τῆς θαλάσσης
שׁאר ישׁוב בו	τὸ <u>κατάλειμμα αὐτῶν</u> σωθήσεται	τὸ <u>ὑπόλειμμα</u> σωθήσεται
כליון חרוץ	λόγον γὰρ συντελῶν	λόγον γὰρ συντελῶν
שׁוטף	καὶ συντέμνων	καὶ συντέμνων
צדקה	ἐν δικαιοσύνῃ	
כי כלה ונחרצה	ὅτι λόγον συντετμημένον	
אדני יהוה צבאות עשׂה	ποιήσει <u>ὁ θεὸς</u>	ποιήσει <u>κύριος</u>
בקרב כל־הארץ	<u>ἐν τῇ οἰκουμένῃ ὅλῃ</u>	<u>ἐπὶ τῆς γῆς</u>

First, although Paul retains the concessive sense of the Isaianic text (ἐὰν, v. 27; Greek Isa 10:22), he replaces ὁ λαὸς Ἰσραηλ with ὁ ἀριθμὸς τῶν υἱῶν Ἰσραὴλ from Hosea 2:1 (ὡς ἡ ἄμμος τῆς θαλάσσης occurs in both texts, providing a segue back into the Isaianic text), likely to avoid equating unbelieving Jews with the Gentile believers who were just designated λαός μου in 9:25.[104] A secondary effect is the irony that whereas Paul favorably applied Hosea 2:1 to the Gentiles (subsequently referred to as the living God's υἱοὶ in 9:26), the echo of Hosea 2:1 in Romans 9:27 unfavorably introduces God's judgment. Similarly, Paul may have omitted ἐν δικαιοσύνῃ ὅτι λόγον συντετμημένον because the sense of *righteous* in the Isaianic context does not fit Paul's usage in Romans, and hence here would have been

---

103. Rom 9:29 follows Greek Isa 1:9 exactly, which simply reflects the Hebrew with the exception of conflating שׂריד כמעט into the single term σπέρμα (perhaps with a view to the hopeful potential inherent in "remnant"?).

104. E.g., Stanley (*Paul*, 115), who advances the position held by most scholars (cf. Schreiner, *Romans*, 528–29; Heil, "Remnant," 711; Shum, *Paul's*, 207) that Paul's use of Hos 2:1, 25; and Isa 10:22–23 in direct sequence forced him to choose between two basically synonymous terms. Gadenz ("Lord," 82–83) notes how the phrase "Israel as the sand of the sea" in Greek Hos 2:1 and Isa 10:22 are the only two occurrences in the entire Greek translation of the Bible, enabling Paul's avoidance of confusing over λαὸς by relating the two traditions according to the rabbinic interpretive rule of *gezerah shawah* (one tradition interpreting another).

distracting.[105] This omission compresses Isaiah 10:22, an effect of which is to forcefully align its rhetoric with its content, thereby underscoring the decisive character of God's judgment. Finally, perhaps Paul changes ἐν τῇ οἰκουμένῃ ὅλῃ to ἐπὶ τῆς γῆς in 9:28 to "tone down the language by removing the universalizing ὅλη and replacing the broader οἰκουμένη with the more neutral γῆ," meaning to emphasize God's reduction of Israel to "a mere shadow of its former self as a result of the coming judgment."[106]

Therefore, in Romans 9:27–28 Paul applies the past in order to prophetically interpret the meaning of the present, in that national Israel is under the same judgment as that faced by historical Israel in Isaiah 10:22–23: "that only a remnant is saved points up the severity and extent of the judgment executed."[107] And Paul's citation formula in 9:29 (καὶ καθὼς προείρηκεν Ἡσαΐας) also highlights that God's judgment is in accordance with his argument regarding Israel's rebellion in Romans 9:6–21 (especially 9:14–21). As with Israel in Isaiah, "because of [national] Israel's unbelief God has judged his people, sparing but a remnant."[108]

As with the Hosean citations in Romans 9:25–26, then, Paul's Isaianic citations in verses 27–29 invert the trajectory described by Isaiah 1:9 and 10:22–23, again increasing their rhetorical power without distorting their meaning. Present national Israel's rejection of the gospel has

---

105. Stanley, *Paul*, 117–18 (noting this may also be a feature of Paul's *Vorlage*); cf. Wright, *Letter*, 643. Stanley is correct in rejecting Dunn's suggestion (*Romans 9–16*, 573) that the omission is due to some kind of "mental haplography" whereby Paul skipped from συντέμνον in Rom 9:22 to συντετμημένον in 9:23.

106. Stanley, *Paul*, 119. Alternatively, the "inhabited world [οἰκουμένη]" of Greek Isaiah may be too narrow to capture God's judgment upon ethnic Israel, for which reason Paul appeals instead to "the earth" of the Hebrew. Or again, perhaps τῆς γῆς invokes "the [promised] land" where judgment takes place in Isa 1–12. In any case, this particular change neither violates the original context nor greatly affects meaning.

Similarly, the text contains several further but inconsequential differences from Isaiah: κατάλειμμα and ὑπόλειμμα were synonymous, even if strong textual support (ℵ A B 81, etc., despite κατάλειμμα in P⁴⁶ ¹ℵ D F G ψ, etc.—the text is *lectio difficilior* and the latter variant reflects a harmonizing impulse despite the fact that Paul here otherwise deviates so extensively from Greek Isaiah) as well as the absence of ὑπόλειμμα in any Greek mss indicate Paul's change was intentional (Stanley, *Paul*, 116, citing Koch). The omission of αὐτῶν in 9:27 may have been rhetorical, though the source of the change is opaque (ibid.). Finally, the substitution of κύριος in 9:28 for ὁ θεός (Isa 10:23) is likewise innocuous. It should not be read as a christological statement, giving Christ agency in executing Isaianic judgment upon national Israel for their rejection of him.

107. Murray, *Epistle*, 2:40–41.

108. Evans, "Paul and the Hermeneutics of 'True Prophecy': A Study of Romans 9–11," *Bib* 65 (1984): 563.

resulted in their terrible reduction to a mere "remnant" (Rom 9:27–28 =
Isa 10:22–23), in accordance with God's forewarned judgment whereby
he turns against his people as "Lord *Sabaoth* [κύριος σαβαωθ]" because
of their rebellion (Rom 9:29 = Isa 1:9). That is, their rebellion consigns
them to God's decisive judgment of becoming an insignificant (in numbers) and dispossessed people, rather than his chosen people among the
nations, just like Israel in Isaiah 1–12.

So in Romans 9:25–29, Paul cites Hosea 2:25 and 2:1 together with
Isaiah 10:22–23 and 1:9 in order to evaluate God's stance toward non-Jewish believers and unbelieving Jews as objects of mercy and wrath, respectively. What function, then, does this evaluation serve within Paul's
argument in the pericope of 9:22–29? In the previous pericope (9:14–18),
Paul assigned to idolatrous national Israel the place of Pharaoh, whom
God raised up to glorify his own name in the deliverance and redemption of his people. Then, in 9:22, springboarding off of his defeat of the
objection in 9:19, Paul rhetorically asks whether God might have endured national Israel's rebellion in order to show forth his glory to the
non-Jews. In answer, in 9:25–29, he points by way of Scripture to both
non-Jewish believers' identification with God's people Israel and God's
judgment upon national Israel, as the present respectively realizes and
repeats the past.

So, Paul's argument in Romans 9:22–29 is that God has used unbelieving Jews' unfaithfulness to his eschatological activity in an ironic
fulfillment of his eschatological promises to Israel. Like Pharaoh, God
was able to use even idolatrous national Israel's rebellion to his purpose. Even though unbelieving Jews rejected the Messiah (who came
from among them; cf. 9:5), God is allowing them to sever as an example to the nations, and they are nevertheless not an impediment to the
gospel—Israel's own story—also being brought to the nations with the
result in their salvation (cf. Rom 1:16).[109] If interpreters are tempted to

---

109. This is not altogether dissimilar from Abasciano, *Romans 9.10–18*, 199, 222–23
(dealing mostly with Exod 9:16 in Rom 9:17). However, Abasciano's understanding of
emphasis is different, reckoning that Paul's concern (and that of the Exodus traditions) is that the purpose of the proclamation of God's grace, mercy and sovereignty
(i.e., his name) is the resultant realization of his redemption purpose of bestowing
mercy and grace (conditionally and non-deterministically) upon those who trust
in Christ; that is as may be in the abstract, but Paul's concern is more properly understood as addressing the *Israelfrage*. That is, Paul is not proposing that national
Israel's unbelief calls for turning to the Gentiles with the gospel. Rather, God's response to their unbelief has as its corollary (if not intention, in this context) the

tie in Genesis 12:1–3 with Romans 9:6–29, then at least in this it can be said that God has indeed used Israel to bless the nations. Furthermore, this flocking of non-Jews to Christ in astounding numbers is the realization of eschatologically oriented Hosea 2:1 and 25, thereby fulfilling God's promises of eschatological restoration—God has indeed blessed his people Israel as well (again, cf. Gen 12:1–3), albeit through his judgment upon *national* Israel. And finally, as God promised in Isaiah, he has responded to idolatry with judgment. As a result of this, the number of Abraham's descendants among his people have been numerically reduced (at least temporarily) to a mere remnant, in the estrangement of the bulk of culled national Israel—God has even remained faithful to his words of judgment. According to Romans 9:22–29, then, God has remained faithful to his according-to-election purpose (Rom 9:11). His judgment upon national Israel is not a failure of his word, but rather indisputable proof of his covenant faithfulness (Rom 9:6a).

SUMMARY OF ROMANS 9:19–29
IN LIGHT OF PAUL'S USE OF SCRIPTURE

In Romans 9:19–29, the final pericope of 9:6–29, Paul first responds to his interlocutor's objection (based on a misinterpretation of Rom 9:14–18) that national Israel never really rebelled against God and so should not be judged for their rejection of Christ and the gospel (Rom 9:19). The answer is Paul's explication that, properly understood, God did indeed harden national Israel as a judgment in response to their idolatry. This is his prerogative, specifically when dealing with idolaters (Rom 9:20–21). Paul then uses this as a launching point for his explanation of how national Israel further compares to Pharaoh in Exodus 4–14: just as God used his judgment upon Pharaoh in the deliverance of Israel, he is now using the same gospel that is the cause of his judgment upon national Israel in the restoration of the humanity of the whole earth. And God is doing so precisely by way of the salvation and identification of non-Jews as his people in fulfillment of his promises regarding Israel's eschatological restoration (Rom 9:22–29). Therefore, as asserted in 9:6a, national Israel's rejection does not prove God unfaithful. In fact, God's response to their very rejection in proves his covenantal faithfulness.

---

nations glorifying Israel's God, such that God's glorification in his judgment upon national Israel also serves to bring salvation to Gentiles.

5

Conclusions

This study has been an attempt to trace Paul's argument in Romans 9:6–29 in light of his use of Scripture. Paul's thesis statement that God has not betrayed his people, along with the meanings of the Scriptures to which he resorts (and the limited extent of available Second Temple and—more frequently—rabbinic witnesses regarding those biblical traditions), together delimit the possibilities of what Paul could coherently be discussing.[1] The soundest interpretation, therefore, is that Paul defends God's covenantal faithfulness by identifying present unbelieving Jews' rejection of the gospel as idolatry, and then explaining how God is using his judgment upon them in fulfillment of his covenantal promises to his people Israel.

For Paul, Israel's very identity is predicated on God's promise and his faithfulness to his own character. He therefore argues that both independently of Israel's moral performance and, in fact, even despite it, God has always remained faithful to his covenantal promises and purpose. Accordingly, it is consistent that at present, as in history, physical descent does not equate with covenantal identity; that fact at present neither refutes nor does not refute God's faithfulness (Rom 9:6–13).

Paul then responds to the resultant objection, that God's apparent rejection now of national Israel entails that he is arbitrarily counting their rebellion against them. In his view, their rejection of God's purposes in Christ is idolatrous. Accordingly, given the nature of idolatry in the biblical tradition, God is judging national Israel by hardening them in their

---

1. This is not to deny an interpretive criterion of dissimilarity (by which Paul is allowed to innovatively argue against contemporary Jewish understanding or interpretation of a given issue). Rather, it is to say that to interpret Paul as understanding the Scriptures that he cites—and/or innovatively finding for them a *sui generis* meaning by which they refer to a doctrine of election and its relationship to soteriology—would be to say that Paul's discussion would not be effective in communicating to a first-century audience who is familiar with and understands the world in terms of Israel's Scriptures and biblical narrative.

idolatry—in order to use his judgment upon them in fulfillment of his covenantal purpose, just as he did Pharaoh in Exodus 4–14 (Rom 9:14–18).

This raises a further possible objection, namely that national Israel did not opt to reject the gospel but were compelled to do so by God. Paul's response is first to correct a misperception regarding the consequences of idolatry: national Israel has surrendered their humanity and are therefore subject to God's judgment, like clay in the potter's hand. Further, Paul argues, just as God used his judgment upon Pharaoh in Israel's deliverance, he is now using his judgment upon national Israel in the redemption of believing Gentiles (Rom 9:19–29). Therefore, through his use of the OT in his argument in Romans 9:6–29, Paul defends God's faithfulness by demonstrating that God has *not* rejected national Israel. Rather, he has used their response to the gospel in fulfillment of his covenantal promises and faithfulness.

This point bears repeating: Paul's strategy in Romans 9:6–29 is *not* to argue that God is faithful even though he has rejected national Israel. Instead, Paul defends God's faithfulness by arguing that he has not rejected them; it is *they* who have rejected *him* by rejecting God's Messiah and gospel. God's judgment upon national Israel may have been unexpected, but it was in response to *their* prior idolatry. The questions of why God has rejected Israel, why this would be acceptable, or what its implications might be are simply not at issue; this is not what he has done. God's seemingly unexpected judgment of his people resulted directly from their tragic, unexpected response to the Christ event. Throughout 9:6–29 Paul never breaks this focus, which supports his claim of God's covenant faithfulness in the thesis of 9:6a. Romans 9:6–29 is a single, coherent, linear argument in response to a particular, occasional concern—namely, unbelieving Jews' rejection of Paul's gospel.

Moreover, Paul's argument *presuppositionally* draws upon rich but complex biblical themes such as election, humans as God's image, idolatry, mercy and judgment, and eschatological restoration. He does not engage in abstract theological discussion, and he is not simply presenting or expositing his position on these issues (even indirectly in order to defend God's faithfulness). And neither is Paul offering interpretation (midrashic or otherwise) of the biblical traditions that he cites. Rather, he selects them because of how they are relevant and apply to the occasion at hand within his own line of thought.

This means that a conclusion like Wright's is accurate but imprecise, when he claims that Paul's focus is "how God's righteousness requires

that he deal properly with sin" along with the related, consequent notion of "how that same righteousness, God's faithfulness to the covenant,
generates [a new Israel] characterized by faith in Jesus."[2] Instead, Paul
argues *from* a biblical understanding of such issues—explaining God's
response to national Israel's rejection of the gospel and what that means
for God's redemptive purposes—in order to defend God's faithfulness.
Similarly, it needs recalling that Paul's point is that God has not broken
his covenant with Israel his people (even if one were to add that that
covenant does now lie broken, with national Israel currently not participating in the christocentric new covenant).

Admittedly, it could be compatible with this to hold that God has rejected unbelieving Jews as belonging to his newly christocentric Israel,
but only if it could also be separately shown that his retroactive judgment upon their idolatrous covenant breaking were to be identified
with his covenantal rejection of them. However, this is only a conditional concession, which is as far as the notion should be pushed, since
it goes beyond the text to identify God's judgment and his covenantal
rejection.[3] That God cannot, by his own character (and by the biblical
definition of *Israel*, in a sense), reject Israel his people is the entire point
of Exodus 33:12-23, upon which Paul draws. And more to the point, both
the prologue to Romans 9-11 in 9:1-5 and its conclusion in 11:25-32 em-
phatically state Paul's agreement with God in hoping for national Israel
to once again identify as God's people by identifying with God in Christ.
Therefore, at least so far as 9:6-29 is concerned, the present and potential future covenantal disposition of national Israel is indeterminate (or
at least unaddressed). Perhaps the most that should be ventured is that
elsewhere in Romans generally it could be inferred (cf., e.g., Rom 3:9-18,
22b-23; 6:23a) that at some future point (the *parousia*?) even those who

---

2. Wright, *Letter*, 644.

3. This should almost go without saying, as it is a commonplace among at least
Hebrew Bible and early Jewish scholars that a primary and in many ways defining
theme of all Jewish literature from at least the Persian period forward—regarding
the exilic and post-exilic eras—is the tension between the fact of the apparently broken covenant between national Israel and God, and the continuity or persistence of
their identity of God's people Israel. Thinking that the advent of the Jewish Messiah
and the eschatological age of the Spirit suddenly breaks continuity—moving from a
post-exilic people who had awaited God's eschatological restoration to an Israel who
now definitively excludes national Israel on a covenantal level—requires a special
kind of theology, one which is thoroughly alien to early Jewish thought and would
be very difficult to ascribe to Paul in any setting, let alone Rom 9-11.

identify as national Israel will lose the opportunity to be reconciled with God and fully restored to his people.

Finally, and on a related note, my reading illustrates that for Paul non-Jews' identification as God's people Israel marks an *ironic* eschatological fulfillment of God's covenantal promises to bless Israel and make them a blessing to the nations. Because national Israel rejected his gospel, Paul brought it to the Gentiles—the nations—where it yielded astounding returns. Although they were formerly dead in *their* idolatry and sin (cf. Rom 1:18-32), they now constitute God's covenant people in an eschatological fulfillment of the promise that Israel would once again become "like the stars of the heavens and the sand on the seashore" (Gen 22:17; cf. Hos 2:1 [Isa 10:22]; Rom 9:26-27).

So Paul is successful in effectively supporting his thesis for both Romans 9:6-29 and (so far) for Romans 9-11 as a whole: "It is not as though the word of God has failed" (9:6a). And this in turn supports Paul's thesis for the argument portion of the letter as a whole (1:16-11:36): that in spite of others' initial impression that national Israel is excluded from his gospel, he is rightly "not ashamed of [that] gospel, for it is the power of God for salvation of all those who believe, to the Jew first and then to the Greek, for in it the righteousness of God is revealed" (1:16-17).

I consider the reading of Romans 9:6-29 presented in this study to be faithful to Paul's own language, his Hellenistic Jewish context and its heritage, and to the biblical traditions (and presuppositional concepts) upon which he draws and the manner in which he appears to be employing them (presuming that his argument is coherent and communicatively effective). Nevertheless, interpreters of a certain strain may consider the reading provided by this study to be a radical *rereading* of Paul. That is, the conclusions of this study may be found objectionable on the basis of their being unpalatable or implausible just because they are untraditional, particularly given the history of interpretation of Romans 9:6-29 (and especially the history of post-Reformation and modern interpretation). But critically speaking, rejection of this reading would require either offering corrective interpretations of the Scriptures that Paul cites but still within their original contexts, or else arguing that the offered interpretations are sound but for some reason(s) do not reflect Paul's own understandings of them. In the latter case, one would either need to produce superior reasons and evidence that Paul employs alternate but equally sound understandings of those Scriptures (that would have been acceptable in an early Jewish setting), or else to conclude that Paul's argument in Romans 9:6–29 is incoherent and that his practice of referencing Scripture is at best haphazard.

PAUL'S ARGUMENT IN ROMANS 9–11 IN LIGHT OF 9:6–29

To further forestall any hesitancy regarding the understanding of Romans 9:6–29 argued in this study, I would like to suggest how it suits Paul's argument in chapters 9–11. Since these chapters lie beyond the scope of the present study, these observations are provisional. Nevertheless, it should be hoped and expected that the coherence of 9:6–29 would lend itself to that of chapters 9–11 as a whole.

Given that in 9:6–29 Paul references national Israel in relation to the issue of God's covenantal faithfulness, this prompts the question: Precisely what is national Israel's failing? It is unsurprising, then, that in the next stage of his argument in Romans 9:30–10:21 Paul specifies the nature of national Israel's idolatry.

The first pericope of this literary sub-unit is Romans 9:30–10:4. The hypothetical interlocutor has challenged Paul by demanding why wicked Gentiles should be righteousized and participate in being God's people while national Israel does not (especially given the fact that they at least attempted Torah faithfulness, even if they transgressed Torah; cf. Hab 2:4 in Rom 1:17, above). Paul's phrasing of this (9:30–31) slightly twists the interlocutor's wording to expose its logical flaw: unbelieving Jews sought not just righteousization generally, but righteousization on their own terms—namely, by way of attaining Torah itself and an exactness of Torah observance, supposing these to be the place where God awaited them. Paul's riposte (9:32) is that national Israel was devoted to Torah rather than God. Or, if they were devoted to God as well, it was only so long as he remained the expected God who related to his people through Torah, righteousizing them on the basis of Torah observance. Insofar as they are self-determined in this, unbelieving Jews' idol is therefore themselves, as they take the prerogative of deciding what is divinely normative.

That is, Paul does not simply find fault in the fact that national Israel did not relate to God on the basis of faith. Instead, the problem is that they still insist on expressing and defining their covenantal trust/faith in terms of Torah observance, whereas for Paul the Christ event means that God's people now live out their trust-based relationship with him by trusting in the teachings, deeds, death, resurrection, and identity of Jesus of Nazareth and God's own involvement in the Christ event (cf. Rom 5). Even if in many quarters of early non-Christian Judaism(s) the distinction may have been incoherent, post-resurrection Paul diagnoses that national Israel was devoted to Torah rather than God and righteousness. And just as with preexilic Israel (Rom 9:33 = Isa 28:16 and 8:14), God both exonerates himself as the true hope and source of life for the faithful—rather than the cause of their woes—and judges the (rebellion and) idolatry of the unfaithful, who are committed to a false version of God. And so, because national Israel are ignorant of God's methods in Christ and are committed to righteousizing themselves via Torah observance, they reject God's covenantal faithfulness in the Christ event and thereby reject God (Rom 10:1–4).[4] It is in punishment for this refusal to acknowledge God's work that God is allowing national Israel to remain uncomprehending of the nature, character, and source of the righteousness that characterizes his people.

Romans 10:5–13 is subordinate to this, an elaboration on Paul's final point of the previous pericope in 10:4. Paul's opening citations from Torah present two horns of a dilemma: if one now (i.e., post–Christ event) chooses to pursue, by means of Torah observance, a life that is characterized by righteousness, then one is committed to that method even if it means no longer trusting God since he is no longer righteousizing by means of Torah observance (Rom 10:5 = Lev 18:5).[5] But it is a repetition of Israel's historical covenantal unfaithfulness (in direct contravention of the Deuteronomic admonition to not disregard God; Rom 10:6–8 = Deut 9:4 and 30:12–14) that national Israel does not repent from obtuseness or recalcitrance, misunderstanding or rationalizing that Christ, God's superlative Word, is distant and inaccessible (as the conquest generation could have wrongly done with Torah). Paul reasons that hearers of the gospel—national Israel included—are obligated to live lives characterized by righteousness on the basis of trusting

---

4. The counterpoint is believers from among the nations (Rom 9:30b; 10:4), who have christocentrically identified as Israel in that they are defined by the trust-based relationship with God that is Israel's defining characteristic. Meadors (*Idolatry*, 121, 139–41) offers the interpretation (relying more upon theological coherence than critical analysis) that hardened unbelieving Jews "are idolaters who have stood in the path of God's plan of salvation and have thereby challenged the working out of God's covenantal promises," based upon "their preexisting devotion to religious observance."
5. Lev 18:5 in Rom 10:5 merits discrete treatment (as does its usage in Gal 3:12), as it does not relate in any fashion to Hab 2:4, either biblically or within the macro-structure or Rom 1:16–11:36—or, arguably, in Gal 3:11 (contra Francis Watson, *Paul and the Hermeneutics of Faith* [London: T&T Clark, 2004]).

God in Jesus. This is because the Christ event realizes the eschatological expectation of Israel's renewal wherein God establishes a universal standard of justice (Rom 10:11 = Isa 28:16[-17]).[6] Surprisingly, the feared Day of Yhwh is primarily one of restoration rather than judgment (Rom 10:12–13 = Joel 3:5).

The final pericope in this literary sub-unit is Romans 10:14–21, in which Paul expands upon his teaching that in Christ God's Word is immediate and accessible to all who hear his gospel. Paul here addresses the worry that unbelieving Jews had neither the opportunity nor the means to receive God's message and his purposes in the Christ event (perhaps because they had not been evangelized, or perhaps because there was something deficient in the means of communication). Paul responds that Scripture records Israel's history as being one of repeatedly receiving and yet refusing God's message and redemptive activity. Romans 10:14–15 makes clear that God has brought the Messiah to his people. Paul has faithfully discharged his prophet-like duty of voicing Jesus' teachings (and the teaching about Jesus) to national Israel, so that in the equation it is only unbelieving Jews' obligation to accept the gospel that has not been met. Romans 10:16–17 expounds that present national Israel is rejecting God's message just as they have frequently (always?) done, historically.[7] Then, having exonerated himself of failing to discharge his duties, in 10:18 Paul turns the focus to one of culpability for unbelieving Jews' rejection of the gospel, providing a catena of Scriptures (Rom 10:18–19 = Greek Psa 19:5; Rom 10:19 = Deut 32:21; Rom 10:20–21 = Isa 65:1–2) that are interpretively presented to state how national Israel's present rejection of the gospel is the pinnacle of Israel's history of rebellion (especially as eschatologically anticipated in

---

6. The scriptural context also carries a reiteration of the warning that—in contrast to Rom 10:9—were one to *not* confess Jesus' lordship, then one would remain in rebellion to God and not participate in either his salvation or Israel's blessing of deliverance and restoration.

7. Rom 10:16 = Isa 53:1, where the New Exodus proclaimed by the (innocent) prophet is ironically brought about by his state execution. Isa 53:1 is dehistoricized and interpreted within Isaiah as an effective redemptive sacrifice on the people's behalf that is given an eschatological referent, after which the chorus are able to recognize the restoration effected by his death. In Rom 10:16, Paul places himself and believers in the role of the chorus while assigning Christ the role of the prophet *qua* sacrificed faithful Servant.

Isaiah—which prophetically applies the Deuteronomic covenant to its own current events).[8]

On this last point, Paul invokes two features. First, then—as now—Israel's rebellion against God and rejection of his prophetic word is accompanied by and/or identified with idolatry. And second, God's judgment upon his people has always in the past—and continuing into the present—included an ironic extension of Israelite identity to non-Israelites at the nation's expense. God has always been clear with Israel. They have always been equipped to recognize and accept God's word and his activity, and have always had a history characterized by their not doing so. In this, God's response has always been to convict and punish them for their rebellion. That this pattern is repeating itself in a somewhat definitive way in national Israel's rejection of the gospel does not implicate either Paul or the gospel. Nor does it provide national Israel a defense of ignorance, since they were made aware of (and were established in their negative response toward) God's policies and purposes long before.

The final portion of Paul's argument in Romans 9–11 is the literary sub-unit of chapter 11. Paul's opening query in Romans 11:1a as to whether God rejected "his people" (to whomever that refers) initially seems redundant to the claims in 9:6a or 9:30–31. However, in 9:6–29 Paul addressed the issue of God's faithfulness (making recourse to God's response toward Israel's idolatry and demonstrating the constancy of his covenantal purposes). In 9:30–10:21, Paul addressed the issue of national Israel's sin against God that would result in their alienation from him (identifying as their idol their simulacrum of God and, ultimately, their own self-determination, specifying how their failure to receive the gospel has been their own). The question now is: What of national Israel's future? In response, in 11:1–32 Paul argues that national Israel's estrangement from God is neither the final snapshot nor the full picture.

Romans 11:1–10 is replete with scriptural references, making its proper analysis much longer than its in fact relatively straightforward meaning would seem to require. Paul's thesis statement here is that Israel's foregoing idolatry does not entail that God has abandoned his people (11:1a, bearing in mind that the identity of "God's people" is debated in both postexilic biblical and postbiblical traditions). This is elaborated

---

8. Wagner (*Heralds*, 182–84) presents a reasonably strong argument that portions of Rom 10:18–19 also echo Isa 40:21.

upon in the example of Paul himself (11:1b–2). This claim is then justified by the applicability to the present of the scriptural precedent (1 Kgs
19:10, 14, 18 = Rom 11:2b–4) of God's people comprising only a remnant of
believing, covenantally faithful Jews within the entire nation of Israel
(11:5). The implication is that "the rest" of national Israel is repeating
the sins of their historical non-remnant forerunners (11:7)—present
Israel has not attained the righteousness and trusting relationship with
God that they had intended. In support of this evaluation, Paul offers
another catena of Scriptures illustrating that, as in Isaiah's time, national Israel is again reaping the covenantal curse of hardening as a consequence for their idolatrous rebellion (Deut 29:3 and Isa 29:10 = Rom 11:8,
in an explicit application of the principle outlined in Rom 9:14–18). This
also illustrates that David joins Moses and Isaiah in inveighing against
national Israel, and that their hardening is the warranted result of their
rebelling against God (in oppressing the repentant psalmist who identifies with God; Greek Psa 68:23–24 = Rom 11:9–10).[9]

In qualification of that final statement in Romans 11:7, the bulky
pericope of 11:11–24 begins an elaboration on the degree to which national Israel is alienated from God and the covenantal blessings that are
their heritage. However, Paul's explanation is not fully fleshed out until
11:25–32. The several thoughts of 11:11–24 cooperate to express the single
main idea of the necessary conditions for Israel's reconciliation with
God. Paul emphasizes that, even as apostle to the Gentiles, his heart (cf.
Rom 9:1–5) is for national Israel. In this and the rich potential to their
submission to the Christ event, he and his Roman audience are in accord (11:11–15). Added to this is that national Israel's natural place is with
God's people, such that it would be easier for their Israelite identity to
be restored than it was for it to be sundered (11:16, 23–24). Along the way,
Paul digresses, relating the object lesson of national Israel to the Gentile
believers among his audience, but which also further details national
Israel's circumstances (having digressed, in 11:23 Paul returns to point):
Particularly, Paul decries (11:17–22) any potential arrogance on the part
of non-Jewish believers (cf. the "strong" and the "weak" in 14:1–15:7),

---

9. Further, it may be suggested that David's voice is messianic in Paul's post-Christ-
event usage, such that this citation is christological and the psalmist's words are
voiced by Christ (cf. Greek Psa 68:22 in the Passion scenes in Gospel traditions),
whereby national Israel is standing against and oppressing the Messiah himself,
causing them to be scandalize and rightly condemned for idolatrous rebellion
against God.

since there but for the grace of God went they, and could do again more easily than national Israel has done. In this fashion, Paul supports his assertion that national Israel has been scandalized but has not completely fallen, whereby the nations' participation in national Israel's blessings may drive them to trust God (who is able to restore them) to their restoration (11:11).[10]

Finally, also in support of Romans 11:7, Paul supplies in 11:25–32 an apocalyptic revelation that fills out the argument of 11:11–24, with the overriding concern that the audience fully understand the landscape (11:25, as in 11:7). An entity referred to as "all Israel" (11:26a) will be saved when the full complement of the nations has become Israelified over the course of the ongoing eschatological present, stretching forward from Paul's time until the final consummation of history.[11] Structurally, the first half of the pericope speaks of why national Israel and believing Jews like Paul (cf. 11:1b–2a) do not presently occupy the same space, as it were. The second half mitigates against concluding the worst for national Israel in the future, lest God's priority of his christocentric people of Israel be misread.

A reserved interpretation is that Romans 11:25–27 disclose how "a part" of Israel has been hardened until that time when the "fullness" of the nations is Israelified. This is tied to the salvation of "all Israel," supported by Paul's Isaianic citations.[12] Then, 11:28–32 take pains to qualify

---

10. The olive tree metaphor of Rom 11:17b–21 presents as an illustration national Israel, whom God has covenantally cut off from the cultivated olive tree (Christ) and its rich root (biblical Israel). However, the larger scheme of Rom 9–11 requires reservation on this point. God not having spared those branches and their having been cut off (by an unspecified agent) from his renewed covenant with his people in Christ does not speak to agency. (Within the overall context, this passage makes most sense and is most coherent if it was by *their* covenant-breaking rejection of God's purposes that national Israel has alienated *themselves* from covenantal identity.) In any case, this passage must not be read *back* into Rom 9:6–29, lest it be misunderstood that when Paul there details God's judgment his strategy ever comes close to identifying that judgment with God's rejection of them and then seeking to justify said rejection. It remains the case that in the first portion of his argument in Rom 9–11, Paul's strategy is to identify national Israel's alienation from God in terms of *their* rejection of *him*.

11. Although nothing in the pericope is suggestive of Paul's understanding of when that may be or details anything about the shape of the intervening eschatological present.

12. Romans 11:26–27 is a conflated citation of Greek Isa 59:20–21a and 27:9a. In both of these traditions, the emphasis is upon God's action. Although Israel's response is not exposited, it is clear in context that God's actions are decisive as regards at

that in terms of the particularity of national Israel, God holds them in his heart far above all other people groups. God will not—nor can anything else—undo (11:29) his calling of them (initial and continued) nor his gifts of promised fidelity, the prophets, the Scriptures, and even the Messiah (cf. 9:3-5). Therefore, as per the principle in 11:32 (by way of forensic metaphor—that God's gift of the gospel is his means of showing mercy equally to all people amid their universal imprisonment; cf. 3:22-25), Paul concludes in 11:30-31 that national Israel may and are hoped to replicate the example of the Gentile audience's experience of salvation in Christ: God desires that they move from disobedience to the acceptance of mercy.[13]

---

least those who are ultimately redeemed from among Israel as his people (with the former especially blurring the identity of God's people in comparison to Israel as a nation). Most important, both Isa 59:20-21a and 27:9a do *not* simply refer to deliverance. Rather, they refer first to God's judgment upon Israel, followed by his relational renewal particularly with his faithful people from among Israel. Paul quotes the latter half of this complex in each case, drawing together their single trajectory regarding eschatological declarations of God's restoration of his people on the Day of the Lord. In so doing, Paul identifies his post-Christ event present as the designated moment, laying claim to the realization of that Isaianic expectation.

13. The referent of "all Israel" in Rom 11:26 and the timing of the salvation to which Paul refers is a notorious crux. The reserved, provisional interpretation of 11:26 offered here does not depend on any particular conclusion regarding its theological implications. However, at the risk of giving hostage to fortune, further specificity may be speculated: It needs recollecting that in many postexilic biblical and post-biblical traditions there is a large degree of introduced ambiguity as to the degree of collocation of national Israel and God's people. It seems to me that the soundest reading takes seriously various relevant aspects of 11:25-27 (the technical nature of *mystery* and the genre of apocalyptic, the full sense of the Isaianic citations [cf. previous note], and the sense of the "fullness of the nations") along with the fact that, to some relevant degree, Paul views the Christ event as having inaugurated the eschatological era. From these, it seems to follow that "all Israel" in 11:26 refers to nothing more or less than those who are now God's people, relative to Christ, without regard to preference according to any now-outdated evaluative frameworks. Paul is making the positive statement that God is presently in the process of reconstituting his people, and this does not entail any negative corollary about national Israel. Therefore, I would entertain the notion that Paul means for "all Israel" in 11:26 to refer to God's corporate christocentric people, apocalyptically revealing that their salvation is taking place in the eschatological present. On the other side of things, nothing is specified with regard to if, when, or how unbelieving Jews will take part in Israel's reconstitution, except perhaps to say that it looks as though Paul has decisively disjoined national Israel from God's people as regards the former's inevitable identity. God (and Paul with him) desires that national Israel will take advantage of the opportunity during the eschatological present to join the nations in being ingathered as part of God's people, but the destiny and composition of God's

Apart from the final doxology of Romans 11:33–36, this is how Paul concludes his answer to the *Israelfrage* and ends his defense of God's covenantal faithfulness in Romans 9–11. Before the audience's very eyes, God is both restoring his people and inviting national Israel to partake of that restoration. Although provisional, this reading of the remainder of Romans 9–11 is to a large degree contingent upon the analysis given in the above study of 9:6–29. Therefore, if there is merit to my reading of Romans 9:6–29, it may have a significant impact on the directions in which Paul's argument may be seen to progress (as well as the method with which the remainder of his argument must be interpreted, given its frequent recourse to and application of Scripture). That is, it may be necessary to recognize that in Romans 9:6–29 Paul identifies national Israel's rejection of the gospel as idolatry in order to account for the coherence of the literary unit of Romans 9–11 within the letter as a whole. In this, the discussion in 9:30 and beyond proceeds directly from that in 9:6–29, in a continuance of his defense of God's faithfulness begun in 9:6a. Although scholars readily recognize the connection between Paul's thesis in 9:6a and the latter stages of his argument in chapters 9–11, the interpretation of Paul's argument in 9:6–29 presented in this study binds the whole together in a new way.

IMPLICATIONS OF THE STUDY

In closing, I would draw attention to the way in which this study speaks to several of the questions that scholars ask of Romans 9:6–29. As mentioned in chapter 1, scholars typically debate: 1) whether 9:6–29 is abstract; 2) what it states about Paul's views on divine sovereignty and human free will; 3) whether it presents a doctrine of the salvation of individuals versus corporate groups; and 4) who are the elect of Israel.

First, as previewed in the introductory chapters, this study strongly suggests that Romans 9:6–29 is occasional and *not* part of a doctrinal treatise of any kind. Any theological implications of Paul's argument

---

people is wholly independent from that of national Israel from this point forward (cf. Gal 3:1–4:7, which is also contested but arguably proceeds from the notion that the pre-Christ event configuration of Israel is over and no longer spiritually/religiously relevant). So in principle, for Paul there is no longer anything theologically relevant about national Israel as a corporate entity or institution. As regards the gospel, those to whom the designation *national Israel* applies are on equal footing before God as other *goyim*.

are just that: derivations rather than explicit statements of or arguments concerning doctrine.

Second, putting aside entirely for the moment the question of whether so-called Reformed or Arminian categories are viable within biblical theologie(s) or Second Temple thought (of which Paul is a representative), it does not appear that in at least Romans 9:6–29 Paul is discussing salvation as such at all, whether of individuals or corporate groups. This study neither argues against nor affirms any conclusion on this spectrum (and is presumably compatible with any conclusion one could wish to draw on that issue). Rather, it simply discovers that whatever scholars may otherwise decide on the question of the doctrine of predestination in Paul, generally, 9:6–29 is irrelevant to the debate.

Third, on questions of agency in election and/or salvation, Paul is completely silent. This would mean that Romans 9:6–29 would be hypothetically congruous with any coherent, biblical theory, all things being equal (e.g., without violating what he is clear on). If Paul does reference the issues of human free will or God's sovereignty at all, then he does so only indirectly as presuppositional supporting points, and under the highly restrictive rubric of the biblical view of idolatry and its dehumanizing consequences. Thus, the question of whether Paul thinks that God compels the behavior of individuals for his purposes is unanswerable from 9:6–29, except to say that here judgment (if it does involve compulsion) is only a factor when God responds *after* his creatures have previously sinned in committing idolatry.

Fourth, in Romans 9:6–29 Paul does not make any explicit statements regarding who is Israel or what are the boundary markers of covenantal membership. He may make relevant statements on this issue in the remainder of Romans 9–11, but it is left to interpreters to infer possible implications of 9:6–29.

In sum, Paul's focus in Romans 9:6–29 is God's present (i.e., first-century) manner of relating to national Israel—that is, the character of God vis-à-vis his people's composition in light of the Christ event. If an "-ology" must be attached to this portion of the letter, then it should not be soteriology—it may be that the only fitting choices are theology proper or perhaps ecclesiology. And so, if a given interpreter's reading of salvation or election in Romans 9 seems distasteful, the best and correct strategy is not to try and out-interpret them with regard to soteriology. Rather, it is to point out their error insofar as this passage does not advocate any view on such topics.

However, touching one last time on the topic of Israel's identity, this study also demonstrates that in Romans 9:6–29 Paul does begin to present his answer to the *Israelfrage*: God has not rejected Israel, nor has he been unfaithful to his covenantal promises, despite national Israel's rejection of the Messiah. Instead, he has shown patience and wisdom in turning their rebellion to his own redemptive purposes. But this is only the first part of Paul's answer to the question of Israel: as frequently in Romans 9–11, Paul details that God still has a heart that national Israel should once again be identified as his covenant people. For this reason, Paul concludes in Romans 11:25–32 with the revelation of the mystery: God will indeed save his entire people, equally offering his mercy to all nations—with Abraham's descendants among them.

Bibliography

Abasciano, Brian J. *Paul's Use of the Old Testament in Romans 9:1–9: An Intertextual and Theological Exegesis.* Library of New Testament Supplement Series 301. Edinburgh: T&T Clark, 2005.

———. *Paul's Use of the Old Testament in Romans 9.10–18: An Intertextual and Theological Exegesis.* Library of New Testament Studies 317. New York: T&T Clark, 2012.

Achtemeier, Elizabeth. *Nahum–Malachi.* Interpretation Bible Commentary. Atlanta: John Knox, 1986.

Ackroyd, Peter R. "Isaia I–XII: Presentation of a Prophet." Pages 16–48 in *Congress Volume: Göttingen, 1977,* edited by Walther Zimmerli. Supplements to Vetus Testamentum 29. Leiden: Brill, 1978.

Aletti, Jean Noël. "L'argumentation Paulinienne en Rm 9." *Biblica* 68 (1987): 41–56.

Alter, Robert. *The Five Books of Moses: A Translation with Commentary.* New York: W. W. Norton, 2004.

———. *Genesis: A Translation and Commentary.* New York: W. W. Norton, 1996.

Allen, James P. *Genesis in Egypt: The Philosophy of Ancient Egyptian Creation Accounts.* New Haven: Yale Egyptological Seminar, 1988.

Andersen, Francis I., and David Noel Freedman. *Hosea: A New Translation.* Anchor Bible 24. New York: Doubleday, 1980.

Assis, Elie. "Structure and Meaning in the Book of Malachi." Pages 354–69 in *Prophecy and the Prophets in Ancient Israel: Proceedings of the Oxford Old Testament Seminar,* edited by John Day. Library of Hebrew Bible/Old Testament Studies 531. New York: T&T Clark, 2010.

Atwell, James E. "An Egyptian Source for Genesis 1." *Journal of Theological Studies* 51 (2000): 441–77.

Baldwin, J. G. "Mal. 1:11 and the Worship of the Nations in the Old Testament." *Tyndale Bulletin* 23 (1972): 117–24.

Beale, G. K., ed. *The Right Doctrine from the Wrong Texts? Essays on the Use of the Old Testament in the New.* Grand Rapids: Baker, 1994.

———. "An Exegetical and Theological Consideration of the Hardening of Pharaoh's Heart in Exodus 4–14 and Romans 9." *Trinity Journal* 5 (1984): 129–54.

———. "Isaiah VI 9–13: A Retributive Taunt Against Idolatry." *Vetus Testamentum* 41 (1991): 257–78.

Bellis, Alice Ogden. "Habakkuk 2:4b: Intertextuality and Hermeneutics." Pages 369–85 in *Jews, Christians, and the Theology of the Hebrew Scriptures,* edited by Alice Ogden Bellis and Joel S. Kaminsky. Society of Biblical Literature Symposium Series 8. Atlanta: SBL, 2000.

Benware, Wilbur A. "Romans 1.17 and Cognitive Grammar." *The Bible Translator* 51 (2000): 330–40.

Bergey, Ronald. "The Song of Moses (Deuteronomy 32.1–43) and Isaianic Prophecies: A Case of Early Intertextuality?" *Journal for the Study of the Old Testament* 28 (2003): 33–54.

Beuken, W. A. M. "Perversion Reverted." Translated by B. Doyle. Pages 43–64 in *Scriptures and the Scrolls: Studies in Honour of A. S. van Der Woude on the Occasion of his 65th Birthday*, edited by F. Garcia Martinez, A. Hilhorst, and C. J. Labuschagne. Leiden: Brill, 1992.

Bird, Phyllis A. "The Harlot as Heroine: Narrative Art and Social Presupposition in Three Old Testament Texts." *Semeia* 46 (1989): 119–39.

Blenkinsopp, Joseph. *Isaiah 1–39: A New Translation with Introduction and Commentary*. Anchor Bible 19. New York: Doubleday, 2000.

Brown, Raymond E. "The Roman Church Near the End of the First Christian Generation (A.D. 58—Paul to the Romans)." Pages 105–127 in *Antioch and Rome: New Testament Cradles of Catholic Christianity*, edited by R. E. Brown and J. P. Meier. New York: Paulist, 1983.

Bruce, F. F. *Romans*. Tyndale New Testament Commentaries. Grand Rapids: Eerdmans, 1985.

Brueggemann, Walter. "Crisis-Evoked, Crisis-Resolving Speech." *Biblical Theology Bulletin* 24 (1994): 95–105.

———. "'Impossibility' and Epistemology in the Faith Tradition of Abraham and Sarah (Gen 18:1–15)." *Zeitschrift für die alttestamentliche Wissenschaft* 94 (1982): 615–34.

———. *Isaiah 1–39*. Westminster Bible Companion. Louisville: Westminster John Knox, 1998.

———. "Pharaoh as Vassal." *Catholic Biblical Quarterly* 57 (1995): 27–51.

Byrne, Brendan. *Romans*. Sacra Pagina 6. Collegeville, MN: Liturgical, 1996.

Calvin, John. *Commentaries on the Epistle of Paul the Apostle to the Romans*. Translated and edited by John Owen. Grand Rapids: Eerdmans, 1955.

Campbell, W. S. "Romans iii as a Key to the Structure and Thought of the Letter." *Novum Testamentum* 23 (1981): 32–34.

Carlson, Richard P. "Whose Faith? Reexamining the Habakkuk 2:4 Citation within the Communicative Act of Romans 1:1–17." Pages 293–324 in *Raising Up a Faithful Exegete: Essays in Honor of Richard D. Nelson*, edited by K. L. Noll and Brooks Schramm. Winona Lake, IN: Eisenbrauns, 2010.

Carson, D. A., and H. G. M. Williamson, eds. *It is Written: Scripture Citing Scripture: Essays in Honour of Barnabas Lindars*. Cambridge: Cambridge University Press, 1988.

Cassuto, U. *A Commentary on the Book of Exodus*. Translated by Israel Abrahams. Jerusalem: Magnes, 1967.

Chan, Michael. "Rhetorical Reversal and Usurpation: Isaiah 10:5–34 and the Use of Neo-Assyrian Royal Idiom in the Construction of an Anti-Assyrian Theology." *Journal of Biblical Literature* 128 (2009): 717–33.

Childs, Brevard. *The Book of Exodus: A Critical Theological Commentary*. Philadelphia: Westminster, 1974.

———. *Isaiah*. Louisville: Westminster John Knox, 2001.

Chisolm, Robert B. Jr. "Divine Hardening in the Old Testament." *Bibliotheca Sacra* 153 (1996): 410-34.

Clines, David J. A. "Hosea 2: Structure and Interpretation." Pages 83-103 in *Studia Biblica 1978. I. Old Testament and Related Themes. Sixth International Congress on Biblical Studies, Oxford, 3-7 April, 1978*, edited by E. A. Livingstone. Journal for the Study of the Old Testament Supplement Series 11. Sheffield: JSOT, 1979.

———. "The Image of God in Man." *Tyndale Bulletin* 19 (1968): 53-103.

Cotter, David W. *Genesis*. Berit Olam. Collegeville, MN: Liturgical: 2003.

Currid, John D. *Ancient Egypt and the Old Testament*. Grand Rapids: Baker, 1997.

———. "Why Did God Harden Pharaoh's Heart?" *Bible Review* 9 (November/December, 1993): 46-51.

Di Lella, Alexander A. "Tobit 4,19 and Romans 9,18: An Intertextual Study." *Biblica* 90 (2009): 260-63.

Donfried, Karl P. "A Short Note on Romans 16." Pages 50-59 in *The Romans Debate*, 50-59, edited by Karl P. Donfried. Minneapolis: Augsburg, 1977.

———, ed. *The Romans Debate*. Minneapolis: Augsburg, 1977.

———, ed. *The Romans Debate*. Rev. and exp. ed. Minneapolis: Augsburg, 1991.

Dumbrell, William J. "Worship in Isaiah 6." *Reformed Theological Review* 43 (1984): 1-8.

Dunn, James D. G. *Romans 1-8*. Word Biblical Commentary 38A. Dallas: Word Books, 1988.

———. *Romans 9-16*. Word Biblical Commentary 38B. Dallas: Word Books, 1988.

Durham, John I. *Exodus*. Word Biblical Commentary 3. Dallas: Word Books, 1987.

Eslinger, Lyle. "Freedom or Knowledge? Perspective and Purpose in the Exodus Narrative (Exodus 1-15)." *Journal for the Study of the Old Testament* 52 (1991): 43-60.

Evans, Craig A., ed. *The Interpretation of Scripture in Early Judaism and Christianity: Studies in Language and Tradition*. Sheffield: Sheffield Academic, 2000.

———. "On Isaiah's Use of Israel's Sacred Tradition." *Biblische Zeitschrift* 30 (1986): 92-99.

———. "Paul and the Hermeneutics of 'True Prophecy': A Study of Romans 9-11." *Biblica* 65 (1984): 560-70.

Exum, J. C. "Isaiah 28-32: A Literary Approach." *Society of Biblical Literature Seminar Papers* 2 (1979): 123-51.

Fee, Gordon D. *God's Empowering Presence: The Holy Spirit in the Letters of Paul*. Peabody, MA: Hendrickson: 1994.

———. "Wisdom Christology in Paul: A Dissenting View." Pages 355-78 in *To What End Exegesis? Essays Textual, Exegetical, and Theological*. Grand Rapids: Eerdmans, 2001.

Fisher, Loren R. "Creation at Ugarit and in the Old Testament." *Vetus Testamentum* 15 (1965): 313-24.

Fitzmyer, Joseph A. *Romans: A New Translation with Introduction and Commentary.* Anchor Bible 33. New York: Doubleday, 1993.

Fokkelman, J. P. "Time and Structure of the Abraham Cycle." Pages 96–109 in *New Avenues in the Study of the Old Testament: A Collection of Old Testament Studies, Published on the Occasion of the Fiftieth Anniversary of the Oudtestamentisch Werkgezelschap and the Retirement of Prof. Dr. M. J. Mulder*, edited by A. S. van der Woude. Leiden: Brill, 1989.

Ford, William. *God, Pharaoh and Moses: Explaining the Lord's Actions in the Exodus Plague Narrative.* Paternoster Biblical Monographs. Milton Keynes, UK: Paternoster, 2006.

Garrett, Duane A. *Hosea.* New American Commentary 19A. Nashville: Broadman and Holman, 1997.

Gaston, Lloyd. "Israel's Enemies in Pauline Theology." Pages 80–99 in *Paul and the Torah.* Vancouver: University of British Columbia Press, 1987.

Glazier-McDonald, Beth. *Malachi: The Divine Messenger.* Society of Biblical Literature Dissertation Series 98. Atlanta: Scholars, 1987.

Glenny, W. Edward. "The 'People of God' in Romans 9:25–26." *Bibliotheca Sacra* 152 (1995): 42–59.

Gowan, Donald E. *Theology in Exodus: Biblical Theology in the Form of a Commentary.* Louisville: Westminster John Knox, 1994.

Greenberg, Moshe. "The Thematic Unity of Exodus 3–11." *World Congress of Jewish Studies* 1 (1967): 146–59.

———. *Understanding Exodus.* New York: Behrman House, 1969.

Grønbæk, Jakob H. "Baal's Battle with Yam: A Canaanite Creation Fight." *Journal for the Study of the Old Testament* 33 (1985): 27–44.

Gunn, David M. "The 'Hardening of Pharaoh's Heart': Plot, Character, and Theology in Exodus 1–14." Pages 72–96 in *Art and Meaning: Rhetoric in Biblical Literature*, edited by David J. A. Clines, et al. Sheffield: JSOT, 1982.

Hafemann, Scott J. "The Glory and the Veil of Moses in 2 Corinthians 3:7–14: An Example of Paul's Contextual Exegesis of the OT—A Proposal." *Horizons in Biblical Theology* 14 (1992): 31–49.

Hamilton, Victor P. *The Book of Genesis Chapters 18–50.* New International Commentary on the Old Testament. Grand Rapids: Eerdmans, 1995.

Hartley, Donald E. *The Wisdom Background and Parabolic Implications of Isaiah 6:9–10 in the Synoptics.* Studies in Biblical Literature 100. New York: Peter Lang, 2006.

Hauge, Martin Randal. *The Descent from the Mountain: Narrative Patterns in Exodus 19–40.* Journal for the Study of the Old Testament Supplement Series 323. Sheffield: Sheffield Academic, 2001.

Hays, Richard B. *Echoes of Scripture in the Letters of Paul.* New Haven, CT: Yale University Press, 1987.

Heil, John Paul. "From Remnant to Seed of Hope for Israel: Romans 9:27–29." *Catholic Biblical Quarterly* 64 (2002): 703–20.

Hess, Richard S. "Genesis 1–2 and Recent Studies of Ancient Texts." *Science and Christian Belief* 7 (1995): 141–49.

Hill, Andrew E. *Malachi.* Anchor Bible 25D. New York: Doubleday, 1998.

Hoffmeier, James K. "Some Thoughts on Genesis 1 & 2 and Egyptian Cosmology."
    Journal of the Ancient Near Eastern Society 15 (1983): 39–49.
Isbell, Charles David. *The Function of Exodus Motifs in Biblical Narratives: Theological
    Didactic Drama.* Studies in the Bible and Early Christianity 52. Lewiston, NY:
    Edwin Mellen, 2002.
Jensen, Joseph. *The Use of* tôrâ *by Isaiah: His Debate with the Wisdom Tradition.*
    Catholic Biblical Quarterly Monograph Series 3. Washington: Catholic
    Biblical Association of America, 1973.
Jewett, Robert. "Ecumenical Theology for the Sake of Mission: Romans 1:1–17 +
    15:14–16:24." *Society of Biblical Literature 1992 Seminar Papers* 2 (1992): 598–612.
————. *Romans: A Commentary.* Hermeneia. Minneapolis: Fortress, 2006.
Johnson, E. Elizabeth. "Romans 9–11: The Faithfulness and Impartiality of God."
    Pages 211–39 in *Pauline Theology*, vol. 3, edited by David M. Hay and E.
    Elizabeth Johnson. Minneapolis: Fortress, 1995.
Johnson, Luke Timothy. *Reading Romans: A Literary and Theological Commentary.*
    New York: Crossroad, 1997.
Keck, Leander E. *Romans.* Abingdon New Testament Commentary. Nashville:
    Abingdon, 2005.
Klein, George L. "Reading Genesis 1." *Southwestern Journal of Theology* 44
    (2001): 22–38.
Knierim, Rolf P. "The Vocation of Isaiah." *Vetus Testamentum* 18 (1968): 47–68.
Lenski, R. C. H. *The Interpretation of St. Paul's Epistle to the Romans.* Minneapolis:
    Augsburg, 1961.
Levenson, Jon D. *Creation and the Persistence of Evil.* San Francisco: Harper, 1988.
Longenecker, R. N. "The Focus of Romans: The Central Role of 5:1–8:39 in the
    Argument of the Letter." Pages 49–69 in *Romans and the People of God: Essays
    in Honor of Gordon D. Fee on the Occasion of His 65th Birthday*, edited by Sven
    K. Soderlund and N. T. Wright. Grand Rapids: Eerdmans, 1999.
Macintosh, A. A. *Hosea.* International Critical Commentary. Edinburgh: T&T
    Clark, 1997.
Mason, Steve. "'For I am Not Ashamed of the Gospel' (Rom. 1.16): The Gospel and
    the First Readers of Romans." Pages 254–87 in *Gospel in Paul: Studies on
    Corinthians, Galatians and Romans for Richard N. Longenecker*, edited by L.
    Ann Jervis and Peter Richardson. Sheffield: Sheffield Academic, 1994.
McComiskey, Thomas. "Hosea." In *The Minor Prophets: An Exegetical and Expository
    Commentary, Volume 1, Hosea, Joel, and Amos.* Grand Rapids: Baker, 1992.
McKane, William. *Prophets and Wise Men.* London: SCM, 1965.
McLaughlin, John L. "Their Hearts Were Hardened: The Use of Isaiah 6,9–10 in the
    Book of Isaiah." *Biblica* 75 (1994): 1–25.
Meadors, Edward P. *Idolatry and the Hardening of the Heart: A Study in Biblical
    Theology.* New York: T&T Clark, 2006.
Merrill, Eugene H. *Haggai, Zechariah, Malachi: An Exegetical Commentary.* Chicago:
    Moody, 1994.
Meyer, Ben F. "Election-Historical Thinking in Romans 9–11, and Ourselves." *Ex
    Auditu* 4 (1988): 1–7.

Miller, James C. *The Obedience of Faith, the Eschatological People of God, and the Purpose of Romans*. Society of Biblical Literature Dissertation Series 177. Atlanta: Society of Biblical Literature, 2000.

Miscall, Peter D. "Biblical Narrative and the Categories of the Fantastic." *Semeia* 60 (1992): 39–51.

Moo, Douglas J. *The Epistle to the Romans*. New International Commentary on the New Testament. Grand Rapids: Eerdmans, 1996.

Morris, Leon. *The Epistle to the Romans*. Grand Rapids: Eerdmans, 1987.

Moyise, Steve, ed. *The Old Testament in the New Testament: Essays in Honour of J. L. North*. Sheffield: Sheffield Academic, 2000.

Murray, D. F. "The Rhetoric of Disputation." *Journal for the Study of the Old Testament* 38 (1987): 95–121.

Murray, John. *The Epistle to the Romans*, 2 vols. New International Commentary on the New Testament. Grand Rapids: Eerdmans, 1968.

Elliott, Neil. *The Rhetoric of Romans: Argumentative Constraint and Strategy and Paul's Dialogue with Judaism*. Journal for the Study of the New Testament Supplement Series 45. Sheffield: JSOT, 1990.

Nielsen, Kirsten. "Is 6:1–8:18 as Dramatic Writing." *Studia Theologica* 40 (1986): 1–16.

Ochsenmeier, Erwin. "Romans 1,11–12: A Clue to the Purpose of Romans?" *Ephemerides theologicae louvanienses* 83 (2007): 395–406.

Omanson, Roger L. Review of *The Justification of God: An Exegetical and Theological Study of Romans 9:1–23*, by John Piper. *Review and Expositor* 82 (1985): 283–84.

Oppenheim, A. L. *Ancient Mesopotamia*. Chicago: University of Chicago, 1970.

Osborne, Grant R. *Romans*. Downers Grove, IL: InterVarsity, 2003.

Oswalt, John N. *The Book of Isaiah, Chapters 1–39*. New International Commentary on the Old Testament. Grand Rapids: Eerdmans, 1986.

Petersen, David L. *Zechariah 9–14 and Malachi: A Commentary*. Louisville: Westminster John Knox, 1995.

Pierce, Ronald W. "Literary Connectors and a Haggai/Zechariah/Malachi Corpus." *Journal of the Evangelical Theological Society* 27 (1984): 277–89.

———. "A Thematic Development of the Haggai/Zechariah/Malachi Corpus." *Journal of the Evangelical Theological Society* 27 (1984): 401–11.

Piper, John. *The Justification of God: An Exegetical and Theological Study of Romans 9:1–23*. Grand Rapids: Baker, 1983.

Porter, Stanley E. "The Use of the Old Testament in the New Testament: A Brief Comment on Method and Terminology." Pages 79–96 in *Early Christian Interpretation of the Scriptures of Israel: Investigations and Proposals*, edited by Craig A. Evans and James A. Sanders. Journal for the Study of the New Testament Supplement Series 148. Sheffield: Sheffield Academic, 1997.

Propp, William H. C. *Exodus 1–18*. Anchor Bible 2. New York: Doubleday, 1999.

Reid, M.L. "A Rhetorical Analysis of Romans 1:1–5:21 with Attention Given to the Rhetorical Function of 5:1–21." *Perspectives in Religious Studies* 19 (1992): 255–72.

Richardson, Neil. *Paul's Language About God*. Journal for the Study of the New Testament Supplement Series 99. Sheffield: Sheffield Academic, 1994.

Robinson, Geoffrey D. "The Motif of Deafness and Blindness in Isaiah 6:9–10: A Contextual, Literary, and Theological Analysis." *Bulletin for Biblical Research* 8 (1998): 167–86.

Robinson, John A. T. *Wrestling with Romans.* London: SCM, 1979.

Rudman, Dominic. "The Theology of the Idol Fabrication Passages in Second Isaiah." *Old Testament Essays* 12 (1999): 114–21.

Sanday, William, and Arthur C. Headlam. *The Epistle to the Romans.* International Critical Commentary. Edinburgh: T&T Clark, 1895.

Sarna, Nahum M. *Exodus: The Traditional Hebrew Text with the New JPS Translation.* Philadelphia: Jewish Publication Society, 1991.

———. *Exploring Exodus: The Heritage of Biblical Israel.* New York: Schocken, 1986.

Schreiner, Thomas R. *Romans.* Baker Exegetical Commentary on the New Testament 6. Grand Rapids: Baker, 1998.

Seitz, Christopher R. *Isaiah 1–39.* Interpretation. Louisville: John Knox, 1993.

Sherwood, Aaron. "The Mixed Multitude in Exodus 12:38: Glorification, Creation, and Yhwh's Plunder of Israel and the Nations," *HBT* 34 (2012): 139–54.

———. *Paul and the Restoration of Humanity in Light of Ancient Jewish Traditions.* Ancient Judaism and Early Christianity 82. Leiden: Brill, 2012.

Sherwood, Yvonne. *The Prostitute and the Prophet: Hosea's Marriage in Literary-Theoretical Perspective.* Journal for the Study of the Old Testament Supplement Series 212. Sheffield: Sheffield Academic, 1996.

Shum, Shui-Lun. *Paul's Use of Isaiah in Romans: A Comparative Study of Paul's Letter to the Romans and the Sibylline and Qumran Sectarian Texts.* Wissenschaftliche Veröffentlichungen zum Neuen Testament 156. Tübingen: Mohr Siebeck, 2002.

Smiga, George. "Romans 12:1–2 and 15:30–32 and the Occasion of the Letter to the Romans." *Catholic Biblical Quarterly* 53 (1991): 257–73.

Snodgrass, Klyne. "The Use of the Old Testament in the New." Pages 407–34 in *Interpreting the New Testament,* edited by David Alan Black and David S. Dockery. Nashville: Broadman and Holman, 2001.

Spero, Shubert. "Jacob and Esau: The Relationship Reconsidered." *Jewish Bible Quarterly* 32 (2004): 245–50.

Stanley, Christopher D. *Paul and the Language of Scripture: Citation Techniques in the Pauline Epistles and Contemporary Literature.* Cambridge: Cambridge University, 1992.

Stansell, Gary. "Isaiah 28–33: Blest Be the Tie that Binds (Isaiah Together)." Pages 68–103 in *New Visions of Isaiah,* edited by Roy F. Melugin and Marvin A. Sweeney. Journal for the Study of the Old Testament Supplement Series 214. Sheffield: Sheffield, 1996.

Stuart, Douglas. *Hosea-Jonah.* Word Biblical Commentary 31. Dallas: Word Books, 1987.

———. "Malachi." In *The Minor Prophets: An Exegetical and Expository Commentary. Vol. 3, Zephaniah, Haggai, Zechariah, Malachi,* edited by Thomas McComiskey. Grand Rapids: Baker, 1992.

Stuhlmacher, Peter. *Paul's Letter to the Romans: A Commentary.* Translated by Scott J. Hafemann. Louisville: Westminster John Knox, 1994.

Sweeney, Marvin A. "Hosea." In *The Twelve Prophets. Vol. 1, Hosea, Joel, Amos, Obadiah, Jonah*. Berit Olam. Collegeville, MN: Liturgical, 2000.

———. *Isaiah 1–4 and the Post-Exilic Understanding of the Isaianic Tradition*. Berlin: Walter de Gruyter, 1988.

———. *Isaiah 1–39: With an Introduction to Prophetic Literature*. Forms of the Old Testament Literature XVI. Grand Rapids: Eerdmans, 1996.

———. *The Twelve Prophets. Vol. 2, Micah, Nahum, Habakkuk, Zephaniah, Haggai, Zechariah, Malachi*. Berit Olam. Collegeville, MN: Liturgical, 2000.

Talstra, Eep. "'I and Your People': Syntax and Dialogue in Exod 33." *Journal of Northwest Semitic Languages* 33 (2007): 89–97.

Tate, Marvin E. "Questions for Priests and People in Malachi 1:2–2:16." *Review and Expositor* 84 (1987): 391–407.

Taylor, John W. "From Faith to Faith: Romans 1.17 in the Light of Greek Idiom." *New Testament Studies* 50 (2004): 337–348.

Taylor, Richard A., and E. Ray Clendenen. *Haggai, Malachi*. New American Commentary 21A. Nashville: Broadman and Holman, 2004.

Terino, Jonathan. "A Text Linguistic Study of the Jacob Narrative." *Vox evangelica* 18 (1988): 45–62.

Thornhill, Anthony Chadwick. *To the Jew First: A Socio-Rhetorical and Biblical-Theological Analysis of the Pauline Teaching of "Election" In Light of Second Temple Jewish Patterns of Thought*. PhD diss., Liberty Baptist Theological Seminary, 2012.

du Toit, Andreas B. "Persuasion in Romans 1:1–17." *Biblische Zeitschrift* 2 (1989): 192–209.

Verhoef, Pieter A. *The Books of Haggai and Malachi*. New International Commentary on the Old Testament. Grand Rapids: Eerdmans, 1987.

Vorster, Johannes N. "Strategies of Persuasion in Romans 1.16–17." Pages 152–70 in *Rhetoric and the New Testament: Essays from the 1992 Heidelberg Conference*, edited by Stanley E. Porter and Thomas H. Olbricht. Journal for the Study of the New Testament Supplement Serties 90. Sheffield: JSOT, 1993.

Wagner, J. Ross. *Heralds of the Good News: Isaiah and Paul "in Concert" in the Letter to the Romans*. Boston: Brill, 2002.

Walters, James C. *Ethnic Issues in Paul's Letter to the Romans: Changing Self-Definitions in Earliest Roman Christianity*. Valley Forge, PA: Trinity Press International, 1993.

Waltke, Bruce K. *Genesis: A Commentary*. Grand Rapids: Zondervan, 2001.

Watson, Francis. *Paul and the Hermeneutics of Faith*. London: T&T Clark, 2004.

Watts, John D. W. *Isaiah 1–33*. Word Biblical Commentary 24. Waco, TX: Word Books, 1985.

Watts, Rikki E. "'For I Am Not Ashamed of the Gospel': Romans 1:16–17 and Habakkuk 2:4." Pages 3–25 in *Romans and the People of God: Essays in Honor of Gordon D. Fee on the Occasion of His 65th Birthday*, edited by Sven K. Soderlund and N. T. Wright. Grand Rapids: Eerdmans, 1999.

———. "On the Edge of the Millennium: Making Sense of Genesis 1." Pages 129–51 in *Living in the LambLight: Christianity and Contemporary Challenges to the Gospel*, edited by Hans Boersma. Vancouver: Regent College, 2001.

———. "The New Exodus/New Creational Restoration of the Image of God." Pages 18–29 in *What Does it Mean to Be Saved? Broadening Evangelical Horizons of Salvations*, edited by John G. Stackhouse, Jr. Grand Rapids: Baker, 2002.

Wedderburn, A. J. M. "Purpose and Occasion of Romans Again." Pages 195–202 in *The Romans Debate*, rev. and exp. ed., edited by Karl P. Donfried. Peabody, MA: Hendrickson, 1991.

———. *Reasons for Romans*. Edinburgh: T&T Clark, 1988.

Wenham, Gordon J. *Genesis 1–15*. Word Biblical Commentary 1. Dallas: Word Books, 1987.

———. *Genesis 16–50*. Word Biblical Commentary 2. Dallas: Word Books, 1994.

Westermann, Claus. *Genesis 1–11: A Commentary*. Translated by J. J. Scullion. Minneapolis: Augsburg, 1984.

———. *Genesis 12–36: A Commentary*. Translated by J. J. Scullion. Minneapolis: Fortress, 1985.

Wildberger, Hans. *Isaiah: A Commentary*. Translated by Thomas H. Trapp. Minneapolis: Fortress Press, 1990.

Williams, Sam K. Review of The Justification of God: An Exegetical and Theological Study of Romans 9:1-23, by John Piper. *Journal of Biblical Literature* 104 (1985): 548–51.

Winn Leith, Mary Joan. "Verse and Reverse: The Transformation of the Woman, Israel, in Hosea 1–3." Pages 95–108 in *Gender and Difference in Ancient Israel*, edited by Peggy L. Day. Minneapolis: Fortress, 1989.

Wire, Antoinette Clark. "'Since God is One': Rhetoric as Theology and History in Paul's Romans." Pages 210–227 in *The New literary criticism and the New Testament*, edited by Elizabeth Struthers Malbon. Journal for the Study of the New Testament Supplement Series 109. Sheffield: Sheffield Academic, 1994.

Witherington, Ben III. *Paul's Letter to the Romans: A Socio-Rhetorical Commentary*. Grand Rapids: Eerdmans, 2004.

Wright, N. T. *The Climax of the Covenant: Christ and the Law in Pauline Theology*. Minneapolis: Fortress, 1992.

———. *The Letter to the Romans*. New Interpreter's Bible 10. Nashville: Abingdon, 2002.

———. *The New Testament and the People of God*. Minneapolis: Fortress, 1992.

———. "Romans and the Theology of Paul." Pages 3–67 in *Pauline Theology, Vol. 3: Romans*, edited by David M. Hay and E. Elizabeth Johnson. Minneapolis: Fortress, 1995.

———. Review of *The Justification of God: An Exegetical and Theological Study of Romans 9:1-23*, by John Piper. *Evangelical Quarterly* 60 (1988): 80–84.

Yee, Gale A. "'She Is Not My Wife and I Am Not Her Husband': A Materialist Analysis of Hosea 1–2." *Biblical Interpretation* 9 (2001): 345–83.

Index of Subjects and Authors

Index of Scripture and Other Ancient Literature

Old Testament

New Testament